Bill; Trust in the [Lord] with all your hea[rt] ... on your own underst[anding] Proverbs 3:5 May God Bless you, Uncle Brian.

ARMAGEDDON

APPOINTMENT
WITH
DESTINY

Grant R. Jeffrey

BANTAM BOOKS
NEW YORK • TORONTO • LONDON • SYDNEY • AUCKLAND

ARMAGEDDON: APPOINTMENT WITH DESTINY

A Bantam Nonfiction Book / published by arrangement with
the author

PRINTING HISTORY
Frontier Research Publications edition published August 1988
Bantam rack edition / July 1990

COMMENTS

"Armageddon - Appointment With Destiny will prove fascinating to the Christian whose special interest in the Bible is eschatology. It is a unique in depth study of the fulfillment of past prophecies and how they offer clues to the future. Much has been written on the subject, but not as exhaustively and available in one volume. Obviously biblical scholars do not agree completely on what the scriptures say about the "end times;" therefore, Mr. Jeffrey's discussion will be challenging to sincere students of the Word."

Dr. Cyrus N. Nelson, Former Chairman of the Board
Gospel Light Publications - Ventura, Ca.

"Grant Jeffrey believes that Jesus Christ is coming soon, and his exhaustive research of God's Word as it applies to today's world of politics, antireligious feeling and the ominous military arms build-up fortifies his urgency to teach Bible Prophecy and the Second Coming of Christ. Grant's prophetic teaching is neither sensational nor daringly speculative, but he believes that the absolutes of biblical prophecy are astounding as written in the Word of God. I have known Grant for many years and have watched his ministry and seen the positive impact of his message upon the personal commitment of the Church. It is with great personal joy that I recommend that you read Armageddon - Appointment With Destiny. Jesus is indeed coming soon and this message needs to be proclaimed."

Neil Enloe
The Couriers - Mechanicsburg, Pa.

ACKNOWLEDGEMENTS

A book like "*Armagedddon - Appointment With Destiny*" reflects the reading and inspiration of thousands of books, articles and commentators, plus countless hours of Bible study over the last 25 years. Although almost one hundred volumes are referred to in the footnotes and selected bibliography, this obviously represents only a fraction of the authors who have influenced and challenged my thinking. However, the inspired word of God has been both the major source and continual guide to my studies.

My parents, Lyle and Florence Jeffrey instilled in me a great love for the Lord and His word and have continually encouraged me in this project.

I would like to dedicate this book to my loving wife, Kaye, who has so faithfully completed the manuscript revisions and proofs. She is a continual encouragement, partner and inspiration in our ministry.

I trust that the information revealed in the following pages will encourage you to study the Word of God and increase your personal faith in the Lord Jesus Christ as your personal Savior.

Grant R. Jeffrey,
Toronto, Ontario
August, 1988

TABLE OF CONTENTS

Introduction

Does the Bible reveal the future events which will vitally affect the lives of each of us in the next decade?

Has God set "appointments with destiny" for Israel, Russia and the nations?

Do the prophecies of the Bible reveal the time of the final Battle of Armageddon?

Will Israel rediscover the lost Ark of the Covenant and rebuild its beloved Temple once more?

The Bible's answer to these questions is a resounding "YES."

All of these questions and more will be discussed in the fascinating light of original biblical and historical research. Unlike some books on prophecy you may have read, this book will challenge you with intriguing new material which has never before been published.

The theme of this book is that God has throughout history set precise, prophetic "appointments with destiny" for Israel, the nations and for individuals. God has manifested His sovereignty and prophetic foreknowledge through these predictions and their fulfillment. These prophecies and their incredibly accurate fulfillment prove the inspiration of Scriptures and strongly suggest that these prophetic appointments set for our generation will also be accomplished "at the time appointed".

As you observe this phenomenon of divine time cycles and amazing biblical anniversaries in the life of Israel and the nations, I believe you will be filled with a sense of wonder that God has exercised such a sovereignty over the rise and fall of empires to accomplish His purposes in human history.

It is fascinating to observe that all of these prophetic time cycles comes together in our generation that is now poised to participate in the most climactic struggle in human history. This struggle for the soul and destiny of mankind has spanned all of the generations since Adam and will see its incredible conclusion in the events of the next decades. It is no exaggeration to state that man is now faced with spiritual, political and military choices upon whose outcome the future of man rests. As we face this intense crisis over the next decade it is important to realize that all of this was foreseen by the prophets of the Bible thousands of years ago. Whether we personally believe it or not, God has His hand upon this world and He has set from the beginning of time an appointment with destiny which cannot be evaded or postponed.

Throughout recorded history, mankind has struggled with a burning desire to know its destiny. We have focused our hopes and fears on our future. Every tribe and culture in history has concerned itself with prophecy, despite the abysmal failure rate of all known prophecies outside of the Bible. In this frightening period, this interest in our destiny is heightened by the fact that for the first time in history, intelligent men can actually envision the catastrophic ending of all our hopes and dreams.

Man stands today on a path that seems to lead step by step towards the worst horrors of all our nightmares. Before us lies an abyss containing worldwide nuclear war, famine, chemical warfare, dictatorship, terrorism and the collapse of those family values which make life worthwhile.

Is there any hope for mankind? Is there any intelligent basis for believing that man will survive and go forth to build a secure, prosperous and just society in which our human potential will finally be realized?

The answer to these questions is yes, there is still hope. It is not a hope based on wishful thinking, but rather a firm confidence that beyond all the frightening prospects lies a land, "a paradise lost," which mankind has searched for with tears through all these generations. There is a basis for a realistic hope for tomorrow. We have not been left in darkness about our future. The prophecies of the Bible indicate why mankind is facing this present crisis, the events which will culminate in the final Battle of Armageddon and the tremendous promises of the Messianic Age which await fulfillment at the return of Christ.

The same God who prophesied so precisely about the details of Israel's history, which have already been fulfilled, has also told us clearly about the disaster that man will face in "the last days." God has revealed through His prophets a great amount of information about the approaching holocaust that all mankind fears and dreads. But God has also revealed the marvelous future that will immediately follow the Battle of Armageddon, when Jesus Christ will bring in the long-promised Kingdom. He prophesied that He will create a paradise on Earth and in Heaven for each of us who will put our trust in Jesus Christ. While it is true that the immediate future contains awesome and tragic events as the culmination of man's sinfulness and God's judgment; this terrible time will be followed by a Millennium of the greatest period of peace, happiness and prosperity that man has ever known.

Prophecy is not simply another branch of theology for a Christian. Our personal view of prophecy is at the heart of our faith. Our perception of God's purpose in human history will reflect our understanding of the revelation of the prophetic truths of the Bible. The overall principles we use to interpret Scripture are intimately linked to the principles we use to interpret the prophetic portions of Scripture.

An important principle to remember is that God has never abandoned His Covenant with Israel; Christ will accomplish His sovereign purpose in returning to usher in the long awaited Messianic Kingdom. Historically, many in the Church have "written off" Israel and the eternal promises which God made to her. They believe that God rejected and abandoned Israel forever because she rejected Jesus Christ, her Messiah. The Apostle Paul warned the Church against this mistake: **"I do not want you to be ignorant of this mystery, brothers, so that you may not be conceited: Israel has experienced a hardening in part until the full number of the Gentiles has come in. And so all Israel will be saved, as it is written:" (Romans 11:25,26, NIV).** God will still accomplish all of His promises to Israel.

The primary focus of this book is to present an interpretation of the unique prophecies concerning Israel and the nations; it does not focus directly on the Church. Naturally, as a committed Christian, I am vitally concerned with Christ's command to each believer to be a witness to the world and to understand His prophecies about the

Church, the Rapture of the saints and our future in heaven. These subjects will be developed at length in a second book.

Armageddon - Appointment With Destiny explores the amazingly accurate fulfillment of past prophecies and examines the prophecies that relate to this time period leading up to the Second Coming of Christ. The book will present evidence that those prophecies of the Bible, which have already been accomplished, were fulfilled to the letter. Since this is true, why is it so difficult for some people to believe that the prophecies regarding future events will also be fulfilled literally? They feel that we should interpret the language of these prophecies as myth or allegory and that nothing definite can or should be concluded regarding the interpretation of these prophecies. It is certainly true that there is a spiritual meaning and principle behind all prophetic portions of Scripture.

However, every single prophecy, which has had its fulfillment recorded in Scripture, has been fulfilled with precise accuracy down to the smallest detail. Therefore, I have taken these prophecies in a literal sense because history and the New Testament indicate that this is the correct method of interpretation. A small sample of these exact fulfillments is detailed in chapter 1.

It is inconsistent and illogical to propose that a new system of non-literal or allegorical interpretation has now been instituted since the New Testament was completed in the First Century. Therefore, we can have confidence that the prophecies about the "last days" will also be fulfilled as precisely as the specific predictions regarding Christ's Life, Death and Resurrection.

As we consider the critical importance of these prophetic events it is natural for us to inquire as to when it will all take place. Does the Bible give any indication of the time when these appointed events shall come to pass? The answer is a resounding yes! As we look back over the history of our civilization's last four thousand years in light of Scripture, we are confronted by a strange phenomenon. Despite the apparent random nature of historical dates and events, a curious pattern of astonishing complexity emerges when we examine the biblical prophecies regarding the nation of Israel and their precise fulfillment. More than forty of the most significant events in Israel's history have occurred on precise anniversaries of the feast days of the biblical calendar.

God's sovereignty over history and His foreknowledge are manifested clearly as He sets these prophetic appointments for Israel. Then, as each time cycle concludes, He keeps the appointment by bringing the prophesied event to pass at the appointed time.

This amazing phenomenon, together with proofs of the precise fulfillment of other prophecies, leads us to believe that we do not have to live in darkness regarding the major events that will occur before the Second Coming of Christ. The Apostle Peter attests to the value of prophecy: **"And we have the word of the prophets made more certain, and you will do well to pay attention to it, as to a light shining in a dark place, until the day dawns and the morning star rises in your hearts"** (2 Peter 1:19, NIV).

Jesus Christ told His disciples about the terrible events that constitute the signs of the times leading up to the Battle of Armageddon and His second coming. He then gave His disciples a clear time prediction of when this would occur. **"Now learn this lesson from the fig tree [symbol of Israel] : As soon as its twigs get tender and its leaves come out, you know that it is near, right at the door. I tell you the truth, this generation will not pass away until all these things have happened"** (Matthew 24:32-34 NIV).

On May 14, 1948, after almost nineteen hundred years of devastation and persecution, Israel was reborn as a nation—precisely to the year as foretold by the prophet Ezekiel . Therefore, based on Christ's promise in Matthew 24:32-34, our generation for the first time has a sound foundation for believing that within our natural life span (forty to seventy years) we will be witnesses to the amazing events described in the following chapters of this book. Ours is the first generation in history that can, with the firm scriptural basis of Matthew 24:32-34, have confidence that, **"When these things begin to take place, stand up and lift up your heads, for your redemption is drawing near"** (Luke 21:27-28, NIV).

CHAPTER 1

The Precision of Prophecy

"I am God, and there is none like me, Declaring the end from the beginning, and from ancient times the things that are not yet done, saying, My counsel shall stand, and I will do all my pleasure" (Isaiah 46:9-10).

One of the strongest evidences of the divine inspiration of Scripture is the phenomenon of fulfilled prophecy. The Bible is unique among the religious books of mankind in that it dares to predict future events in great detail. Other religious writings, such as the Koran or the Veda, do not contain detailed, specific prophecies. The reason for this is that it is impossible to consistently prophecy specific future events with real accuracy unless you are God. It is only when we come to examine the Bible that we find hundreds of detailed prophecies concerning various nations, events and individuals covering thousands of years.

Modern day secular prophets do dare to make predictions but they have a very poor record of accuracy. The more specific their prediction, the more certain it is to be wrong. Anyone who attempts to prophesy specific events will be confronted by the staggering odds against success created by the inescapable "laws of mathematical probability". Human wisdom will fail to accurately predict even a simple 50-50 proposition, such as who will win a football game.

To appreciate fully the difficulty of making detailed prophecies such as those found in the Bible, let us consider the comparatively simple task of predicting the precise score of tomorrow's football game between the Los Angeles Rams and the New York Jets.

There is one chance in two that the L.A. Rams will beat the N.Y. Jets. That's fairly easy to guess correctly. But what will the final score be? Assuming that most football scores are between 1 and 50, the chances of guessing correctly that the L.A.. Rams will have a particular final score (say 42 Points) at the end of the game are one chance in fifty. The odds are the same one chance in fifty of course, for predicting the N.Y. Jets' final score. Therefore, to sum up the risk of basing our reputation on predicting tomorrow's exact football score, we simply multiply the probabilities: 2 x 50 x 50 = 5000 possible score totals. This analysis shows that there is only one chance in 5000 that you will correctly pick the precise final score; that is why you would not bet a month's pay, let alone your reputation, that you would make such an exact prediction.

When you consider the difficulty of predicting accurately such a simple thing as the final score of tomorrow's football game, you can readily understand why no one, except God Himself, would dare to risk His claim to the divine inspiration of His Word, – the Bible, on such a risky undertaking—humanly speaking—as predicting future events in great detail.

Current so-called "prophets," such as those you read about in magazines, understand the odds against making such accurate predictions. They are too "wise" to risk their reputation for psychic ability by an attempt to publicly predict the actual score of a football game. Such "prophets" are content to predict that "someone who is either a member or friend of the Royal family will come close to death or injury in the next few years." Considering that there are perhaps as many as twenty people within the Royal family ,the odds are perhaps one in three of such an event transpiring with such a vague prediction.

If anyone connected with the Royal family, even a friend, is injured, the newspapers will claim this to be "an amazing psychic success" and the "seer's" reputation will remain secure for those who are easily impressed. If these "prophets" could truly predict events with any degree of accuracy, any stockbroker would be delighted to show them how they could easily earn millions of dollars each month on the stock market.

David Hocking, in his April 8, 1985, radio broadcast, "Biola Bible Class," reported on a fascinating article entitled

"The Shattered Crystal Ball." This study analyzed the accuracy of the ten top psychics whose prophecies were published over a three-year period, 1976 - 1979. The study compared all of the published predictions with their subsequent success or failure rate. The results are certainly intriguing: 98 percent of all of their predictions were totally incorrect! Only 2 percent of their predictions were fulfilled. However, some predictors were much less accurate than their colleagues: six out of the ten psychics were wrong 100 percent of the time as recorded in the study.

The four really "amazingly accurate psychics" made only one correct prediction each during the three-year study. Their crystal ball is indeed shattered. Yet, despite this hopelessly poor record, literally millions of citizens spend hard earned dollars on psychics and channellers, looking for guidance in their confused lives. These inaccurate prophets not only deceive their clients, but almost invariably promote false, cultic beliefs such as spiritualism, channelling, and other New Age occult systems.

However, when we examine the prophecies in the Bible we are confronted with a different phenomenon of staggering mathematical proportions. The Bible contains hundreds of incredibly accurate predictions of events which historians and archeologists have verified. God declares boldly in His Word that these prophecies and their fulfillments are His signature upon the Bible and His verification that the Bible is truly the inspired (God-breathed) Word of God.

God hurled forth His challenge to false prophets and false religions that has remained unanswered for over twenty-five hundred years:

"'Present your case', says the Lord. 'Set forth your arguments,' says Jacob's King. 'Bring in your idols, to tell us what is going to happen. Tell us what the former things were, so that we may consider them and know their final outcome. Or *declare to us the things to come, tell us what the future holds, so we may know that you are gods*" (Isaiah 41:22,23 NIV).

The Lord declares that accurate prophecy belongs to God alone and that He alone can prophesy accurately the future of mankind. The precision of fulfilled prophecy thus becomes not only an irrefutable proof of God's foreknowledge and sovereignty, but it also proves conclusively that the Bible is the revelation of God's truth regarding man's sinfulness and need for salvation. We are confronted with the claims of Christ regarding our sinful rebellion and His pardon which He purchased for us by His death and resurrection.

"Remember the former things of old: for I am God, and there is none else; I am God, and there is none like me, declaring the end from the beginning, and from ancient times the things that are not yet done, saying, My counsel shall stand" (Isaiah 46: 9-10).

The Laws of Probability

Statistical theory shows that if the probability of one event occurring is one in five and the probability of another event occurring is one in ten, then the probability of both events being fulfilled in sequence is five multiplied by ten. Thus, the chance of both events occurring is one in fifty.

Consider one area of specific prophecy and its fulfillment. Throughout the Old Testament, there are hundreds of prophecies in which God promised that He would send a Messiah to save humanity from their sins. To illustrate the precision of biblical prophecy, let us examine three specific predictions made by three different prophets and their detailed fulfillment in the life of Jesus Christ hundreds of years later. We also present the probability or odds of these events occurring by chance alone so that you can see how impossible it is that these prophecies were made by man's wisdom.

The Prediction and the Event	Probability
A. The Messiah would come from the tribe of Judah, one of the 12 tribes descended from Jacob **(Genesis 49:10; – Luke 3: 23-24)**	1 chance in 12
B. He would be born in Bethlehem **(Micah 5:2; – Matthew 2:1)**	1 chance in 200

C. He would be betrayed for 30
   pieces of silver
   (Zechariah 11:12; –
   Matthew 26:15)   1 chance in 50

The Combined Probability: 12 Times 200 Times
50 Equals <u>One Chance in 120 Thousand</u>

Thus, there is only one chance in 120 thousand that any man would fulfill all three prophecies by chance. For those who believe that Jesus simply arranged the events of His life to fulfill these predictions, I would respectfully point out the difficulty most of us would have in arranging our ancestors, the particular city of our birth, and the exact price in silver of our betrayal.

The Prophecies about the Messiah and the Laws of Probability

Out of many hundreds of prophecies concerning the promised Messiah, some four dozen are quite specific. Including the three we have already mentioned, the following is an analysis of eleven Messianic predictions made more than four hundred years before they were fulfilled.

The odds I have assigned in this chapter are obviously arbitrary estimates. Some of my readers will find that the odds I have suggested are too liberal or too conservative in some cases. What odds would you assign for the accuracy of these predictions coming true by chance, rather than Divine sovereignty? If you have other suggestions for the odds for any particular predictions; work out the math along with me and develop your own mathematical probabilities for these eleven prophecies being fulfilled by chance alone. Regardless of your estimates, the combined mathematical probability is staggering.

The Eleven Predictions: The Odds Against This Occurring:

The promised Messiah would:

 1. Be born in Bethlehem Probability: **1 in 200**

Old Testament Prediction:
"But thou, Bethlehem Ephratah, though thou be little

among the thousands of Judah, yet out of thee shall he come forth unto me that is to be ruler in Israel" (Micah 5:2).

New Testament Fulfillment:
"Jesus was born in Bethlehem of Judea in the days of Herod the King" (Matthew 2:1).

2. Be preceded by a messenger   Probability: 1 in 20

Old Testament Prediction:
"The voice of him that crieth in the wilderness, Prepare ye the way of the Lord, make straight in the desert a highway for our God" (Isaiah 40:3).

New Testament Fulfillment:
"In those days came John the Baptist, preaching in the wilderness of Judea, and saying, Repent ye: for the kingdom of heaven is at hand" (Matthew 3:1-2).

3. Enter Jerusalem on a colt   Probability: 1 in 50

Old Testament Prediction:
"Rejoice greatly, O daughter of Zion; shout, O daughter of Jerusalem: behold, thy King cometh unto thee: he is just, and having salvation; lowly, and riding upon an ass, and upon a colt the foal of an ass" (Zechariah 9:9).

New Testament Fulfillment:
"And they brought him to Jesus: and they cast their garments upon the colt, and they set Jesus thereon. And as he went, they spread their clothes in the way. And when he was come nigh, even now at the descent of the mount of Olives, the whole multitude of the disciples began to rejoice and praise God with a loud voice for all mighty works that they had seen" (Luke 19:35-37).

4. Be betrayed by a friend   Probability: 1 in 10

Old Testament Prediction:
"Yea, mine own familiar friend, in whom I trusted, which did eat of my bread, hath lifted up his heel against me" (Psalms 41:9).

New Testament Fulfillment:
"And while he yet spake, lo, Judas, one of the twelve, came, and with him a great multitude with swords and staves, from the chief priests and elders of the people. Now he that betrayed him gave them a sign, saying, Whomsoever I shall kiss, that same is he; hold him

fast.... and Jesus said unto him, 'Friend, wherefore art thou come?'" (Matthew 26:47-50)

5. Have His hands and feet pierced   Probability: 1 in 100

Old Testament Prediction:
"The assembly of the wicked have inclosed me: they pierced my hands and my feet" (Psalm 22:16).

New Testament Fulfillment:
"And when they were come to the place, which is called Calvary, there they crucified him, and the malefactors, one on the right hand, and the other on the left" (Luke 23:33).

6. Be Wounded and Whipped by His Enemies
Probability: 1 in 25

Old Testament Prediction:
"But he was wounded for our transgressions, he was bruised for our iniquities: the chastisement of our peace was upon him; and by his stripes we are healed" (Isaiah 53:5).

New Testament Fulfillment:
"Then released he Barabbas unto them: and when he had scourged Jesus, he delivered him to be crucified" (Matthew 27:26).

7. Be Sold for Thirty Pieces of Silver   Probability: 1 in 100

Old Testament Prediction:
"And I said unto them, If ye think good, give me my price; and if not, forbear. So they weighed for my price thirty pieces of silver" (Zechariah 11:12).

New Testament Fulfillment:
"What will ye give me, and I will deliver him unto you? And they covenanted with him for thirty pieces of silver" (Matthew 26:15).

8. Be spit upon and beaten   Probability: 1 in 10

Old Testament Prediction:
"I gave my back to the smiters, and my cheeks to them that plucked off the hair: I hid not my face from shame and spitting" (Isaiah 50:6).

New Testament Fulfillment:
"Then did they spit in his face, and buffeted him; and others smote him with the palms of their hands" (Matthew 26:67).

9. **Have His betrayal money thrown in the Temple and given for a potter's field** **Probability 1 in 200**

Old Testament Prediction:

"And the Lord said unto me, Cast it unto the potter: a goodly price that I was prized at of them. And I took the thirty pieces of silver and cast them to the potter in the house of the Lord" (Zechariah 11:13).

New Testament Fulfillment:

"And he cast down the pieces of silver in the temple, and departed, and went and hanged himself. And the chief priests took the silver pieces, and said, It is not lawful for to put them into the treasury, because it is the price of blood. And they took counsel, and bought with them the potter's field, to bury strangers in" (Matthew 27: 5-7).

10. **Be silent before His accusers** **Probability: 1 in 100**

Old Testament Prediction:

"He was oppressed, and he was afflicted, yet he opened not his mouth: he is brought as a lamb to the slaughter, and as a sheep before her shearers is dumb, so he openeth not his mouth" (Isaiah 53:7).

New Testament Fulfillment:

"And when he was accused of the chief priests and elders, he answered nothing. Then said Pilate unto him, Hearest thou not how many things they witness against thee? And he answered him never a word; insomuch that the governor marvelled greatly" (Matthew 27:12-14).

11. **Be crucified with thieves** **Probability: 1 in 100**

Old Testament Prediction:

"He hath poured out his soul unto death: and he was numbered with the transgressors; and he bare the sin of many and made intercession for the transgressors" (Isaiah 53:12).

New Testament Fulfillment:

"Then were there two thieves crucified with him, one on the right hand, and another on the left" (Matthew 27:38).

The Combined Probability Is Equal To
One Chance in 10 to the 19th power

In other words, there is only one chance in 10 billion times a billion that the prophets could have accurately predicted these eleven specific prophecies by chance alone, or that any one man's life could fulfill these detailed prophecies by chance alone; in fact, it is obviously impossible!

Regarding the estimates I have given for the probability of these specific events occurring purely by chance, let us consider the first prophecy of Micah's that was written more than seven hundred years before its fulfillment, that the promised Messiah would be born in the insignificant village of Bethlehem. I have assigned a probability of one chance in two- hundred to the possibility of Israel's King being born in this little village by chance alone. In Israel, as in all other countries with monarchies, virtually all of the kings were born in palaces in their capital, Jerusalem, and almost never in a small agricultural village. Let us assume then that the odds of a king being born in the country rather than in the capital city is one in ten, which is a very conservative estimate. Since Israel had thousands of small villages, the odds against picking the correct village by chance alone, is conservatively one in one thousand. Therefore, to be realistic, the odds against correctly predicting the birthplace of the promised King is one in ten; (the odds on the capital versus a rural village) to which we multiply one chance in one thousand; (the odds on picking the right village) which produces a combined probability on one chance in ten thousand. However, in an attempt to be very conservative, I have assigned the probability as only one chance in two hundred; not using the figure of one chance in ten thousand, which could easily be justified.

The prophecy of Jesus having "his hands and feet pierced", for example, is given odds of 1 in 100. This prediction in the Psalms was made more than 500 years before the Roman Empire invented crucifixion as an unusual and barbaric method of execution. The prophecy that He would be wounded and whipped by his enemies is given odds of 1 in 25. This also is very conservative in that few kings in history have been subjected to whipping by their enemies. The prophecy of His silence before His

21

accusers is given odds of 1 in 100. The number of leaders and teachers who have been unjustly accused and executed, who have chosen to remain silent and not defend themselves is miniscule. Most of us would loudly defend ourselves against our accusers if we were faced with torture, whipping and death by agonizing crucifixion, even if we were guilty, much less if we, like Christ, were innocent of the charges.

Another point should be considered by those who are mathematically inclined and who feel that my assigned probabilities are too high. Go ahead and assign the most conservative numbers possible to these combined prophetic probabilities about the life of Jesus the Messiah. You will still be confronted with a probability so staggering in its magnitude that it is impossible to honestly convince yourself that these things occurred by chance. In the unlikely event that you are still not convinced, you should consider that we have listed only eleven of the forty-eight major prophecies given in the Old Testament about the promised Messiah.

The Bible's Precise Prophecies Prove That It Alone is the Word of God

When we consider all forty-eight of the specific Messianic prophecies, the odds against any one life fulfilling these predictions by chance alone are simply astronomical. In order that we might grasp the reality of this prophetic proof that Jesus Christ is, in absolute certainty, the promised Messiah and Son of God, consider the following illustration:

1. The odds of the prophets of the Bible correctly guessing all eleven prophecies is: 1 chance in 10 to the 19th power.

Only one chance in 10 billion times 1 billion

2. Let each chance in 1 to the 19th power (10 billion times a billion) represent an area of the ocean floor only 1/20th of an inch square (the size of one printed letter on this page). The entire remaining parts of the earth's ocean floor will represent all of the other chances against Jesus fulfilling these eleven prophecies by chance.

22

3. To see just how "lucky" the biblical prophets had to be to predict those eleven significant events; imagine that someone dropped a diamond ring from a plane somewhere over one of the oceans. You enter a bet that you can locate it with just one try, using a long line and a fishhook. You can wander over earth's oceans (197,000,000 square miles of surface) in your boat for as long as you like. When you feel lucky, stop, drop the line and try to hook the diamond ring that is lying thousands of feet below you on the ocean floor. You only get one try.

Your odds of finding the lost ring are precisely equal to the odds against the biblical prophets correctly predicting those eleven specific details in the life of Jesus Christ, the promised Messiah.

With such odds against you, would you bet one month's salary that you would find the ring? I doubt that you would risk your money on such impossible odds. Yet, sadly, every year millions will die who have bet their lives and their eternal destinies on the "chance" that fulfilled prophecy and the Bible are not reliable, and they can therefore safely ignore the claims of Christ upon their lives.

"For God so loved the world, that he gave his only begotten Son, that whosoever believeth in him should not perish, but have everlasting life. He that believeth on him is not condemned: but he that believeth not is condemned already, because he hath not believed in the name of the only begotten Son of God" (John 3:16,18).

This book will focus primarily on the interpretation of the predictive elements of the message of the biblical prophets. However, the role of the prophet and his message is much broader than simply the prediction of spiritually significant future events. There are three words used in the Bible to describe a prophet – Ro'eh, Hozeh and Nabi. In combination, they reveal that his role includes both that of the seer as well as an exhortation to personal and national righteousness. Prophecy includes a declaration of God's sovereign design as it unfolds itself in human history and His call to our obedience to that revealed will, both individually and corporately. In summary, the message of the prophet is twofold: First, God's coming judgment of sin, but secondly, it declares the hope in the immediate and ultimate triumph of God's truth and purpose. Both the past and the future are united together in the message of the prophet through the prophetic revelation that God is guiding human history toward that day when the kingdoms of this world will truly become the kingdoms of Christ.

Several important principles of Biblical prophetic interpretation are reflected in this book and have developed from my twenty-five years of Bible study and teaching: (1) Take all Scripture in its ordinary, usual and common sense meaning unless the context makes it clear that the statement is symbolic. (2) Symbolic language is usually interpreted in a clear fashion in another biblical passage. (3) God has consistently prophesied and set appointed times for Israel and the nations which have been fulfilled to the exact day as predicted. The Lord has always dealt with Israel in terms of specifically appointed time periods and the Promised Land. (4) However, in dealing with the Church, Scripture reveals no appointed time period pinpointing the "day or the hour" of the Rapture, when Christ takes the believers to heaven. (5) The message of the prophet is both for his own time and for all the generations which will follow him. It's purpose is not simply to provide information, but rather to challenge our behavior and our life priorities in light of Christ's lordship of our present as well as our future.

While it is certainly true that many details in the unfolding plan of God in history will not be known until they come to pass, four factors encourage us to examine those prophecies which point to the events leading up to the time of Christ's return to set up His Kingdom: (1) the importance that God puts on His prophecies - over one quarter of the Bible is prophetic and He directs us to study it; (2) Fulfilled prophecies, such as the ones in this chapter, encourage us to believe that future prophecies will be fulfilled in a similar, "literal" manner; (3) Christ criticized the religious leaders of His day for failing to pay attention to the prophecies and failing to "discern the signs of the times"; (4) the Apostle Paul specifically reminds Christians that while it is true that, "the Day of the Lord so cometh as a thief in the night" to unbelievers, he immediately goes on to declare an important truth: *"But ye, brethren, are not in darkness, that that day should overtake you as a thief. Ye are all the children of light, and the children of the day: we are not of the night, nor of darkness. Therefore let us not* sleep, as do others: *but let us watch and be sober*" *(1 Thessalonians 5: 4-6).*

These factors encourage us to carefully and prudently examine those prophecies which clearly relate to our generation.

In the following chapters we will look into some exciting prophecies that have already been fulfilled to the exact day. However, the final chapters should prove very interesting as we look into those prophecies that still remain to be fulfilled in our generation.

God will continue to fulfill His ancient prophecies as He has in the past. The Lord Himself says, **"For I am the Lord, I change not" (Malachi 3:6).** We will also analyze those appointments with destiny that God has set for Israel and the nations, based on the ancient biblical calendar, and discover indications of when these final events will come to pass.

CHAPTER 2

Daniel's Prophecy of the Seventy Weeks of Years

"Seventy weeks [490 Years] are determined upon thy people and upon thy holy city, to finish the transgression and to make an end of sins, and to make reconciliation for iniquity, and to bring in everlasting righteousness and to seal up the vision and prophecy, and to anoint the most Holy. Know therefore and understand, that from the going forth of the commandment to restore and to build Jerusalem unto the Messiah the Prince shall be seven weeks, and threescore and two weeks: the street shall be built again, and the wall, even in troublous times. And after threescore and two weeks shall Messiah be cut off but not for himself: and the people of the prince that shall come shall destroy the city and the sanctuary; and the end thereof shall be with a flood, and unto the end of the war desolations are determined. And he shall confirm the covenant with many for one week: and in the midst of the week he shall cause the sacrifice and the oblation to cease" (Daniel 9:24-27).

Nebuchadnezzar, King of Babylon, conquered Jerusalem in 606 B.C. and returned home with a group of royal captives, including a young man named Daniel. These Jewish captives were to be trained in all of the wisdom of this pagan empire so that they could eventually serve as royal advisors. Daniel distinguished himself by his exemplary character, his wisdom and the tremendous prophetic gifts which God had bestowed upon him due to his faithfulness. As a result of these prophetic abilities Daniel was elevated from the position of a captive slave to ultimately become the First Minister of this great Babylonian Empire which ruled the known world.

While Daniel was taken to Babylon with the other captives, his contemporary, the prophet Jeremiah, continued to prophecy to the remainder of the Jewish people living under the Babylonian army of occupation in Jerusalem. Jeremiah declared that **"this whole land shall be a desolation, and an astonishment; and these nations shall serve the king of Babylon seventy years"** (Jeremiah 25:11).

In 538 B.C. Daniel was reading this prediction and knew that the seventy years of the Babylonian Captivity would end within two years in 536 B.C. He began to pray and ask God to reveal to him the future of the Jewish people. While he was interceding on behalf of his people and Jerusalem, God answered by sending His angel Gabriel to give him "skill and understanding" about the future course of history. Daniel received one of the most amazing visions ever given to man. This vision of the Seventy Weeks of years foretold to the precise day when Israel would reject and "cut off" their Messiah and then looks forward almost two thousand years to His Second Coming to set up His everlasting kingdom. It is an unusual prophecy because the time element is given so specifically and clearly. Daniel 9:24-27, recorded at the beginning of this chapter, provides the details of this revelation.

In 1895, Sir Robert Anderson, a gifted biblical scholar and the head of Scotland Yard, wrote a fascinating review of this prophecy to Daniel. In a masterful work, he proved that the portion of that prophecy that begins with, **"From the going forth of the commandment to restore and to build Jerusalem unto the Messiah the Prince shall be seven weeks [sevens], and threescore and two weeks [sevens]"** was fulfilled to the exact day 483 biblical years (each year equalling 360 days) after it commenced.

An important but often overlooked point in considering the chronology of prophecy is that of the length of the prophetic year. The Jewish year of biblical times was lunar-solar and had only 360 days. The solar year, which we live by, of 365.25 days was unknown to the nations in the Old Testament. According to the *Encyclopedia Britannica* and *Smith's Bible Dictionary* on Chronolgy, Abraham continued to use a year of 360 days in his original Chaldean homeland. The record of the history of Noah's flood confirms that a thirty day month was used in the book of Genesis (150 days are recorded as the five month interval between the seventeenth day of the second month to the seventeenth day of the seventh month). Sir Isaac Newton relates that "all nations, before the just length of the solar year was known, reckoned months by the course of the moon, and years by the return of winter and summer, spring and autumn; and in making calendars for their festivals, they reckoned thirty days to a lunar month, and twelve lunar months to a year, taking the nearest round numbers, whence came the division of the ecliptic into 360 degrees." *(see the Appendix section on the 360 day Biblical year.)*

Therefore, if we wish to understand the precise times involved in the fulfillment of prophecy, we still need to use the same biblical lunar-solar year of 360 days which the prophets themselves used. If the prophet Daniel made an appointment to meet someone in one year, he would arrive in 360 days, not 365 days. The failure to understand and utilize the true biblical year of 360 days has prevented a clear understanding of Daniel's vision of the Seventy Weeks and many other prophecies which contain a time element. This is borne out in the book of Revelation where John's vision refers to the Great Tribulation. It describes the last three and one-half years as precisely 1260 days (Revelation 12:6), "a time, times and half a time" where a "time" in Hebrew stands for a year of 360 days (verse 14), and "forty-two months" of thirty days each (13:5). All of these references reaffirm that the 360-day biblical year, is the one by which we must calculate biblical prophecy.

Summary of Anderson's Calculation of Daniel's Seventy Weeks

First, Anderson stated that the commencement point of the vision is **"the commandment to rebuild the walls of Jerusalem,"** which begins in Daniel 9:25. This decree was issued by the Persian King Artaxerxes Longimanus "in the month of Nisan, in the twentieth year" of his reign according to Nehemiah 2:1. "The first day of the month of Nisan," according to the *Talmud* (a collection of writings that constitute Jewish civil and religious law), "is the New Year for the computation of the reign of kings and for festivals. "The 1st of Nisan in King Artaxerxes' twentieth year was computed by the Royal Observatory , Greenwich United Kingdom, as March 14, 445 BC."

Second, "**from the commandment to restore and to build Jerusalem**" given on March 14, 445 B.C., there is a period of seven "weeks" (7 x 7 = 49 years), and sixty-two "weeks" (62 x 7 = 434 years) which total 69 weeks of years (69 x 7 years = 483 Biblical years). This period of 483 Biblical years equals 173,880 days.

$$(483 \times 360 \text{ days} = 173,880 \text{ days})$$

Third, at the end of the sixty-nine "weeks" (483 years), or 173,880 days there would be a time when, according to Daniel, the "**Messiah will be cut off**". On the tenth day of Nisan, April 6, A.D. 32, on Palm Sunday, in fulfillment of this prophecy, Jesus Christ entered Jerusalem and presented Himself as "the Messiah". (See "The Date of Christ's Ministry and Crucifixion" in the Appendix.)

On that joy-filled day the Messiah rode into Jerusalem on the back of a foal and his disciples recognized Him as the Messiah, proclaiming, "**Blessed be the King that cometh in the name of the Lord: peace in heaven, and glory in the highest**" (Luke 19:38). However, the Pharisees and most of the people refused to acknowledge Him as their Messiah. They called out to Jesus, "**Master, rebuke thy disciples**" (verse 39).

But Jesus replied to the Pharisees that "if these should hold their peace, the stones would immediately cry out". Then Luke describes the scene as Jesus approached Jerusalem "**he beheld the city, and wept over it, saying, If thou hadst known, even thou, at least *in this thy day*, the things which belong unto thy peace! but now they are hid from thine eyes. For the days shall come upon thee, that thine enemies shall cast a trench about thee, and compass thee round, and keep thee in on every side, and shall lay thee even with the ground, and thy children within thee; and they shall not leave in thee one stone upon another; *because thou knewest not the time of thy visitation*" (Luke 19:41-44)**

In the preceding passage, Jesus emphasized the fact that this day, the tenth day of Nisan, April 6, A.D. 32, was an incredibly important day for Israel. This was the "time of thy visitation," their decision day, in which they had to decide whether or not to accept Jesus as their prophesied Messiah-King. Despite the acclaim of Jesus' disciples and some of the country's citizens, the reaction of the nation's religious and political leaders to their time of visitation was to reject their Messiah. Five days later this rejection culminated in the crucifixion of Jesus and their promised kingdom has now been postponed for almost two thousand years.

In A.D. 70, less than forty years after Christ's prophecy, the Roman army besieged Jerusalem, killed more than one million of her inhabitants, and totally fulfilled Christ's prophecy that **"they shall not leave in thee one stone upon another"(Luke 19:44).** The fearsome cry of the people, **"Let him be crucified" (Matthew 27:23)** and, **"His blood be on us, and on our children" (Matthew 27:25)** had its tragic fulfillment, according to Flavius Josephus in his *Wars Of The Jews*, Book 5, chapter 11, section 2, when he describes the hills surrounding Jerusalem that were studded with thousands of crosses as far as the eye could see during the tragic final siege of Jerusalem in A.D. 70.

To sum up these calculations; Daniel's vision spoke of a total of seventy "sevens" or seventy "weeks" of years, equalling 490 biblical years. This period of time, beginning with the command to rebuild the walls of Jerusalem (March 14, 445 B.C.) until the Messiah is "cut off" (April 6, A.D. 32, the tenth of Nisan) is seven "sevens" plus sixty-two "sevens," equal to sixty-nine "weeks of years" (173,880 days). This prophecy was fulfilled to the exact day. (Note: In calculating the duration in years between any date in B.C. - Before Christ, to any date in A.D. - Anno Domini-In the year of our Lord, one year must always be omitted. Therefore, the time lapse between Passover in 1 B.C. and the next passover in A.D.1 is only one year; not two years. There is no such year as 0 B.C.)

For those who want to confirm these calculations for the period of the 69 "weeks" by working back from our calendar dates; follow this through with a calculator. From March 14, 445 B.C. (the date of the command to rebuild Jerusalem) to March 14, A.D. 32 is 476 years of 365 days each -- 173,740 days. Add the 24 days from March 14, A.D. 32 until April 6 A.D.32 (Palm Sunday - the "cutting off" of Messiah)-- twenty-four days. Then add the 116 leap days which occurred during that period (calculated by the Royal Observatory, Greenwich, United Kingdom) = 116 days. Add together (173,740 + 24 + 116 = 173,880) and you will get

30

the total of 173,880 days, the exact duration of Daniel's 69 "weeks" of years = 173,880 days.

The first sixty-nine "weeks" of Daniel's vision have been fulfilled to the very day. The last seventieth "week" of seven critical years remains to be fulfilled in our generation. *(see figure 1)*

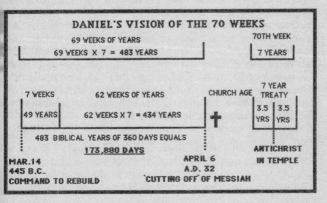

Figure 1

When we thoughtfully and fairly consider the incredible accuracy of Daniel's prophecy, how could we possibly doubt that the remaining "week" of seven years, the seventieth "week" of years, will be fulfilled just as precisely?

The final week of Daniel 9:27, is the climactic seven years towards which all of Jewish and Gentile human history has been inexorably focused. When Israel rejected Jesus Christ as their promised Messiah on Palm Sunday, April 6, A.D. 32, "the time of thy visitation" on the last day of Daniel's sixty-ninth week of prophecy, one part of God's prophetic clock was stopped and the Lord postponed their prophesied Kingdom for almost two thousand years.

An analogy of this postponement of the promised Kingdom can be found in the parallel situation some fifteen hundred years earlier when Israel stopped at the very edge of the Promised Land and awaited the report of the 12 tribal leaders who spied out Canaan. If Israel had believed and obeyed God at that time, they could have immediately gone in to possess the Promised Land. However, the tragic history in Exodus tells us that through their disobedience and disbelief in God's promises, the people rejected both God's Word and His leader, Moses, and sought to stone him and Aaron. The rejection by the people led to the forty years in the wilderness and the loss of that entire generation who died without seeing the fulfillment of the original conditional promise of the land of Canaan. The entry into the Promised Land was postponed until a new generation appeared who were ready to believe God's promises and receive the prophesied Kingdom. In an analogous way, the nation of Israel missed their time of visitation and their Messiah in A.D. 32 and have now had to wait almost two thousand years to once more return to that point where they can begin to hear the steps of their Messiah approaching to finally usher in their long awaited Kingdom.

During this interval between Daniel's sixty-ninth week and the final seventieth week, God has created a Church of both Jews and Gentiles from all nations whose purpose is to witness to all the world and to offer God's salvation to any who would accept Jesus Christ as Lord and Savior.

Also during this period, the prophecy that "war and desolations" would continue until the end has been tragically fulfilled. Yet, God also promised that although **"blindness in part is happened to Israel, until the fullness of the Gentiles be come in. And so all Israel shall be saved" (Romans 11:25-26).**

Daniel 9:24 specifically tells us that "seventy weeks" are decreed for your people, the Jews. The first sixty-nine weeks of years focused upon God's dealing with the Jewish people and on His witnessing to the world through His "chosen people." In the same manner, the central focus of this final seventieth "week" of seven years will again be on God's dealing directly with Israel and His witnessing through them to the world of His coming kingdom, as we will describe in chapter 11.

God will never leave the world without a witness. Once the Church has been raptured (miraculously resurrected to join Christ in heaven), God will turn His focus once more to His people, Israel, now back in the Holy Land with a rebuilt Temple. Christ promised that **"this gospel of the kingdom shall be preached in all the world for a witness unto all** nations; and then shall the end come" (Matthew 24:14). This "gospel of the kingdom" will be the same message that both John the Baptist and Jesus preached during His three and one-half years of ministry, which ended on Palm Sunday, the end of the sixty-ninth week of years.

John the Baptist preached, **"Repent ye: for the kingdom of heaven is at hand. For this is He that was spoken of by the prophet Esaias, [Isaiah], saying, The voice of one crying in the wilderness, Prepare ye the way of the Lord, make his paths straight"** (Matthew 3: 2-3). And, **"From that time Jesus began to preach, and to say, 'Repent: for the kingdom of heaven is at hand'"** (Matthew 4:17).

CHAPTER 3

Ezekiel's Vision of the Rebirth of Israel in 1948

"This shall be a sign to the house of Israel. Lie thou also upon thy left side, and lay the iniquity of the house of Israel upon it: according to the number of the days that thou shalt lie upon it thou shalt bear their iniquity. For I have laid upon thee the years of their iniquity, according to the number of the days, three hundred and ninety days: so shalt thou bear the iniquity of the house of Israel. And when thou hast accomplished them, lie again on thy right side, and thou shalt bear the iniquity of the house of Judah forty days: I have appointed thee each day for a year" (Ezekiel 4:3-6).

It appears that in God's divine purpose, many of the details of the last days were sealed in visions in such a way that they could not be clearly discerned prior to their accomplishment. Each prophecy must be interpreted carefully in the light of the rest of Scripture. A sincere student of the Word must be very careful when he moves from the clear, broad outlines of prophecy (e.g. the restoration of Israel and the revival of a ten-fold division of the Roman Empire) into the specific forecasting of exact times and the sequences of events of the latter days.

To illustrate the problem: consider the four different prophecies about the earthly home of Jesus Christ. He is described in the Old Testament as (1) being born in Bethlehem (2) coming forth out of Egypt (3) being a Nazarene and (4) being presented as the King of the Jews in Jerusalem. On the face of it, these four prophecies seem totally contradictory, and yet each one of them was fulfilled to the letter in Christ's life. He was born in Bethlehem, spent several years in Egypt, was raised in Nazareth and was presented in Jerusalem as their King.

From the viewpoint of looking back to the time when Jesus Christ came to earth, Bible scholars can clearly see something of the nature of prophecy. While there was some expectation and knowledge of details surrounding Christ's birth before that day, (for example, that it would take place in Bethlehem), it was only after the events had occurred that believers could search the Old Testament and see how a truly incredible amount of detailed prophecy had been fulfilled to the letter in the life, death and resurrection of Jesus.

In this chapter, I will confine my observations to a single event that has taken place in recent history which has tremendous implications. **"Henceforth there is laid up for me a crown of righteousness, which the Lord, the righteous judge, shall give me at that day: and not to me only, but unto all them also that love his appearing"** (2 Timothy 4:8).

A basic principle of scripture is that times are always specified in great detail for Israel, but are never given for the Church. We would look in vain for any date or calculation that will reveal the time of the Rapture. God has specifically hidden this time from all but Himself. It is the failure to appreciate this fact that has led to so much error in prophetic interpretation.

Israel's relationship to the land is a major focus of prophecy, both fulfilled and unfulfilled. God prophesied precisely when Israel would return to the Promised Land on the past two occasions – after her captivity in Egypt and in Babylon.

Israel's First Captivity and Return

On the 14th day of Nisan, the exact day that would become the date of Passover, the Lord appeared to Abraham to give him the Covenant for the Promised Land. God also prophesied that Abraham's descendents would be in affliction and bondage for a period of 430 years.

"And he said unto Abraham, Know of a surety that thy seed shall be a stranger in a land that is not their's, and shall serve them, and they shall afflict them four hundred years" (Genesis 15:13). The mistreatment of the seed of

Abraham (his descendants) began just thirty years after God gave Abraham the promise of the "land." **"And the child [Ishmael] grew, and was weaned: and Abraham made a great feast the same day that Isaac was weaned. And Sarah saw the son of Hagar the Egyptian, which she had born unto Abraham, mocking. Wherefore she said unto Abraham, Cast out this bondwoman and her son: for the son of this bondwoman shall not be heir with my son, even with Isaac" (Genesis 21:8-10).** This mocking began the affliction of Abraham's seed in Canaan and eventually ended in the bondage in Egypt and in the killing of male infants (Abraham's descendants) by the Egyptians. **"Now the sojourning of the children of Israel, who dwelt in Egypt, was four hundred and thirty years. And it came to pass *at the end of the four hundred and thirty years, even the selfsame day it came to pass,* that all the hosts of the Lord went out from the land of Egypt" (Exodus 12:40-41).**

On Passover, on the exact day that the 430 years ended, God fulfilled His promise and brought Israel out of the bondage of Egypt to become a mighty nation. (see figure 1) The Apostle Paul, in his letter to the Galatians, confirmed that God fulfilled His promise of ending the captivity precisely 430 years after the promise was given to Abraham (Galatians 3:17).

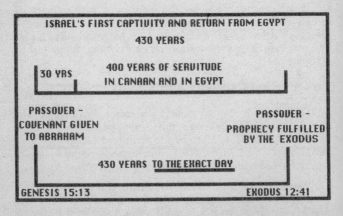

ISRAEL'S FIRST CAPTIVITY AND RETURN FROM EGYPT

430 YEARS

30 YRS

400 YEARS OF SERVITUDE
IN CANAAN AND IN EGYPT

PASSOVER –
COVENANT GIVEN
TO ABRAHAM

PASSOVER –
PROPHECY FULFILLED
BY THE EXODUS

430 YEARS TO THE EXACT DAY

GENESIS 15:13

EXODUS 12:41

Figure 1

Israel's Second Captivity and Return

When the Israelites finally reached the Promised Land after their Exodus from Egypt--and after an additional forty years of wandering as punishment for their disbelief; there followed a period of time when Israel followed the leadership of God, with only a few lapses during the time of the Judges, the descendants of Abraham. This lasted until the kingdom was divided after the death of King Solomon.

Years of rebellion against God followed during which the people, led by some of their worst kings, turned to idol worship and other gods. God's constant warnings to His people through His prophets were ignored. The people of the ten northern tribes, called Israel, were the first to be conquered in 721 B.C.: **"In the ninth year of Hoshea the king of Assyria took Samaria, and carried Israel away into Assyria" (2 Kings 17:6)**. Then, from the kingdom of Judah, Jeremiah gave the final prophecy before the people of Judah were also removed from their Promised Land and taken captive in 606 B.C.: **"And this whole land shall be a desolation, and an astonishment; and these nations shall serve the king of Babylon seventy years" (Jeremiah 25:11)**.

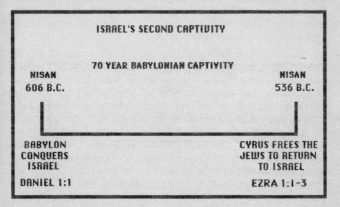

Figure 2

Seventy years later, true to Jeremiah's prophecy, King Cyrus of Persia overthrew the Babylonian Empire and released the Jews, just as Jeremiah had prophesied. History records that the captivity began in the month of Nisan, 606 B.C. and ended seventy years later exactly as prophesied on the first day of Nisan, 536 B.C. (see figure 2.) Ezra records the decree of King Cyrus: **"Who is there among you of all his people? his God be with him, and let him go up to Jerusalem, which is in Judah, and build the house of the Lord God of Israel,(he is the God) which is in Jerusalem"** (Ezra 1:3).

However, only a remnant of the Jews took advantage of the opportunity to leave the Babylonian captivity and return to Israel (fewer than fifty thousand). The vast majority never returned, choosing rather to live in the nation of their captivity.

Israel's Third and Worldwide Captivity

Throughout the Old Testament there are prophecies of a final return of the exiles to the Promised Land in the "last days." Consider the precision with which God revealed the duration of the earlier dispersions and captivities. It seemed probable to me, as a student of biblical history and prophecy, that hidden somewhere in Scripture, there would be a clue revealing the time when the Jews would return from their final worldwide captivity, to their Promised Land and once again establish a nation.

The prophet Ezekiel, like Daniel, was carried off to Babylon as a captive. He prophesied there for about twenty years. Also, like Daniel, he was aware from the prophecies of Jeremiah; that the captivity in Babylon would last seventy years. All three prophets were contemporaries of each other. Then the Lord appeared to Ezekiel in a vision and gave him the prophecy we quoted at the beginning of this chapter: **"This shall be a sign to the house of Israel. Lie thou also upon thy left side, and lay the iniquity of the house of Israel upon it: according to the number of the days that thou shalt lie upon it thou shalt bear their iniquity. For I have laid upon thee the years of their iniquity, according to the number of the days, three hundred and ninety days: so shalt thou bear the iniquity of the house of Israel. And when thou hast accomplished them, lie again on thy right side, and thou shalt bear the iniquity of the house of Judah forty days: I have appointed thee each day for a year"** (Ezekiel 4:3-6).

In this prophecy we are given a sign and a clear interpretation that each day represents one biblical year. Ezekiel was told that Israel would be punished for 390 years and for 40 years. As prophesied, at the end of the seventy years of captivity in Babylon, in the spring of 536 B.C., in the month Nisan, under the decree of the Persian king, Cyrus, a small remnant of the house of Judah returned to Jerusalem.

The vast majority were content to remain in the pagan Persian Empire as colonists. Out of a total decreed punishment of 430 years for Israel's and Judah's sin (390 years plus 40 years = 430 years); once you deduct the 70 years of the Babylonian captivity which ended in 536 B.C.; there is a total of 360 years of further punishment beyond 536 B.C., the end of the Babylonian Captivity. *(see figure 3.)*

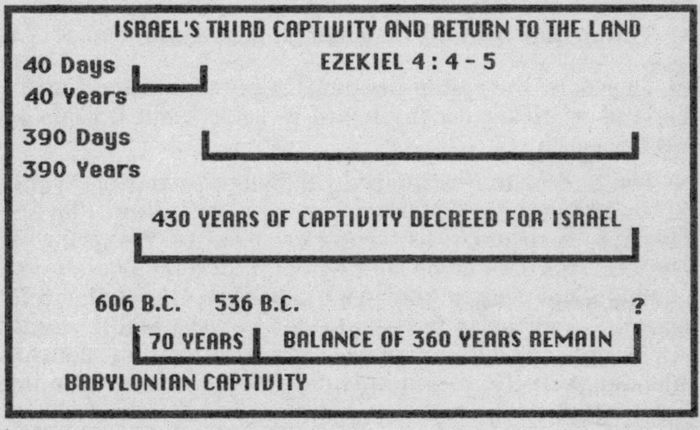

ISRAEL'S THIRD CAPTIVITY AND RETURN TO THE LAND
EZEKIEL 4 : 4 – 5

40 Days
40 Years

390 Days
390 Years

430 YEARS OF CAPTIVITY DECREED FOR ISRAEL

606 B.C.   536 B.C.   ?

70 YEARS   BALANCE OF 360 YEARS REMAIN

BABYLONIAN CAPTIVITY

Figure 3

However, a close scrutiny of Israel's history fails to yield any significant period that corresponds to this period of 360 years of additional punishment, either at the end of the 430 years or at the end of the 360 years. It should be noted that, historically, Israel did <u>not</u> repent of its sin at the end of the seventy years in Babylon. In fact, even the minority of fifty thousand who chose to return with Ezra to the Promised Land did so with little faith . The larger part of the nation failed to repent of their sin and disobedience, which caused

God to send them into captivity. The majority simply settled down as colonists in what is now Iraq-Iran.

The solution to the mystery of the duration of Israel's worldwide dispersion and return is found in a divine principle revealed to Israel in Leviticus 26. In this chapter the Lord established promises and punishments for Israel based on her obedience and her disobedience. On four different occasions in this passage, God told Israel that if, after being punished for her sins, she still did not repent, the punishments previously specified would be multiplied by seven (the number of completion). **"And if ye will not yet for all this hearken unto me, then I will punish you seven times more for your sins" (Leviticus 26:18; see also Leviticus 26:21, 23-24, 27-28).** In other words, if Israel did not repent; the punishments already promised would be prolonged seven times:

$$360 \text{ years} \times 7 = 2{,}520 \text{ biblical years}$$

Therefore, the end of the punishment and restoration to the land would be accomplished in 2,520 biblical years of 360 days each.

The end of the captivity in Babylon, according to the Bible and other historical sources--including Flavius Josephus, is recorded as having occurred in the spring of 536 B.C. This date is the starting point for our calculations: **2,520 biblical years x 360 = 907,200 days.** Converting this figure into our calendar year of 365.25 days and dividing 365.25 into 907,200 days we reach a total of **2,483.8 calendar years.** (In these calculations we must keep in mind that there is only one year between 1 B.C. and A.D. 1). Therefore, the end of Israel's worldwide captivity would occur after a total of 2,483.8 years had elapsed from the Spring of 536 B.C.

End of Babylonian Captivity in the Spring of 536 B.C.	**536 B.C.**
PLUS	+
The Duration of Worldwide Captivity	**2483.8 Calendar Years**

The End of Third Captivity	
The Rebirth of Israel	**1948 May 14th**

On May 14th, 1948, an event transpired which shocked foreign governments around the world. The Jews proclaimed the Independence of the reborn state of Israel and the next day six Arab armies simultaneously invaded the tiny country to try to destroy it at its birth. As an old Jewish Rabbi blew on the traditional "shofar," or ram's horn, the Jewish people celebrated the end of their tragic worldwide dispersion and captivity at the exact time prophesied thousands of years earlier by the prophet Ezekiel. (see figure 4.)

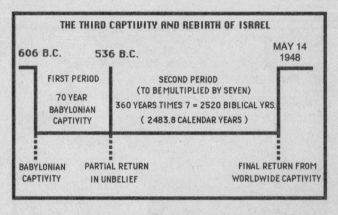

Figure 4

This great day marked the first time since the days of Solomon that a united Israel took its place as a sovereign, independent state among the nations of the world. As far as I have been able to determine in my research, this interpretation of Ezekiel's prophecy, showing its exact fulfillment on May 14, 1948, has never before been published (see figure 5).

Here is a fulfillment of prophecy in our time of such incredible precision that one is forced to marvel at the power of God to foresee and precisely control man's plans and their outcomes.

What does this fact mean to you and me? First, it means that despite the apparent anarchy of the events of our time, God is still on the throne of this universe and is still in full control of events. The universe is unfolding precisely as our Lord ordained and foresaw millenniums ago. Second, this revelation renews our interest in the words of Jesus Christ recorded in Matthew 24:32-34: **"Now learn a parable of the fig tree; When his branch is yet tender, and putteth forth leaves, ye know that summer is nigh: So likewise ye, when ye shall see all these things, know that it is near, even at the doors. Verily I say unto you, This generation shall not pass, till all these things be fulfilled."**

ISRAEL IN THE PROMISED LAND

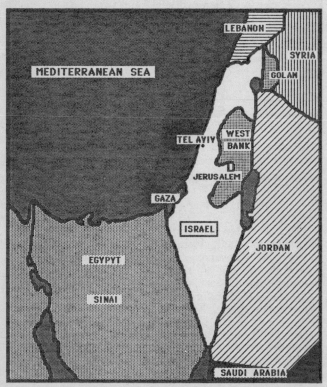

Figure 5

What is the Significance of the Rebirth of Israel?

Perhaps a few lines from an article By Dr. N. Rabinovich can put this event in a Jewish perspective. After discussing the horrors of the holocaust and the unexplainable silence of God during the annihilation of 6 million Jews, he goes on to speak of the meaning of Israel. "The rebirth of Israel is not an indemnity for the unspeakable horrors of the Nazi era and certainly not for the accumulated anguish of seventy-five generations of suffering. The reestablishment of the Jewish state does not solve the dread perplexity of Exile, nor does it spell the quick end of the persistent hatred of the Jew which is the mark of civilization unredeemed.

Is the State of Israel the long awaited fulfillment of the prophecies? Surely only a prophet can tell. Are the footsteps of the Messiah resounding over the hills? Who among us can presume to recognize the signs? There is one simple basic fact which is there for all the world to see. It is so utterly simple and so totally obvious that thousands of millions of people all over the globe know it and see it. Israel is, and it bears God's Name and it has restored God's Crown! In the light of this radical truth, all other questions take on a different meaning....The challenges are very great indeed. It has been pointed out that the existence of the state makes possible the fulfillment of two great aims of Torah: the Ingathering of the Exiles and the building of a just society. The achievement of these ends will require all the dedication and ingenuity that all Jews everywhere are capable of, and we hope that their accomplishment may initiate the Messianic era."

The fig tree (Israel) has put forth it's leaves (been reborn), and we who read these words are of " this generation," the one that is alive to see the fig tree budding its leaves. Ours is the generation that has seen the miracle of Israel's rebirth from **"the valley which was full of dry bones"(see Ezekiel 37:1).** In light of these events, we may join with the prophet John in his closing prayer in the book of Revelation chapter 22:20: **"He which testifieth these things saith, Surely I come quickly. Amen. Even so, come, Lord Jesus."**

CHAPTER 4

The Appointed Feasts

"And Moses declared unto the children of Israel the feasts of the Lord" (Leviticus 23:44).

"Also in the day of your gladness, and in your solemn days, and in the beginnings of your months, ye shall blow with the trumpets over your burnt offerings, and over the sacrifices of your peace offerings; that they may be to you for a memorial before your God: I am the Lord your God" (Numbers 10:10).

In giving the laws for His people, God set several appointed "feasts of the Lord" for Israel to observe at specific times during the year (Leviticus 23). These feasts were to be celebrated from that time in the wilderness when God gave the law and would carry on into the future. The first feast day God set aside is the Sabbath day, which is to be observed every week. The following seven feasts in Leviticus 23 were to be celebrated annually: Passover; Unleavened Bread; First Fruits; Pentecost; Trumpets; Atonement; Tabernacles.

Each feast commemorated a specific event. But that is not all. Looking back from the vantage point of our history, we discover also that additional specific prophesied events were fulfilled on the exact feast days that God instituted to commemorate the events. For example, the Feast of Passover commemorated the deliverance of the Hebrew people from the "destroyer" that passed over their blood-sprinkled homes as he visited the homes of the Egyptians, taking the lives of the firstborn of every family--human and cattle.

The blood that the people were told to put on their doorposts was from a sacrificial lamb. The event that was prefigured, of course, was the offering of the Lamb of God on Calvary. Four of the seven feasts we will discuss in the next few chapters have already been fulfilled, each one on the same day of the month on which God commanded that the feast should be commemorated.

Therefore, because of this phenomenon, we can expect those prophecies which are still in our future to also be fulfilled on the exact calendar day these feasts are to be celebrated.

The Appointed Feast Days — "A Shadow of Things to Come"

Paul spoke of the importance of these special days in his epistle to the church at Colosse. **"Let no man therefore judge you in meat, or in drink, or in respect of an holyday, or of the new moon, or of the sabbath days: Which are a shadow of things to come; but the body is of Christ" (Colossians 2:16-17).** In these verses Paul was primarily admonishing the church to free itself of legalisms. However, he also clearly revealed that a holyday feast, a new moon celebration or a sabbath day were intended by the Lord as prophetic signs of future events.

As we contemplate the sovereignty of God in this precise alignment of feast days and significant events in Israel's history and future, we should feel a profound sense of wonder. God is in charge. He knows the end from the beginning, and He is concerned that we seek to understand His will as He unfolds His plan in human history.

I realize that in the view of some critics many of the events of the Bible have been arbitrarily given dates to correspond to the liturgical festival calendar. However, after years of personal research and the tremendous confirmation of the historical truthfulness of the Bible as proven by the archeology of the last century, I have taken the position that the Biblical accounts are inspired by God and can be taken as accurate records of historical events. Therefore I have accepted the dates as revealed in the Bible as being the correct and literal dates of these events.

In addition to the seven annual feast days that were proclaimed "as holy convocations," we will look at other historically important calendar dates throughout the Jewish biblical year. We choose these dates because they have also had significant events happen more than once on their exact calendar day, and in some cases we can expect prophetic events to be fulfilled on some of these exact dates in the future.

But, before we get into an in-depth study of these dates and events, we need to look at the chart (figure 1.) that compares the Jewish calendar to our modern calendar. These revelations of God become more meaningful if we can see them from our perspective.

THE BIBLICAL CALENDAR

JEWISH MONTH		OUR EQUIVALENT MONTH
ORDER	NAME	
1.	Nisan, or Abib	Mar - April
2.	Zif, or Iyar	April - May
3.	Sivan	May - June
4.	Tammuz	June - July
5.	Ab, or Av	July - Aug
6.	Elul	Aug - Sept
7.	Tishri	Sept - Oct
8.	Bul	Oct - Nov
9.	Chisleu	Nov - Dec
10.	Tebeth	Dec - Jan
11.	Sebat	Jan - Feb
12.	Adar	Feb - Mar

Ve-Adar (the Intercalary Month)

Figure 1

In this study we will be concerned only with those months in which there are those feast days which God commanded should be kept when He gave the Mosaic Law (Exodus 40 and Leviticus 23) and those fast days recorded in the biblical history of Israel. These months are the following: Nisan, Sivan, Tammuz, Av, Tishri, and Chisleu.

The first four of the feasts--Feast of Unleavened Bread, Feast of Passover, Feast of First-Fruits, and Feast of Pentecost--were fulfilled at the first advent of our Lord Jesus Christ. The final three feasts - the Feast of Trumpets, the Feast of Atonement and the Feast of Tabernacles--will be fulfilled, it is believed, at our Lord's second coming. In the

46

following chapters we will study each of these feasts and the prophecy it symbolizes, as well as the events that have occurred already in Israel's history on the exact calendar day of the Feast.

On Rosh Hodesh, the first day of each month of the Jewish calendar, the appearance of even a tiny sliver of the new moon signaled the beginning of the month. This first day was announced through the blowing of the Shofar, the ram's horn, in the cities and by signal fires on each mountain top which fanned out the news to the most distant villages in Israel: **"Blow up the trumpet in the new moon, in the time appointed, on our solemn feast day. For this was a statute for Israel, and a law of the God of Jacob" (Psalm 81:3-5).** During the first temple period, in King Solomon's day, the high priest announced the appearance of the new moon. Later, the Sanhedrin (the highest legal authority) announced the first day of the first month to set the calendar for the new year and set the dates for the seven feasts.

First Day of Nisan

The theme of the first day of the month Nisan was a time for ritual cleansing and new beginnings for the Jews. From the time of the Exodus, God declared that Israel would change their New Year's day from the fall to a new system where the first day of Nisan, in the spring (March-April) became the beginning of the calendar year. Nisan, then, became the first month in the Jewish calendar. Four events have already transpired in Israel's history on this first important biblical anniversary that have to do with cleansing and new beginnings. One still remains to be fulfilled. *(see figure 2.)*

1. The Dedication of the Tabernacle in the Wilderness

Two years after escaping from Egypt, Moses was instructed by God to build the Tabernacle. When Moses had followed God's instructions for building and furnishing the Tabernacle, **"it came to pass in the first month in the second year, on the first day of the month, that the tabernacle was reared up" (Exodus 40:17).** God told Moses that He would fill the Tabernacle with His presence and "Shekinah" glory to guide Israel. (Exodus 40:2,33-34).

```
┌─────────────────────────────────────────────────────┐
│              THE FIRST DAY OF NISAN                  │
│          THEME: CLEANSING AND NEW BEGINNINGS        │
│                                                      │
│  1. THE DEDICATION OF THE TABERNACLE DURING EXODUS  │
│                                                      │
│  2. THE CLEANSING OF THE TEMPLE BY HEZEKIAH         │
│                                                      │
│  3. EZRA AND THE EXILES BEGIN THEIR RETURN FROM     │
│     BABYLON                                          │
│                                                      │
│  4. THE DECREE IS GIVEN TO NEHEMIAH TO REBUILD THE  │
│     WALLS OF JERUSALEM                               │
│                                                      │
│  5. THE CLEANSING OF THE MILLENNIAL TEMPLE          │
└─────────────────────────────────────────────────────┘
```

Figure 2

2. The Cleansing of the Temple by King Hezekiah

After King Solomon died, a series of kings led the divided nations of Israel and Judah. Most of them, however, were evil and practiced idol worship. Finally God raised up a righteous leader, King Hezekiah, who, **"did that which was right in the sight of the Lord, according to all that David his father had done. He in the first year of his reign, in the first month, opened the doors of the house of the Lord, and repaired them"** (2 Chronicles 29:2-3).

The House of the Lord was in such ruins that it took weeks to cleanse it fully. **"Now they began on the first day of the first month to sanctify"** (2 Chronicles 29:17). Two weeks later all Israel gathered to celebrate the Feast of Passover.

3. Ezra Began his Journey to Jerusalem to help Rebuild the Second Commonwealth

On the first day of Nisan, 457 B.C., the Jewish leader, Ezra, began his journey to Israel, bringing an additional group of returning captives, to help lead the rebuilding of the Second Commonwealth. **"for upon the first day of the first month began he to go up from Babylon"** (Ezra 7:9).

God had commanded him to provide additional leadership to the returned exiles. **"And thou, Ezra, after the wisdom of thy God, that is in thine hand, set magistrates and judges, which may judge all the people that are beyond** the river, all such as know the laws of thy God; and teach ye them that knew them not" (Ezra 7:25). Nehemiah joined him thirteen years later. (Ezra 7:9)

4. The Decree is Given to Rebuild the Walls of Jerusalem

As we mentioned in chapter 2, concerning Daniel's vision of the seventy weeks, the Persian King Artaxerxes Longimanus issued a decree which sent Nehemiah to Jerusalem to rebuild the walls of the city. According to Sir Robert Anderson in his book, *The Coming Prince*, this decree was issued on the first day of the month of Nisan, or March 14, 445 B.C. (see Nehemiah 2:1-8). This important date was the beginning point of Daniel's vision of the seventy weeks of years.

5. The Cleansing of the Millennial Temple

This is an annual prophetic event which will take place on the first day of Nisan once the Temple is rebuilt in the future. In the prophet Ezekiel's writings he speaks of the Millennial Kingdom. In chapter 45, Ezekiel talks about offerings and holy days in the new, Millennial Temple. **"Thus saith the Lord God; In the first month, in the first day of the month, thou shalt take a young bullock without blemish, and cleanse the sanctuary" (Ezekiel 45:18).**

Each of these important biblical anniversary events occurred on the first of Nisan, which is the first day of their first month.

The Tenth Day Of Nisan

Sanctification is the theme associated with the tenth day of Nisan. It was the day connected with the setting apart of the Passover Lamb for a holy purpose. There are four major events associated with this special day: *(see figure 3.)*

1. The Sanctification of the Passover Lamb during the Exodus

The first incident in which we read about this day occurred at the beginning of the Exodus and, in fact, this action in setting aside their unblemished lamb was the first act of rebellion against the bondage of Egypt. Four days before the great night in which Israel's Passover occurred, Moses had instructed them: **"In the tenth day of this month they shall take to them every man a lamb,...a lamb for an** house;...your lamb shall be without blemish,...And ye shall keep it up until the fourteenth day of the same month" (Exodus 12:3-6).

THE TENTH DAY OF NISAN

THEME: SANCTIFICATION

1. THE SANCTIFICATION OF THE PASSOVER LAMB DURING THE EXODUS

2. ISRAEL CROSSES THE JORDAN RIVER AND ENTERS THE PROMISE LAND

3. CHRIST "OUR PASSOVER LAMB" WAS "CUT OFF" ON PALM SUNDAY

4. EZEKIEL'S VISION OF THE MILLENNIAL TEMPLE

Figure 3

This sanctified lamb was the one that was to be sacrificed on the night of Passover. This lamb became the perfect symbol that **"Christ our Passover is sacrificed for us" (I Corinthians 5:7).** The Jewish Rabbis taught that the four days (between the setting aside of the lamb on the tenth day and the sacrifice on the fourteenth of Nisan) symbolize the four generations that Israel was set apart in Egypt before Passover and deliverance.

2. Israel Crossed the Jordan River and Entered the Promised Land

The second notable incident that took place on the tenth day of Nisan is described in the book of Joshua. At the end of forty years of wandering in the wilderness, the Israelites were finally ready to cross the Jordan River into the Promised Land.

Joshua told the people, **"Sanctify yourselves: for tomorrow the Lord will do wonders among you" (Joshua 3:5).** Then the story continues, describing how, during this flood season, God caused the Jordan River to stop flowing above the place of crossing so that **"the waters which came down from above stood and rose up upon an heap...and the**

people passed over right against Jordan" (Joshua 3:16).
Scripture goes on to state that **"the people came up out of
Jordan on the tenth day of the first month"** (Nisan; **Joshua
4:19)** just forty years after God had miraculously delivered
them through the parting of the waters of the Red Sea.

3. Christ our Passover Lamb was "cut off" on Palm Sunday

As we discussed in a previous chapter, Palm Sunday,
the tenth day of Nisan, A.D. 32, is the exact day in which
Jesus Christ was finally, irrevocably presented to Israel as
their long-awaited Messiah. This truly was Israel's **"time of
visitation"** and although His disciples and some citizens of
Jerusalem acknowledged His Kingship, the religious and
political leaders (together with the vast majority of the
population of Israel) rejected His claim and the **"Messiah"**
was **"cut off" (Daniel 9: 26).** This rejection resulted
inevitably in His trial and crucifixion on Passover and thus
fulfilled the type of the Passover Lamb that was set aside on
the tenth day of Nisan and later sacrificed at the Passover
Feast.

4. Ezekiel's Vision of the Millennial Temple

The fourth incident that took place on the tenth day of
Nisan is the magnificent vision that was given to the
prophet Ezekiel (40:1-2). He had just received an amazing
prophecy regarding a cataclysmic battle between the
invading forces of Gog and Magog (Russia) and Israel.

God shows Ezekiel that He will supernaturally defeat
this invasion; and then a vision is opened to the prophet
that reveals the building of a tremendous future Temple. He
sees Israel finally enjoying, in peace, all of the Promised
Land which God originally granted to Abraham and his
descendents forever (see Genesis 15: 18 - 21).

The Fourteenth day of Nisan – the Passover Supper

**"These are the Lord's appointed feasts, the sacred
assemblies you are to proclaim at their appointed times:
The Lord's Passover begins at twilight on the fourteenth
day of the first month"** (Leviticus 23:4-5, NIV).

Passover always falls on a full moon, the first full moon
of Spring. All Jewish males were required by God to go to

Jerusalem three times each year to commemorate these feasts – Passover, Pentecost and the Feast of Tabernacles. Passover was the first of these feasts.

The biblical calendar reckons the beginning of a new day from sunset as God did at creation, **"And the evening and the morning were the first day"** (Genesis 1:5). The Passover begins at 6:00 P.M. **"In the fourteenth day of the first month at even [at 6:00 P.M.] is the Lord's passover"** (Leviticus 23:5).

The *Haggadah*, the Jewish liturgy, says: "In every generation, each person should feel as though she or he were personally redeemed from Egypt." In the sacred cycle of festivals, the Passover Supper on the evening of the fourteenth of Nisan, allows all Jews in all the generations since the Exodus to participate personally in the miracle of God's redemption of the enslaved Israelites. The Passover holds forth the promise of that final redemption when the Messiah will redeem all those who look to Him for salvation.

Passover is probably the most significant of all the festivals which Israel celebrates. For almost thirty-five hundred years, Jewish families have gathered to commemorate what God did for them when He delivered them from hundreds of years of slavery in Egypt.

Six times in their history on this day, the fourteenth day of Nisan, the evening Passover Supper has marked a milestone in the spiritual and national life of Israel. (see figure 4.)

1. God makes a Covenant with Abraham regarding the Promised Land

"In the same day the Lord made a covenant with Abram, saying, unto thy seed have I given this land, from the river of Egypt unto the great river, the river Euphrates" (Genesis 15:18).

Abraham, the father of the Chosen People, was removed from his home and led to a strange land which God promised He would "deed" to Abraham's descendants forever. Aside from the obvious obstacle of the strong nations occupying this territory, an even greater obstacle seemed to stand in the way of God's promise of giving a land to Abraham's "descendants": Abraham and his wife were long past the normal age for childbearing. But, as God's messengers later told Abraham, **"Is anything too hard for the Lord?"** (Genesis 18:14).

**THE FOURTEENTH DAY OF NISAN
THE PASSOVER SUPPER**

THEME: THE COVENANT RELATIONSHIP WITH GOD

1. **GOD MAKES A COVENANT WITH ABRAHAM – THE PROMISED LAND**

2. **THE PASSOVER SUPPER EATEN IN PREPARING FOR THE EXODUS**

3. **THE FIRST PASSOVER IN CANAAN – THE COVENANT RENEWED**

4. **THE BOOK OF THE LAW FOUND AND REAFFIRMED UNDER JOSIAH**

5. **THE DEDICATION OF THE SECOND TEMPLE**

6. **THE LAST SUPPER – A NEW COVENANT IS OFFERED BY CHRIST**

Figure 4

The Lord confirmed His covenant with Abraham by this first **"passover."** God had instructed Abraham to bring a heifer, a goat, a ram, a dove and a young pigeon and cut them in half (except for the birds). When Abraham had obeyed, he fell into a deep sleep.

Although there are several verses in Genesis which indicate that this crucial event took place on Passover, the fourteenth of Nisan, God has confirmed this fact by His account in Exodus 12:41 which clearly states that the Passover Exodus, on the fourteenth of Nisan, occurs on the exact anniversary of the giving of the Abrahamic Covenant, four hundred and thirty years earlier.

Then the Lord said to him: **"And he said unto Abram, Know of a surety that thy seed shall be a stranger in a land that is not theirs, and shall serve them; and they shall afflict them four hundred years. And also that nation, whom they shall serve, will I judge: and afterward shall they come out with great substance"** (Genesis 15:13-14). **"And it came to pass, that, when the sun went down, and it was dark, behold a smoking furnace, and a burning lamp that passed between those pieces"** (verse 17). Due to the spiritual death that results from sin, a physical death and the shedding of blood was necessary for this covenant to be ratified and made effective.

2. The Exodus Passover Supper

On this night God concluded the last and most terrible of the ten plagues against Egypt with the "destroyer" killing the firstborn of Egypt. The Jews had Divine protection during this plague due to their sacrifice of the passover lamb and the application of its blood to their door posts.

The next morning, exactly 430 years from the day when God made His Covenant with Abraham, the Lord brought the children of Israel out of their slavery in Egypt. **"And it came to pass at the end of the four hundred and thirty years,** *even the selfsame day it came to pass,* **that all the hosts of the Lord went out from the land of Egypt"** *(Exodus 12:41).*

3. The First Passover in Canaan

God had told Abraham that **"this is my covenant, which ye shall keep, between me and you and thy seed after thee; Every man child among you shall be circumcised. And ye shall circumcise the flesh of your foreskin; and it shall be a token of the covenant between me and you" (Genesis 17:10-11).** This Abraham did **"the selfsame day"** (verse 23), when every male in his household was circumcised.

Then, when God gave Moses regulations for celebrating the Passover, He reconfirmed that no male could participate in the Passover Feast unless he had been circumcised. However, none of the male children born during the forty years of wandering in the wilderness had been circumcised. Joshua, Moses' successor, knowing God's commandment to Moses concerning circumcision and the partaking of the Passover Feast, **"made him sharp knives and circumcised the children of Israel at the hill of the foreskins...And it came to pass, when they had done circumcising all the people, that they abode in their places in the camp, till they were whole" (Joshua 5: 3, 8).**

On the evening of the fourteenth of Nisan, all the Israelites celebrated their first Passover Feast in the Promised Land. The Bible tells us **"And they did eat of the old corn of the land on the morrow after the passover, unleavened cakes, and parched corn in the selfsame day.**

And the manna ceased on the morrow after they had eaten of the old corn of the land; neither had the children of Israel manna any more; but they did eat of the fruit of the land of Canaan that year" (Joshua 5: 11-12). The people celebrated their great national deliverance from Egypt, which was only a foretaste of their ultimate deliverance when Messiah would set up the final kingdom of God.

4. The Book of Law was Discovered

Of all the kings that reigned over the divided kingdom of Judah, King Josiah was one of the most righteous. He began to reign when he was eight years old and "he did that which was right in the sight of the Lord, and walked in the ways of David his father, and declined neither to the right hand, nor to the left...he began to seek after the God of David his father" (2 Chronicles 34:2-3). In the eighteenth year of his reign, he ordered the cleansing and repair of the Temple, which had been neglected by his predecessors.

During the restoration, "Hilkiah the priest found a book of the law of the Lord given by Moses" (verse 14). When the book (scroll) was read to the king, he took it and read it to the people. He was captivated and convicted by the words: "And the king stood in his place, and made a covenant before the Lord, to walk after the Lord, and to keep his commandments, and his testimonies, and his statutes, with all his heart, and with all his soul, to perform the words of the covenant which are written in this book" (verse 31). One of the things that he did in obedience to God was to immediately celebrate the Passover Feast on the fourteenth day of Nisan.

5. The Dedication of the Second Temple

When the Jewish captives returned to Jerusalem under the decree of Cyrus the Great in 536 B.C., they found that when Nebuchadnezzar's soldiers invaded the city in 587 B.C., "They burnt the house of God, and brake down the wall of Jerusalem, and burnt all the palaces thereof with fire, and destroyed all the goodly vessels thereof" (2 Chronicles 36:19).

In 520 B.C., the Israelites began to rebuild the Temple, against great opposition from the Samaritans who had moved into Israel as colonists for Babylon. Finally, after five years of hard work and God's blessing, the Temple was finished in the month Adar. On the fourteenth day of Nisan,

515 B.C., the exiles celebrated the Passover by dedicating the rebuilt Temple under Ezra and the high priest, Joshua (see Ezra 6:16-19).

6. The Last Supper

After Jesus' disciples had sacrificed their Passover Lamb in the Temple, they met in a large upper room, all furnished, to prepare for the feast. However, this supper was like no other they had ever celebrated. **"And he took bread, and gave thanks, and brake it, and gave unto them, saying, This is my body which is given for you: this do in remembrance of me. Likewise also the cup, after supper, saying, This cup is the new testament in my blood, which is shed for you"** (Luke 22:19-20).

In response to the Lord's commandment to **"do this in remembrance of me,"** for some two thousand years Christians have met in catacombs, homes and churches to celebrate His completed sacrifice: **"Ye do shew the Lord's death till he come"** (I Corinthians 11:26). It is interesting to note that, even in this most solemn remembering of His Cross, our faith is focused on the fact that we will commemorate this event only until He comes to wear His rightful Crown of Glory.

The Fifteenth Day of Nisan – The Feast of Unleavened Bread

"And on the fifteenth day of the same month is the feast of unleavened bread unto the Lord: seven days ye must eat unleavened bread. In the first day ye shall have an holy convocation: ye shall do no servile work therein....When ye are come into the land which I give unto you, and shall reap the harvest thereof, then ye shall bring a sheaf of the firstfruits of your harvest unto the priest: And he shall wave the sheaf before the Lord, to be accepted for you: _on the morrow after the sabbath the priest shall wave it"_ (Leviticus 23:6-7,10-11).

Although the Feast of Unleavened Bread (Hag-Ha-Matzot) is quite distinct from the Passover Feast, it occurs at the same time and lasts seven days from the fifteenth day of Nisan through the twenty-first. During these seven days, Israel was to eat bread without leaven (leaven symbolized sin) in remembrance of their baking unleavened bread in their haste to escape Egypt. The Jews in the Old and New Testament usually treated the first day of Unleavened Bread and the Passover as one, due to its historical connection and proximity.

The Matzoh (unleavened bread) that is eaten reminds Israel of that terrible but hopeful night when Jews ate the sacrificial lamb and unleavened bread in obedience to God's command. After 430 years they were faced with either imminent disaster or salvation from the slavery and bondage of Egypt. The unleavened bread symbolized the purging out of the sins of pagan Egypt.

The Apostle Paul was thinking of this unleavened bread when he told the church at Corinth to **"purge out therefore the old leaven, that ye may be a new lump, as ye are unleavened. For even Christ our passover is sacrificed for us: Therefore let us keep the feast, not with old leaven, neither with the leaven of malice and wickedness; but with the unleavened bread of sincerity and truth"** (1 Corinthians 5: 7-8).

During Passover, while the Lord sent the "destroyer" to slay all the first born of Egypt, the children of Israel prepared to leave Egypt in great haste. There was no time for the leaven to cause the dough to rise, so they were forced to carry unleavened bread--Matzoh--as their only food. This became a symbol of their slavery that was transformed into their freedom by the miraculous redemptive act of God, known forever as the Exodus.

There have been three notable anniversary events on the Feast of Unleavened Bread. *(see figure 5.)*

1. The Exodus from Egypt

"And it came to pass at the end of the four hundred and thirty years, even the selfsame day it came to pass, that all the hosts of the Lord went out from the land of Egypt" (Exodus 12:41).

On this day, God brought the children of Israel out of the bondage of Egypt on the exact day their father Abraham had prophesied it would happen some 430 years earlier. After the conclusion of the ten plagues, the Egyptian Pharaoh finally let the people go. In Deuteronomy 16:3, the bread eaten during the Feast of Unleavened Bread is called **"the bread of affliction; for thou camest forth out of the land of**

Egypt in haste: that thou mayest remember the day when thou camest forth out of the land of Egypt all the days of thy life".

THE FIFTEENTH DAY OF NISAN
THE FEAST OF UNLEAVENED BREAD

THEME: THE PURGING OUT OF THE LEAVEN OF SIN

1. THE EXODUS JOURNEY FROM THE BONDAGE OF EGYPT BEGAN

2. THE CRUCIFIXION OF CHRIST, "OUR PASSOVER LAMB"

3. THE FINAL FALL OF THE JEWISH RESISTANCE AT MASSADA

Figure 5

This unpleasant tasting bread symbolized all the burden and affliction in Egypt. Once Israel was free, this bread reminded them that they had left behind them the leaven and sinfulness of pagan Egypt, so it now represented freedom. The transformation of a symbol of bondage into one of freedom is paralleled for a Christian in the transformation of the cross as a tragic symbol of death into the glorious reminder of Christ's victorious resurrection over death.

2. The Crucifixion of Christ, "our Passover Lamb"

Jesus described Himself, **"I am the bread of life"** (John 6:35). Much of His life and ministry centered around the image of bread. Even Bethlehem , where he was born, means the "house of bread" in Hebrew. One time, when Jesus was talking to His disciples, He said: **"The hour is come, that the Son of man should be glorified. Verily, verily, I say unto you, Except a corn of wheat fall into the ground and die, it abideth alone: but if it die, it bringeth forth much fruit.... Now is my soul troubled, and what shall I say? Father, save me from this hour: but for this cause came I unto this hour. Father, glorify thy name. Then came there a voice from**

heaven, saying, I have both glorified it, and will glorify it again" (John 12: 23-24, 27-28).

Christ, the kernel of wheat--the basis for bread--did indeed have to die to be buried on the Feast of Unleavened Bread, the fifteenth day of Nisan, and He rose three days later on the Feast of Firstfruits to become "the firstfruits" of our resurrection.

3. The Final Fall of the Jewish Resistance at Massada

For two years following the destruction of Jerusalem and the Temple, the remaining Jewish resistance, under the command of Eleazar, retreated to the mountain fortress of Massada. This impregnable fortress sits on a mountain top overlooking the Dead Sea. It could only be approached by a narrow "snakepath" which wound its way up the steep cliffs. A small group of soldiers was able to bravely hold off the Roman legions for almost two years until the Roman general Silva built a huge earthen ramp up the western side to enable their battering rams to break through. When the ramp was completed, the Jewish defenders knew that the war was lost and that by early morning the Roman soldiers would overcome the 960 men, women and children who were the last remnant of a free Israel. They knew, from grim experience, that their fate at the hands of the Romans included rape, torture and death for every last one of them.

Rather then submit their wives and children to the cruelties of Roman victory, the defenders decided to take their own lives and die as free men. On my recent trip to Massada, I was able to stand in the ruins of the actual room where the Jews chose by lot those who would mercifully end the lives of the men, after each had ended the life of his family. Several years ago, archeologists discovered in this room the pottery shards upon which the names of the men where written for the lots to be drawn. When the Romans stormed through the gates in the morning, they were stunned to find that they had been robbed of their slaughter. The Jewish historian, Flavius Josephus, in his *War of the Jews*, book 5, chapter 9, section 1, records, "They came within the palace, and so met with the multitude of the slain,....nor could they do other than wonder at the courage of their resolution, and at the immovable contempt of death which so great a number of them had shown, when they went through such an action as that was." He states, "This calamitous slaughter was made on the fifteenth day of the month Nisan" (the Feast of Unleavened Bread).

The Seventeenth Day of Nisan —
The Feast of Firstfruits

The third of the seven feasts is celebrated on the seventeenth day of Nisan, the Feast of Firstfruits. This was the time for the harvesting of the early crops of spring . God wanted Israel to acknowledge that they owed Him not only the firstfruits, but that all they had was from God, a daily gift from His gracious hand.

"The first of the firstfruits of thy land thou shalt bring into the house of the Lord thy God" (Exodus 23:19).

Four historically important anniversary events have happened on the Feast of Firstfruits, the seventeenth day of Nisan. *(see figure 6.)*

**THE SEVENTEENTH DAY OF NISAN
THE FEAST OF FIRSTFRUITS**

THEME: RESURRECTION

1. NOAH'S ARK RESTS ON MOUNT ARARAT

2. ISRAEL MIRACULOUSLY CROSSES OVER THE RED SEA

3. ISRAEL EATS THE FIRSTFRUITS OF THE PROMISED LAND

4. THE RESURRECTION OF JESUS CHRIST

Figure 5

1. Noah's Ark Rested on Mount Ararat

After the flood destroyed all of humanity except for Noah and his family, the ark floated above the endless waters until, by God's mercy, it finally came to rest, on the seventeenth day of Nisan, on Mount Ararat in Turkey. These eight survivors were witnesses to the total destruction of all land life because of the enormous sin, perversion and violence of mankind: **"And God saw that the wickedness of man was great in the earth, and that every imagination of the thoughts of his heart was only evil continually" (Genesis 6:5).**

For a year Noah and his family had floated upon the waters, no doubt wondering if they would ever see land again. Imagine their gratitude when they felt their ship rest on solid rock after nearly a year of not knowing when they would walk again upon the earth. The book of Genesis records this date precisely as the seventeenth day of Nisan (Genesis 8:4) and one can easily imagine the descendants of Noah celebrating for generations on this day, the "firstfruits" of their ultimate safe landing on the hills of the earth.

Most ancient nations, including Israel, began their calendar year in the fall (Sept.- Oct.). However, God changed Israel's calendar by rotating it six months so that, from the time of the Exodus, their New Year's Day began in the Spring on the first day of the month of Nisan (March-April). In order to commemorate Israel's miraculous deliverance from the bondage of Egypt in the month of Nisan, God instructed Moses to change the order of the month of their Exodus, Nisan, which had formerly been their seventh month of the year, into their first month of their year (see Exodus 12:1-2).

Thus, when Genesis 8:4 describes Noah's ark resting on Mount Ararat on the seventeenth day of the ancient calendar's seventh month (Nisan-March), it is the same day exactly as the seventeenth day of the new calendar's first month (Nisan-March) which ultimately became the Feast of Firstfruits.

2. Israel Miraculously Crossed Over the Red Sea

On the night of Passover, when the Pharaoh of Egypt was finally forced by God to let Israel leave Egypt, some 600 thousand refugees started out toward freedom. When they arrived on the shores of the Red Sea, after camping in the desert, they looked back and saw the dust of the approaching Egyptian army. Then they began the first of many complaints to Moses: **"Because there were no graves in Egypt, hast thou taken us away to die in the wilderness? wherefore hast thou dealt thus with us, to carry us forth out** of Egypt? Is not this the word that we did tell thee in Egypt, saying, Let us alone, that we may serve the Egyptians? For it had been better for us to serve the Egyptians, than that we should die in the wilderness" (Exodus 14: 11-12). Their situation appeared utterly hopeless – the enemy behind them and the seemingly impossible barrier of the Red Sea before them.

As it was for Israel, so it often is for us. After a tremendous struggle and a great victory, we move forward with the assurance that we are in the will of God. Then, just as soon as we think the road ahead will be smooth and straight, we run up against the biggest challenge of all. Yet, "our extremity is God's opportunity."

To the east was the impassable Red Sea (which extended much farther to the north at that time); to the west was the enormous Egyptian army; surrounding him was a frightened multitude. Moses turned to the only sure help that exists for any of us. **"And Moses said unto the people, Fear ye not, stand still, and see the salvation of the Lord, which he will shew to you today: for the Egyptians whom ye have seen today, ye shall see them again no more for ever. The Lord shall fight for you, and ye shall hold your peace" (Exodus 14: 13-14).** Then, before their eyes, God parted the waters of this sea of certain death and the multitude of Israelites crossed over into a new life as a resurrected nation on the Feast of Firstfruits, the seventeenth of Nisan, to become the "firstfruits"of a nation reborn from the bondage of Egypt.

3. Israel Eats the Firstfruits of the Promised Land

"The children of Israel encamped in Gilgal, and kept the passover on the fourteenth day of the month at even in the plains of Jericho. And they did eat of the old corn of the land on the morrow after the passover, unleavened cakes, and parched corn in the selfsame day. And the manna ceased on the morrow after they had eaten of the old corn of the land; neither had the children of Israel manna any more; but they did eat of the fruit of the land of Canaan that year" (Joshua 5:10-12).

Throughout the forty years that Israel wandered in the desert, God provided supernatural food--manna--to feed the mighty growing nation. The Bible records that after they crossed over the Jordan River they ate the Passover Supper on the fourteenth of Nisan. The next day, on the fifteenth day of Nisan, the day after the Passover Supper, they ate of the old corn of the land on the morrow after the Passover. The next day, the sixteenth Nisan, was the last day in which God provided the supernatural manna.

Note that the manna ceased on the sixteenth, the day after they ate of the old corn of the land. The day following was the seventeenth day of Nisan, the Feast of Firstfruits, and with no more manna available, the people began to eat of the fruit of the land of Canaan that year – the firstfruits of the land. One can easily imagine their joy at eating the first natural and varied fruits in their forty years of life since the Exodus began. The Jews still celebrate this Feast of Firstfruits every year at this time.

4. Resurrection of Jesus Christ

As Jesus hung on the cross in death, Satan, the Romans, the Pharisees, those who called for His death, and even His followers looked at Him and saw only defeat and death; the death of a great vision. Yet, as Jesus Himself had said, **"Except a corn of wheat fall into the ground and die, it abideth alone: but if it die, it bringeth forth much fruit" (John 12:24).** But when it falls to the ground and takes root it is soon transformed into new life. It was essential for Jesus to die in order to triumph over death, sin and Satan.

The most significant event that took place on the seventeenth day of Nisan is the resurrection of Jesus Christ, the "firstfruits" of all future resurrections into eternal life. **"But now is Christ risen from the dead, and become the firstfruits of them that slept" (1 Corinthians 15:20).** Jesus celebrated this feast by first conquering death Himself, then by offering the firstfruits to all future resurrections when **"the graves were opened; and many bodies of the saints which slept arose, and came out of the graves after his resurrection, and went into the holy city, and appeared unto many" (Matthew 27:52-53).** Christ proved that His power over death was not limited to Himself by resurrecting many of the Old Testament saints on this Feast of Firstfruits. Other ancient writers, including Clement of Alexandria in his Stromata refer to this miraculous resurrection of the dead which, together with more than five hundred eyewitnesses to the risen Christ, assisted in the rapid, early spread of the Christian faith (1 Corinthians 15:4-6).

What an impressive way to present to God the

"firstfruits" of the harvest. **Jesus the firstfruits,** then **"they also which are fallen asleep in Christ,"** (verse 18) and finally all believers who are alive at His second advent at the Rapture, raised imperishable and immortal. **"Death is swallowed up in victory"** (1 Corinthians 15:54).

CHAPTER 5

The Feast of Pentecost and the Fasts of Mourning

The Sixth Day of Sivan – The Feast of Pentecost

"And ye shall count unto you from the morrow after the sabbath, from the day that ye brought the sheaf of the wave offering; seven sabbaths shall be complete. Even unto the morrow after the seventh sabbath shall ye number fifty days; and ye shall offer a new meat offering unto the Lord....And ye shall proclaim on the selfsame day, that it may be an holy convocation unto you: ye shall do no servile work therein: it shall be a statute for ever in all your dwellings throughout your generations" (Leviticus 23:15-16,21).

The fourth of the seven required feasts of Israel took place exactly fifty days after the Feast of the Firstfruits-- hence the name Pentecost, "penta" meaning fifty. This feast is very significant to Christians as well as to Jews. Pentecost, or Shavuot to the Jews, celebrated the end of the grain harvest, the summer harvest. It is also known as the Zeman Matan Tortenu, the "giving of the Law" to Israel. The Feast of Pentecost is the second of the three great feasts that all male Jews were required to celebrate at the Temple in Jerusalem every year.

Two major events took place on the sixth day of Sivan; each one introduced a special time of spiritual stewardship to a specific revelation of God: The giving of the Ten Commandments and the giving of the Holy Spirit. *(see figure 1.)*

65

THE SIXTH DAY OF SIVAN THE FEAST OF PENTECOST THEME: A NEW REVELATION OF GOD'S WILL 1. THE GIVING OF THE LAW TO MOSES ON MOUNT SINAI 2. THE GIVING OF THE HOLY SPIRIT TO THE CHURCH

Figure 1

1. The Giving of the Ten Commandments

After leaving Egypt, the Jews completed fifty days of journeying from Rameses into the wilderness of Sinai; and on the third day of the third month, Sivan, the Israelites arrived at Mount Sinai. Israel now waited for three days at the base of Mount Sinai for Moses to return from conversing with God. The Lord told the people, **"Be ready against the third day: for the third day the Lord will come down in the sight of all the people upon Mount Sinai" (Exodus 19:11).** Although God had chosen Israel by His grace through Abraham, He now confirmed this covenant, four hundred and thirty years later, by the presentation of His Law on the Feast of Pentecost, the sixth of Sivan.

This entire era, from the giving of the Law on Pentecost until Christ, is known as the Dispensation of Law, which transformed human moral law. It began a new period of spiritual stewardship to this further revelation of the will of God. The Jewish rabbinical teachings confirm that it was on the sixth day of Sivan that Moses received the Ten Commandments. Also, *The Jewish Almanac* records that "historically, it (the sixth day of Sivan--Pentecost) commemorates the revelation on Mount Sinai when God gave the Torah to the children of Israel."

The book, *The Jewish Holidays--A Guide and Commentary*, describes this Feast of Pentecost as follows:

"Shavuot (Pentecost--Feast of Weeks) occurs on the sixth day of Sivan. It celebrates the giving of the Torah, God's gift to the Jewish people."

After describing the offerings which the people were to present to God at Pentecost, God tells Moses: **"And when ye reap the harvest of your land, thou shalt not make clean riddance of the corners of thy field when thou reapest, neither shall thou gather any gleaning of thy harvest: thou shalt leave them unto the poor, and to the stranger: I am the Lord your God"** (Leviticus 23:22).

The book of Ruth, which describes Boaz ordering his servants to leave the gleaning of the harvest for Ruth and her mother, is read in synagogues on this day of Pentecost. This harvest-time story records Ruth's conversion to Judaism: **"And Ruth said, Entreat me not to leave thee, or to return from following after thee: for whither thou goest, I will go; and where thou lodgest, I will lodge: thy people shall be my people, and thy God my God"** (Ruth 1:16). The book ends with the genealogy of Ruth, showing that King David and, therefore, Jesus Christ, "the son of David", are descended from Ruth and Boaz (see Matthew 1:5-6). An old Jewish tradition claims that King David was born and also died on the Feast of Pentecost.

2. The Giving of the Holy Spirit

Precisely fifty days after the Feast of Firstfruits, the day the Lord Jesus Christ rose from the dead, 120 disciples gathered **"together in one place"** to await the promise of Christ. He prophesied that they would be baptized with the Holy Spirit, **"But ye shall receive power, after that the Holy Ghost is come upon you: and ye shall be witnesses unto me both in Jerusalem, and in all Judea, and in Samaria and unto the uttermost part of the earth"** (Acts 1:8).

"And when the day of Pentecost was fully come, they were all with one accord in one place" (Acts 2:1). On the sixth day of Sivan the Holy Spirit manifested Himself and **"they were all filled with the Holy Ghost, and began to speak with other tongues, as the Spirit gave them utterance" (verse 4)**. Those ordinary people, His disciples were transformed on that day into men and women of extraordinary spiritual power who would challenge their world of abject paganism with a dynamic Christian movement which not even the might of Rome could stop.

Within days some three thousand Jews became believers and reliable reports suggest that, despite horrible persecutions, tortures and massive executions, within seventy years over 10 million believers had joined the underground Christian Church.

It is no coincidence that, on the same day of Pentecost in which God appeared to Moses in the wilderness of Sinai and revealed to man a new relationship based upon His sacred Law, He again revealed to man a new relationship based on the Holy Spirit. The mystical union of God and Israel that occurred on the Feast of Pentecost at the foot of Mount Sinai is exactly mirrored in the union of God's Holy Spirit with Christ's Bride, the Church, on Pentecost, fifty days after Christ rose from the dead.

Enoch, the first prophet and teacher of righteousness, lived in the seventh generation from Adam and first revealed the prophecy of the coming of Messiah to set up His kingdom (Jude verse 14). A Jewish writer, H.L. Ginzberg, wrote in *The Legends of the Jews*, that according to Israel's oral tradition, Enoch was raptured--taken into heaven on this very day of Pentecost, the sixth day of Sivan. **"And Enoch walked with God: and he was not; for God took him"** (Genesis 5:24).

The Seventeenth Day of Tammuz

"Thus saith the Lord of hosts; The fast of the fourth month, and the fast of the fifth, and the fast of the seventh, and the fast of the tenth, shall be to the house of Judah joy and gladness, and cheerful feasts" (Zechariah 8:19).

Each of the four fasts mentioned by the prophet Zechariah were in commemoration of some tragic event connected with the destruction of the Temple, Jerusalem and the independence of Israel when the Babylonian army conquered Israel successively from 606 B.C. to 587 B.C. Zechariah promises that, once the Messiah has come to set up His Kingdom, these four tragic fasts will be transformed into feasts of joy and gladness to celebrate the eternal peace and blessings of the Messianic Age. The fast of the fourth month – Tammuz, occurred on the seventeenth day of Tammuz (July). The fast of the fifth month – Av, occurred on the ninth day of Av (August).

The next historically important anniversary is not a feast day but rather is a day of fasting and mourning. Nevertheless, this day has been significant in God's dealing with Israel. It is the seventeenth day of Tammuz and occurs in the month of July on our calendar.

The seventeenth day of Tammuz begins a three-week period of national mourning leading up to the fast of Tisha Be-av, the ninth day of Av. Three spiritually significant events have happened on the seventeenth day of Tammuz and each involved the breaking of a spiritual symbol which signified that God's disfavor had been incurred as a result of national disobedience. (see figure 2.) The mourning followed due to the people's consciousness of their sin and their recognition that God's punishment would follow.

THE SEVENTEENTH DAY OF TAMMUZ
THE FAST OF MOURNING
[BEGINS THE THREE WEEKS OF MOURNING TILL 9TH AV]
THEME: THE BREAKING OF A SPIRITUAL SYMBOL OF GOD'S FAVOR

1. MOSES BREAKS THE TABLETS OF THE LAW WHEN HE SEES THE IDOLATRY OF THE GOLDEN CALF

2. THE BABYLONIAN ARMY BREAKS THROUGH THE WALLS OF JERUSAELM AND CAUSES THE DAILY SACRIFICE TO CEASE

3. THE ROMAN ARMIES ATTACK ON THE TEMPLE MOUNT FORCES THE PRIESTS TO STOP THE DAILY SACRIFICE

Figure 2

1. Moses Breaks the Tablets of the Law

As discussed earlier in this chapter, the Lord gave the Law to Moses on the Feast of Pentecost and revealed Himself to the people of Israel in a dramatic and awesome display of divine power on the sixth day of Sivan. The Bible recounts the event: **"Mount Sinai was altogether on a smoke, because the Lord descended upon it in fire: and the smoke thereof ascended as the smoke of a furnace, and the whole mount quaked greatly" (Exodus 19:18).** Instead of recognizing God's authority and power, the very opposite occurred.

On the seventh day of Sivan, Moses returned to Mount Sinai to receive the complete Law which he later recorded in the Torah, the first five books of the Bible. He was on the mountain for forty days, time enough for the memory of God's power to fade in the minds of the people and for them to begin to crave their false idols which they had worshiped in Egypt. While Moses was absent, the people rebelled against God and built a golden calf idol for them to worship. Moses had received the Ten Commandments chiseled on stone tablets from the hand of God and was now descending the mountain to bring his people the greatest advance in law and morality since the world began.

As Moses came down to the plain on the seventeenth of Tammuz, he saw the golden calf and the people's lewd pagan dancing. He was filled with righteous anger at their sinful rebellion and contempt for the God who had miraculously saved them from slavery and death. His anger burned within him and he broke into pieces the sacred Tablets of the Law at the foot of the mountain (Exodus 32:19). This is discussed in great detail in the rabbinical writings, including Ta'anit 28b.

Moses called out, **"Who is on the Lord's side?"** (Exodus 32 : 26) and the priestly tribe of Levites rallied to him. The Lord commanded them to destroy the worst of the offenders and more than three thousand died as a result of their stubborn rebellion.

2. The Babylonians Broke Through the Walls of Jerusalem and Caused the Daily Sacrifice to Cease

The second important event to occur on the seventeenth of Tammuz was the ceasing of the daily Morning and Evening Sacrifice (the Korban Tamid). The city was about to fall after a two-year siege because the army of King Nebuchadnezzar finally broke through the city walls. In an attempt to continue the Daily Sacrifice, during the two year siege, the priests had lowered a basket of gold coins from the walls of the city each day and the Babylonian soldiers had put sheep for the sacrifice in the basket as trade.

When the outer walls on the city fell to the invaders on the seventeenth of Tammuz, the Babylonian soldiers refused to continue the trade because they knew that the whole city would fall to them in a matter of days. Rabbi Y. Culi records in his commentary, Meam Lo'ez that the priests mourned in despair because, for the first time in more than four hundred years, they could no longer continue the Daily Sacrifice as required by God's Law.

This ceasing of the Daily Sacrifice on the seventeenth of Tammuz marked the beginning of the end for Jerusalem. It clearly symbolized that God's divine protection was being withdrawn from Israel as a result of their national sin and rebellion. This day, the seventeenth of Tammuz, became an annual fast of mourning for the Jews which commenced a twenty-one day period of mourning leading to the final loss of their Temple.

3. The Roman Army Forces the Cessation of the Daily Sacrifice

Almost forty years after the crucifixion of Christ, the Roman army besieged Jerusalem to terminate the Jewish War of Independence against the Roman Empire which began in A.D. 66. The Romans fought to destroy Israel because she represented a potentially successful rebellion against the oppression of the Roman Empire upon all her captive peoples.

In A.D. 70 General Titus besieged Jerusalem successfully and famine raged within the city. The Roman army catapults were able to move close enough to the Temple on the seventeenth of Tammuz to be able to continuously catapult large boulders onto the Temple, killing enormous numbers of priests. The writings of Flavius Josephus, the Jewish historian who was an eyewitness to these tragic events, tell us that this bombardment plus the internal chaos of the city forced the priests to discontinue the Daily Sacrifice on the seventeenth of Tammuz, the anniversary of the exact day on which the Babylonian army accomplished the same thing 656 years earlier. This event totally demoralized the Jewish defenders and demonstrated to them that once more God's protection was departing. The final destruction of Jerusalem and the Temple was imminent.

It is surely significant that on this day, the seventeenth of Tammuz, three important historical events should occur that were each characterized by God permitting the destruction of a religious covenant symbol to show that He had turned away from Israel at that moment because of their national disobedience. (See Flavius Josephus, *Wars of The Jews*, book b, chap. 2:1).

An Intriguing Historical Footnote –
The American Declaration of Independence

One additional anniversary event occurred on July 4, 1776, when the American Declaration of Independence was announced. This broke America's bonds to Britain and opened up a potential home for Jewish refugees, fleeing from thousands of years of religious and racial persecution which had oppressed their life in Europe and Russia. This day, the seventeenth of Tammuz, finally saw an event which portended great favor for both Jews as individuals and ultimately, for support of the newly reborn state of Israel in 1948.

The Ninth Day of Av –
A Fast of Mourning

When ye fasted and mourned in the fifth [Av] and seventh month" (Zechariah 7:5).

This day of fasting, known as Tisha Be-Av, is a day of mourning and remembrance of Israel's loss of their sacred Temple. It is one of the most historically significant anniversaries in the life of their nation and is commemorated by Jews throughout the world as the tragic day when God withdrew His Presence and they wept as their precious Temple burned to the ground.

Throughout Israel's history, the ninth of Av (in our August), has witnessed eight of the greatest disasters (see figure 3.) in their nation's history. It has become a day when Jews not only mourn their loss but also look to that great day when their Messiah will finally appear to end their centuries of suffering.

This phenomenon of eight major events of the same nature, namely national disasters, all occurring on the same anniversary date is unprecedented in the history of nations. Tisha Be Av, Israel's fast of mourning on the ninth day of Av has seen more disasters than any other date in history. The prophet Zechariah refers to this day, **"when ye fasted and mourned in the fifth [Av] and seventh month" (Zechariah 7:5).** He goes on to state that when Messiah has come and the long promised Kingdom comes, all of their fasts, including this one, **"shall be to the house of Judah joy and gladness, and cheerful feasts" (Zechariah 8:19).**

72

```
┌─────────────────────────────────────────────────────┐
│              THE NINTH DAY OF AV                     │
│            THE FAST OF TISHA BE-AV                   │
│            THEME: A FAST OF MOURNING                 │
│                                                      │
│  1. THE TWELVE SPIES RETURN WITH THEIR REPORT –      │
│     ISRAEL LOSES FAITH AND IS CONDEMNED TO DIE IN THE│
│     WILDERNESS                                       │
│                                                      │
│  2. THE DESTRUCTION OF SOLOMON'S TEMPLE BY THE       │
│     BABYLONIANS IN 587 B.C.                          │
│                                                      │
│  3. THE DESTRUCTION OF THE SECOND TEMPLE BY THE      │
│     ROMANS IN A.D. 70                                │
│                                                      │
│  4. THE ROMAN ARMY PLOWED JERUSALEM WITH SALT IN     │
│     A.D. 71                                          │
│                                                      │
│  5. THE DESTRUCTION OF SIMEON BAR COCHBA'S ARMY IN   │
│     135 A.D.                                         │
│                                                      │
│  6. ENGLAND EXPELLED ALL OF THE JEWS IN 1290 A.D.    │
│                                                      │
│  7. SPAIN EXPELLED ALL THE JEWS IN 1492 A.D.         │
│                                                      │
│  8. WORLD WAR ONE IS DECLARED ON THE NINTH OF AV,    │
│     1914 RUSSIA MOBILIZED FOR WORLD WAR ONE AND      │
│     LAUNCHED PERSECUTIONS AGAINST THE JEWS IN        │
│     EASTERN RUSSIA.                                  │
└─────────────────────────────────────────────────────┘
```

Figure 3

1. The Twelve Spies Return with their Report

Moses sent out the twelve tribal leaders to spy out the Promised Land for forty days prior to entering Canaan. However, due to unbelief, ten of the twelve spies returned with pessimistic reports about how impossible it would be to conquer the land, even though God had promised them victory. The ancient Jewish commentary, the Mishna, records that the people believed the evil report, mourned all night in fear and turned against Moses and the two faithful spies on the ninth day of the month Av (Ta'anit 29a). The result, according to Numbers 14:1-10, was a total rebellion and led to an attempt to stone Moses and return to the bondage of Egypt on the ninth of Av, 1490 B.C.

If this rebellion had been successful, this violation of God's Covenant with Abraham would have led to the death and assimilation of the Jewish people into Egypt. God judged the rebel leaders and told Israel that this sinful rebellion would result in that whole generation wandering in the wilderness of Sinai for forty years, even as the spies had searched out the land for forty days. The result of this awful rebellion and unbelief in God's promises was the loss of the Promised Land for this entire generation, save for the two faithful spies, Joshua and Caleb. The Bible records that **"Moses told these sayings unto all the children of Israel: and the people mourned greatly"** (Numbers 14 : 39).

Thus, the ninth of Av became a fast of mourning as Israel wept over their lack of obedience to God and the tragedies which would follow so many times during the next thirty-five centuries.

2. The Destruction of Solomon's Temple by the Babylonians

The Babylonian army under Nebuchadnezzar besieged Jerusalem in 589 B.C. After a two year siege they breached the walls on the seventeenth of Tammuz, as recounted earlier. Twenty-one days later, the Babylonian army fought through the city to directly attack the Jews' final defenses on the massive Temple Mount on the ninth of Av, 587 B.C.

According to the Jewish commentary, Me'am Lo'ez by Rabbi Yaakov Culi and Rabbi Aguiti, and other historical sources, including Ta'anit 29a from the Jerusalem Talmud, the Babylonian army fought their way into the Temple on the seventh day of Av. "His men ate, drank and caroused there until the ninth of Av. Toward evening, they set the Temple on fire. It burned all night and through the next day, the tenth day of Av." Jeremiah, who was an eyewitness to the terrible destruction of the city, records that, after the conquering of the city and the capture of King Zedekiah, the Temple was burned by the Babylonian captain of the guard, Nebuzaradan, and confirms that, with no attempts being made to fight the enormous fire, the huge Temple complex was still burning through until the next day, the tenth of Av (Jeremiah 52 : 5-14).

This tragedy has been commemorated ever since by a solemn fast on the ninth of Av, known as Tisha Be Av. For more than two thousand years, on this day, the Jews have read the book of Lamentations in which Jeremiah laments the destruction of Jerusalem and the great Temple of Solomon. **"The Lord hath cast off His altar, He hath** abhorred His sanctuary, He hath given up into the hand of the enemy the walls of the palaces; they have made a noise in the House of the Lord, as in the day of a solemn feast" (Lamentations 2:7 and Zechariah 8:9).

3. The Destruction of the Second Temple by the Romans

As mentioned earlier, the Romans had been at war with the Jews since A.D. 66, and finally were about to crush the revolt by destroying their capital, Jerusalem in A.D. 70. Over one million, two hundred and fifty thousand people were trapped inside the city by the encircling Roman legions. The original attack had occurred on the Feast of Passover when a huge number of pilgrims came to Jerusalem to celebrate the Passover and were caught by the encircling Roman legions.

The Daily Sacrifice had ceased on the seventeenth Tammuz and now, twenty-one days later, on the ninth day of the month of Av, the army reached the edge of the Temple compound. The Roman general, Titus, gave strict orders that the beautiful Temple, the greatest building in the Roman Empire, should not be destroyed. He implored the Jewish defenders to surrender on terms so that their city and their beloved Temple would not have to be destroyed. However, the judgment of God had been delivered almost forty years earlier by Jesus Christ and this terrible appointment with destiny could not be avoided (Luke 19:41-44). The Jewish leaders rejected the offers of General Titus and the final pitched battle for the Temple Mount began.

Despite his firm orders to the Roman centurions, the enraged soldiers threw torches into the Temple and, within minutes, the Holy Place became an inferno of fire.

An eyewitness, Flavius Josephus, reported that General Titus stood in the great entrance to the Holy Place beating back his soldiers with his sword in a vain attempt to save at least the Inner Temple from their act of destruction. It is also reported that when Titus saw that the flames had reached the inner sanctuary, he fell to his knees and cried out, "As God is my witness, this was not done by my order."

Neither General Titus nor his soldiers realized that they were unconsciously fulfilling two very specific scriptural prophecies. First, the prophet Daniel, more than six hundred years earlier, had predicted, in his great prophecy of the Seventy Weeks, that **"after threescore and two weeks shall Messiah be cut off, but not for himself: and** the people of the prince that shall come shall destroy the city and the sanctuary; and the end thereof shall be with a flood, and unto the end of the war desolations are determined" (Daniel 9:26).

This strange phrase reveals two facts: (1) the people, the Roman soldiers, would be responsible for the destruction, not their leader **"the prince"**; and (2) **"the prince that shall come"** refers to the "prince" of the Roman Empire. When General Titus initially began the Jewish war, he was not of royal blood. However, his father, General Vespasian, became emperor in A.D. 69. When the final siege was undertaken in A.D. 70, Titus, his son had become the **prince"** and thus perfectly fulfilled the ancient prophecy.

A future and final fulfillment of this prophecy will see the Antichrist and his revived Roman Empire again attack the city of Jerusalem and the rebuilt Temple in reenactment of this amazing history of Jerusalem and Israel.

The second major prophecy regarding the destruction of the Temple was given by Jesus Christ in Luke 19:41-44. After the Pharisees had told Jesus to restrain His disciples from their joyful praise of God, **"He answered and said unto them, I tell you that, if these should hold their peace, the stones would immediately cry out" (Luke 19:40).** As the crowd drew near to Jerusalem, Jesus looked at the city and its Temple and wept over it.

He said: **"For the days shall come upon thee, that thine enemies shall cast a trench about thee, and compass thee round, and keep thee in on every side, and shall lay thee even with the ground, and thy children within thee; and they shall not leave in thee one stone upon another; because thou knewest not the time of thy visitation" (verses 43-44).**

This prophecy was fulfilled to the smallest detail in A.D. 70. As the Romans burned the Temple, the tremendous heat of the fire melted the sheets of gold that covered much of the Temple building. The molten gold ran down into every crack between the foundation stones. When the fire finally died down, the Roman soldiers used wedges and crowbars to overturn every stone to search for this gold, thus fulfilling Christ's words.

4. The Romans Plowed Jerusalem and the Temple

In A.D. 71, one year after the destruction of the city of Jerusalem and the burning of the Temple, on the ninth of Av, the Roman army plowed the Temple Mount and the city. This was a complete fulfillment of the prophecy of Micah: **"Therefore shall Zion for your sakes be plowed as a field, and Jerusalem shall become heaps, and the mountain of the house as the high places of the forest" (Micah 3:12).** The rabbinical source, Ta'anit 26b records that this was done in preparation of making the city into a Roman colony.

5. The Destruction of Bar Kochba's Army

After the fall of Jerusalem in A.D. 70, there was a period of enforced peace. In Matthew 24, Jesus spoke about Daniel's prophecy of the destruction of the Temple. Then He said, **"If any man shall say unto you, Lo, here is Christ, or there; believe it not. For there shall arise false Christs, and false prophets, and shall shew great signs and wonders; insomuch that, if it were possible, they shall deceive the very elect" (Matthew 24: 23-24).**

Among those false prophets was a dynamic Jewish leader named Simon Bar Kochba. As Jesus had predicted, many people, including the famous Jewish scholar Rabbi Akiba, acclaimed him as the "Messiah." Jesus prophesied before His rejection: **"I am come in my Father's name, and ye receive me not; if another shall come in his own name, him ye will receive" (John 5:43).** How sad that after rejecting the true Messiah they would now accept a counterfeit.

For two years Simon Bar Kochba and his followers were successful in repelling the Romans. Finally, Emperor Hadrian came with an enormous army that attacked and destroyed the Jewish rebels at Beitar, southwest of Jerusalem. On that tragic ninth of Av, A.D. 135, the last great army of an independent Israel was slaughtered without mercy.

Dio Cassius, the Roman historian, says that 580 thousand Jewish soldiers fell by the sword alone, not counting those who fell by fire and famine. The horses of the Romans, he says, were wading in blood up to their girths in the mud and mire of the valley battleground. Sixty-five years to the day after the city of Jerusalem and the Temple were destroyed, another rebellion against Rome ended in tragedy for the Jews.

The prophet Isaiah said, **"Within sixty-five years Ephraim [Israel] will be too shattered to be a people" (Isaiah 7:8 NIV).** The primary reference of Isaiah's prophecy was fulfilled sixty-five years after it was given by the Assyrian Captivity of the northern tribes of Israel in 721 B.C. However, it would seem that Isaiah may also have been referring to this final shattering of the people of Israel in 135 A.D., which also occurred on the sixty-fifth anniversary of the burning of the Temple, the ninth of Av.

6. England Expelled all Jews in A.D. 1290

On July 18, A.D. 1290, the ninth of Av, King Edward I ordered the expulsion of all Jews from England. It would be hundreds of years before they would be legally allowed back into the country. Almost four hundred years later, Oliver Cromwell, Lord Protector of England granted the Jews the right of settlement in A.D. 1657. It is interesting to note that the British Empire's prosperity and world power can be traced to its beginning in the reign of Lord Cromwell. The Jews returned and prospered in England and all her colonies.

"And I will bless them that bless thee, and curse him that curseth thee: and in thee shall all the families of the earth be blessed." (Genesis 12:3)

On November 2, 1917 Lord Balfour gave his historic declaration endorsing the setting up of a national homeland for the Jews. This was partly in response to the tremendous scientific contribution to England's war effort made by Chaim Weizmann, who later became Israel's first President. At the end of World War I, a victorious England held power through its British Empire over one quarter of the world. Tragically, at the same time Lawrence of Arabia was promising the Arabs that England would give them the lands that were being occupied by the Turkish Empire, in return for their help in defeating Germany and Turkey in the War. However, in these negotiations, the area of Israel itself was never conceded or demanded by the Arabs. The reason for this lack of interest is that few Arabs lived there because of the barren land. Also, the Arabs ultimately received over 5 million square miles of territory (comprising 21 countries and the Jews received only 8000 square miles (less than one fifth of 1% of what the Arabs received).

In the 1920's and throughout the period until 1948, England again and again reversed its promises to the Jews for a national homeland. Israel ultimately received only 17.5 percent of the territory promised her by the Balfour Declaration and the League of Nations British Mandate. Britain stopped Jewish immigration to Palestine throughout the period which contributed tragically to the fact that the Jews of Europe had no homeland to flee to when the savage persecution of Adolf Hitler began. The six million who died in the death camps could have fled to Israel if the British had not broken their word and stopped Jewish immigration to Palestine.

It is not improbable that the decline of Britain from its exalted status as the preeminent superpower that "ruled the seas" to the position of a second level power is somehow connected to her abandonment of support for the Jews and their national homeland. In this same period, 1917 until 1948, England lost her complete Empire, one quarter of the globe, and even lost the southern part of Ireland. The history of the rise and fall of many nations can be found stated succinctly by God over four thousand years ago, **"I will bless them that bless thee, and curse him that curseth thee." (Genesis 12:3)**

7. Spain Expelled all Jews in A.D. 1492

On August 2, A.D.1492, the ninth of Av, the Spanish government ordered the expulsion of some 800 thousand Jews. This event marked a watershed in the rise of the Spanish Empire, and from this point the empire's fortunes began to decrease, possibly in fulfillment of God's promise to Abraham that **"I will bless them that bless thee, and curse him that curseth thee" (Genesis 12:3)**. The rise and fall of many nations and empires can be traced to this prophecy and God's intervention in history.

It is interesting to note that this ninth of Av, A.D. 1492 was the same day that Christopher Columbus left Spain to discover the New World. This pivotal event was of tremendous importance to the Jews, for America ultimately provided a place of refuge for the Jews, and when the new nation of Israel was reborn in 1948, the United States of America became Israel's strongest protector and supporter.

There is some evidence to suggest that Columbus may have been of Jewish ancestry and that the ninth of Av, 1492, was therefore a propitious day for him to leave Spain.

8. Russia Mobilized for World War 1 and Launched Persecutions against the Jews

On the ninth of Av, August 1, 1914, as the Jews fasted and mourned, World War 1 was declared. This war involved the greatest military struggle in history to this point as **"nation shall rise against nation and kingdom against kingdom" (Matthew 24:7)**. As Russia mobilized its army, this triggered persecution and attacks against the Jews in eastern Russia and forced many of them to emigrate to the Holy Land. These Russian and eastern European Jewish immigrants joined the native born "Sabras" in building the agricultural settlements and infrastructure of the embryonic state. This immigration helped set the stage for the dramatic events of the creation of Israel in 1948.

As mentioned earlier the phenomenon of eight major historical disasters affecting one nation over thirty-five centuries happening on the same anniversary day is totally unprecedented in human history. As a student of history for the last twenty years I can assure you that I have looked, without success, for any such pattern of historical anniversaries or "coincidences" in the history of any nation other than Israel, God's Chosen People.

In fact, if any of my readers are mathematically inclined, I would suggest that they check the probability that these eight historical tragedies could have occurred by chance rather than by God's foreknowledge and sovereignty. *(see figure 3.)* Because there are 365 days in a year, the chance that even a second significant historical tragedy could occur by chance alone on the anniversary date of a previous tragedy on a given day, say, the ninth day of Av (August), is one chance in 365. The odds against a third similar event occurring on the exact same day, the ninth day of Av, is:

$$1 \text{ times } 365 \text{ times } 365 = 133,225$$

In other words, the odds against only three of these disasters occurring by chance alone on the ninth day of Av is only:

$$1 \text{ Chance in } 133,225$$

The odds that all eight events would occur by chance alone on the ninth day of Av, rather than by God's design, is equal to:

$$1 \times 365 \times 365 \times 365 \times 365 \times 365 \times 365 \times 365 \times 365 =$$

one chance in 863,078,009,300,000,000

or

1 Chance in 863 Zillion

It is important to remember that the above probability analysis only considers eight of the anniversary events, those which occurred on the ninth day of the biblical month Av. In all, there are more than forty anniversary events in Israel's history that we are examining in this chapter. If we were to add these additional dates to our probability figures, the numbers would be so astronomically high that no rational person could conclude that these events have happened on their respective dates by chance alone.

The consideration of these facts will lead many to believe, with this author, that the only rational explanation for this phenomenon is that God has His hand upon the Jews and Israel and that the Bible, which reveals these staggering, historically verified events, is truly the inspired Word of God.

NOTES TO CHAPTER 5

1. Michael Strassfeld, The Jewish Holidays — A Guide and Commentary (New York: Harper and Row, 1985), p. 69

CHAPTER 6

The Feast of Trumpets, Day of Atonement and the Feast of Tabernacles

"And the Lord spake unto Moses, saying, Speak unto the children of Israel, saying, In the seventh month, in the first day of the month, shall ye have a sabbath, a memorial of blowing of trumpets, an holy convocation" (Leviticus 23:23-24).

Of the seven "holy convocations" or appointed **"Feasts of the Lord"** mentioned in Leviticus 23, it is fascinating to note that four of them have had a prophetic fulfillment in the major significant events in the life of Jesus Christ. These are:

1. The fourteenth of Nisan, the Passover Supper – the Last Supper

2. The fifteenth of Nisan, the Feast of Unleavened Bread – the Crucifixion

3. The seventeenth of Nisan, the Feast of Firstfruits – the Resurrection

4. The sixth of Sivan, the Feast of Pentecost – the Giving of the Holy Spirit

There are still three appointed feasts to consider. Some scholars believe that the final three festivals: the Feast of Trumpets, the Day of Atonement and the Feast of Tabernacles will be fulfilled at the climactic Battle of Armageddon and the ushering in of the Millennium.

The First Day of Tishri – The Feast of Trumpets

The Feast of Trumpets occurs on the first of Tishri, in the fall (September-October). As soon as the new moon was sighted in eastern Israel, the watchers would trumpet the signal from hill to hill until the signal finally reached the Temple. Then the High Priest would blow the ram's horn (the Shofar) and announce the beginning of the New Year.

Rosh Ha'shanah, the ancient New Year's day for Israel as well as most middle eastern cultures, is celebrated on the first day of Tishri. Jewish tradition reveals its four-fold meaning: (1) New Year's day; (2) the day of Remembrance; (3) the day of Judgment; (4) the day of blowing the Shofar (the ram's horn).

On this day the synagogue lesson of Isaiah, chapters 60 and 61, teaches of that long-awaited day when the Lord is revealed as King and He will be accepted as the ruler of the world. Two spiritually important events have already occurred on the anniversary of the Feast of Trumpets. One still remains to be fulfilled in our future. *(see figure 1.)*

THE FIRST DAY OF TISHRI
THE FEAST OF TRUMPETS

ROSH HA'SHANA – THE ANCIENT NEW YEARS DAY
THEME: A DAY OF NEW BEGINNINGS

1. **JOSHUA BROUGHT THE FIRST OFFERING TO THE REBUILT ALTAR**

2. **EZRA READ THE LAW TO THE RETURNED EXILES TO AFFIRM THE COVENANT**

3. **THE POSSIBLE ANNIVERSARY DATE FOR THE BATTLE OF ARMAGEDDON**

Figure 1

1. Joshua Brought the First Offering to the New Altar

When King Cyrus of Persia decreed in 536 B.C. that the Jewish exiles could return to Jerusalem to rebuild the Temple, he sent with them fifty-four hundred articles of gold and silver that had been taken from the Temple when the Jews were captured and exiled. More than forty-two thousand people settled in towns around Jerusalem. The first thing the leaders of the people did was to rebuild the altar of God (Ezra 3:1-6).

Even before the foundation of the Temple was built, the priests began to offer burnt offerings to the Lord--on the first day of Tishri. The High Priest, Joshua (Jeshua-in Hebrew) presented this offering on the rebuilt altar. The name Joshua is "Jesus" in the Greek language. Therefore, Joshua has been seen as a type of Christ, our great High Priest.

2. Ezra Read the Law to the Returned Exiles

The rebuilding of the Temple was completed, before the people were able to rebuild the walls of the city to keep out invaders.

"And Ezra the priest brought the law before the congregation both of men and women, and all that could hear with understanding, upon the first day of the seventh month. And he read therein before the street that was before the water gate from the morning until midday, before the men and the women, and those that could understand; and the ears of all the people were attentive unto the book of the law" (Nehemiah 8: 2-3).

This day, the Feast of Trumpets, marked a new beginning for Israel as they accepted once again God's Covenant.

3. The Possible Day for the Battle of Armageddon

The prophet Joel seems to connect the great Day of the Lord – the Battle of Armageddon – with this day, the Feast of Trumpets. Consider the prophecy of Joel: *"Sanctify ye a fast, call a solemn assembly,* gather the elders and all the inhabitants of the land into the house of the Lord your God, and cry unto the Lord, Alas for the day! *for the day of the Lord is at hand,* and as a destruction from the Almighty shall it come" (Joel 1:14-15).

"Blow ye the trumpet in Zion, and sound an alarm in my holy mountain: let all the inhabitants of the land tremble: *for the day of the Lord cometh, for it is nigh at hand"* (Joel 2:1-2).

The prophet Jeremiah may also be referring to Armageddon and the Feast of Trumpets when he says, "Declare ye in Judah, and publish in Jerusalem; and say, *Blow ye the trumpet in the land:* cry, gather together, and say, Assemble yourselves, and let us go into the defenced cities, Set up the standard toward Zion: retire, stay not: for

I will bring evil from the north, and a great destruction" (Jeremiah 4:5-6).

Time alone will prove whether this interpretation is correct and whether or not the Battle of Armageddon will begin on Rosh Ha'Shanah, the Feast of Trumpets. However, one additional fact supports this interpretation. Both Daniel (9:27) and the book of Revelation (12:6) confirm that the period of the Great Tribulation commences with the Antichrist profaning the rebuilt Temple and concludes exactly 1260 days later with the destruction of Antichrist at the Battle of Armageddon by the Second Coming of Jesus Christ.

In his attempt to deceive Israel about his messiahship, it is possible that the Antichrist will enter the Temple, be killed and raised from the dead by Satan on Passover to try and "fulfill" the prophecies and prove his claims (Revelation 13:2-8,14). It is remarkable that it is exactly 1260 days from Passover until the Feast of Trumpets, three and a half years later.

The ancient oral tradition of Israel suggests several other notable events that occurred on the first day of Tishri (Rosh Ha'Shanah): the creation of Adam and Eve (see Sanhedrin 38b); Adam and Eve were expelled from the Garden of Eden; the waters from the flood were dried up and Noah removed the covering from the ark (see Genesis 8:13); Sarah, Rachel and Hannah all prayed and had their prayers answered on the first day of Tishri (Yevamot 64b); Joseph was released after spending sixteen years in an Egyptian prison (Rosh Ha'Shanah 10b).

Two more "appointed feasts" are yet to be fulfilled: The Day of Atonement and the Feast of Tabernacles.

The Tenth Day of Tishri –
The Day of Atonement

"And the Lord spake unto Moses, saying, Also *on the tenth day of this seventh month there shall be a day of atonement:* it shall be an holy convocation unto you; and ye shall afflict your souls, and offer an offering made by fire unto the Lord. And we shall do no work in that same day: for it is a day of atonement, to make an atonement for you before the Lord your God." (Leviticus 23:26-32).

The prophetic fulfillment of the final two "appointed feasts," the Day of Atonement and the Feast of Tabernacles, may also occur during the events leading up to the Millennium when Christ returns in glory to set up His Kingdom.

The Day of Atonement – Yom Kippur

Yom Kippur, the Day of Atonement, is the holiest day in the Jewish calendar. It is the day when all Israel mourns for their sins. On this day, the tenth day of Tishri, and only on this day (see Hebrews 9:7), the High Priest would enter the Most Holy of Holies in the Temple, the place where the Shekinah glory dwelt. He was to wear special clothing, a "sacred linen tunic," and enter the Holy of Holies with the blood from the sacrificial animals, and sprinkle the blood before the mercy seat. For twenty-four hours the people were to do no work, but were to spend the entire time confessing their sins that they had committed during the past year.

The writer of the book of Hebrews describes Christ as our great High Priest who **"Neither by the blood of goats and calves, but by his own blood he entered in once into the holy place, having obtained eternal redemption for us....How much more shall the blood of Christ, who through the eternal Spirit offered himself without spot to God, purge your conscience from dead works to serve the living God?" (Hebrews 9:12,14).**

The Day of Atonement was to be observed every year. However, every fiftieth year was the Year of Jubilee. Leviticus 25 describes this celebration: *"Then shalt thou cause the trumpet of the jubilee to sound on the tenth day of the seventh month, in the day of atonement shall ye make the trumpet sound throughout all your land. And ye shall hallow the fiftieth year, and proclaim liberty throughout all the land unto all the inhabitants thereof: it shall be a jubilee unto you; and ye shall return every man unto his possession, and ye shall return every man unto his family"* (Leviticus 25:9-10).

In this Year of Jubilee, on the Day of Atonement, all debts were cancelled, slaves were set free, and family lands that had been sold would be returned to their original owners. This was a year of celebration and renewal.

Modern Jews refer to the Day of Atonement as Yom Kippur. The word Kippur comes from the Hebrew word Kapper, which means "to cover over." God covers over the sins of His people through the blood of the sacrifice. When Christ was crucified, His blood "covered over" our sins so that when God looks at a repentant sinner, He no longer sees the sin, rather, He sees the blood of His righteous Son. We have miraculously become righteousness before our God because of the price which Jesus Christ paid when He died upon the cross. **"For he hath made him to be sin for us, who knew no sin; that we might be made the righteousness of God in him" (2 Corinthians 5:21).**

The blood sprinkled in the Holy of Holies on the Day of Atonement was a prefigurement of that ultimate sacrifice, God's only begotten Son, that had to be paid to atone for your sins and mine forever.

The Talmud of the Jews states, "There is no atonement except with blood" (Yoma 5a). Hebrews 9:22 says, **"Without shedding of blood is no remission."** As the first and only sinless man, Jesus was the only person in history who did not deserve the judgment of eternal separation from God that the Bible calls hell. Thus, as a perfect sacrifice, He could stand in our place and pay the price of physical and spiritual death which each one of us deserves for our sinful rebellion. Then, by His triumph over death and Hell, He won for us that righteousness which allows us to enter heaven.

Two historically important events have already occurred on the tenth day of Tishri, and one future event will possibly transpire on this date (see figure 2.)

1. Aaron, the High Priest, made Atonement for Israel for the First Time in the Wilderness

On the tenth day of Tishri, Aaron in the wilderness sacrificed for the sins of his people. This of course, was the first time God commanded it should be done. This first Day of Atonement is recorded during the Exodus in Leviticus 16:1-28.

2. Israel Saved from Annihilation in 1973 Yom Kippur War

On Yom Kippur, the tenth day of Tishri, the holiest day of the Jewish Year the Arab armies attacked Israel without warning. More than one hundred thousand Egyptian soldiers invaded Sinai against some three thousand Jewish defenders of the Bar Lev line on the Canal. In a miracle as great as any in Bible times, the enemies of Israel paused to regroup at a point when they could easily have overrun the Jewish state. God intervened in this war of Yom Kippur and Israel turned the tide of battle to win against Syria and Egypt.

THE TENTH DAY OF TISHRI
THE DAY OF ATONEMENT

THEME: MOURNING AND ATONEMENT FOR SIN

1. AARON, THE FIRST HIGH PRIEST, MAKES ATONEMENT FOR ISRAEL

2. ISRAEL WAS SAVED FROM ANNIHILATION WHEN THE ARABS OVERRAN THEIR DEFENSES IN THE YOM KIPPUR WAR OCTOBER, 1973

3. THE POSSIBLE DATE WHEN ISRAEL WILL MOURN AS THEY SEE THEIR MESSIAH WHOM THEY HAVE PIERCED

Figure 2

3. Israel will Mourn when they see their Messiah whom they Pierced

The prophet Zechariah, after describing the Battle of Armageddon, goes on to describe a supernatural outflowing of grace to the Jewish remnant several days after their Messiah defends them at the Battle of Armageddon (which possibly occurs on the first of Tishri):

"And I will pour upon the house of David, and upon the inhabitants of Jerusalem, the spirit of grace and of supplications: *and they shall look upon me whom they have pierced, and they shall mourn for him, as one mourneth for his only son,* and shall be in bitterness for him, as one that is in bitterness for his firstborn. *In that day shall there be a great mourning in Jerusalem,* as the mourning of Hadadrimmon in the valley of Megiddon" (Zechariah 12:10-11).

Then in chapter 13 we read: **"In that day there shall be a fountain opened to the house of David and to the inhabitants of Jerusalem for sin and for uncleanness"** (verse 1).

It is probable that this final reconciliation will take place on the tenth day of Tishri, the appointed Day of Atonement. On this day, Israel's rejected Messiah will finally be accepted by the nation He chose.

The prophet Ezekiel tells of a great day of restoration for Israel: **"A new heart also will I give you, and a new spirit will I put within you: and I will take away the stony heart out of your flesh, and I will give you an heart of flesh....Thus saith the Lord God; In the day that I shall have cleansed you from all your iniquities I will also cause you to dwell in the cities, and the wastes shall be builded"** (Ezekiel 36:26,33).

Paul prophesied of Israel's greatest Day of Atonement when he declared, **"And it shall come to pass, that in the place where it was said unto them, Ye are not my people; there shall they be called the children of the living God"** (Romans 9:26).

The Fifteenth Day of Tishri –
The Feast of Tabernacles

"And the Lord spake unto Moses, saying, Speak unto the children of Israel, saying, *The fifteenth day of this seventh month shall be the feast of tabernacles for seven days unto the Lord....***Ye shall dwell in booths seven days; all that are Isaelites born shall dwell in booths: that your generations may know that I made the children of Israel to dwell in booths, when I brought them out of the land of Egypt: I am the Lord your God"** (Leviticus 23:33-34,42-43).

The Feast of Tabernacles was the third of the three annual feasts which all Jewish men were required to attend in Jerusalem each year.

This feast, known as Sukkot was instituted by God in the wilderness of Sinai. It begins on the fifteenth day of Tishri, five days after the solemn Day of Atonement. It is sometimes referred to as the great "Harvest Home," which occurred at the end of the fruit harvest (Sept.-Oct.).

During this feast of seven days, the people were to live in booths—temporary dwellings made of branches—to commemorate their dwelling in tents for forty years in the wilderness. It is interesting that, on each of the seven days, they were to offer fourteen lambs without blemish (Numbers 29:15, 32). There is an interesting parallel in the Gospel of Matthew where he lists the genealogy of Jesus, the Lamb of God. The generations from Abraham to David are fourteen, from David to the Babylonian captivity are fourteen, and from the captivity to Christ are fourteen.

Although there is no clear, scriptural proof of the exact date of the birth of Christ, John's Gospel is very suggestive that the day was in fact the Feast of Tabernacles when he uses the unusual word "tabernacled" to describe the birth of Christ. **"the Word was made flesh, and dwelt [tabernacled – in the Greek] among us" (John 1:14).**

Christ's age of thirty-three and a half years at His death on the Feast of Passover, as evidenced by the historical data in Appendix B, would correspond precisely to this birth date of the fifteenth day of Tishri, the Feast of Tabernacles . Considering the phenomenon that over forty major events in Israel's spiritual history have occurred on the anniversary dates of biblical feast or fast days, it is more than probable that the birth of our Lord Jesus Christ also followed this pattern and occurred on the anniversary of the Feast of Tabernacles. If this supposition is correct, then each major event in the life of our Lord followed one of the three main Feast Days which required all male Jews to come up to the Jerusalem Temple to worship the Lord. He would have been born on the Feast of Tabernacles (the fifteenth of Tishri): crucified on the Feast of Passover (the fifteenth of Nisan) and His promised Comforter, the Holy Spirit, baptized His church with power on the Feast of Pentecost (the sixth of Sivan).

It is a well attested phenomenon reported by many Christian scholars, including Donald Guthrie in his New Testament Introduction (page 282), that the gospel of John is arranged to illustrate the life of Christ in the sequence of the Jewish liturgical seasons and feast days. The Introduction to Saint John in the authoritative Jerusalem Bible (page 141) states, "Moreover, this gospel is far more interested than the Synoptics [Matthew, Mark and Luke] in worship and sacraments. It relates the life of Jesus to the

Jewish liturgical year, and associates his miracles with the principal feasts: the Temple is often given as the setting both for them and for Christ's discourses." Regarding the analysis and division of John it states, "In the first place there is no doubt that he attaches special importance to the Jewish liturgical feasts which he uses to punctuate his narrative. These are: three feasts of Passover, 2:13, 6:4, 11:55, etc....Secondly, the evangelist on several occasions very deliberately calculates the number of days with a view to divide the life of Christ into set periods" On page 142 it states, "This division suggest that Christ not only fulfilled the Jewish liturgy but by doing so brought it to an end."

R. H. Lightfoot in his St. Johns Gospel – A Commentary also describes this gospel's focus on this phenomenon on page 20, "Finally, each of the sections is connected, more or less closely, with a festival of the Jewish sacred year. From the first it was a recognized part of the tradition that the Lord's death had taken place at Passover time, and in thus spreading the incidents of the Jewish feasts throughout the ministry, St John...invites the reader to see the Lord's whole work in close connection with the Jewish festival, especially the Passover....In St. John's view all these festivals in different ways have pointed forward to the coming of the Lord, and in that coming they have now been fulfilled.

There are two notable historical anniversary events connected with the Feast of Tabernacles and one possible future fulfillment. (see figure 3.)

1. The Dedication of Solomon's Temple on the Feast of Tabernacles

The dedication took place on the fifteenth day of Tishri, the Feast of Tabernacles, 1005 B.C. Second Chronicles records that on this day: **"Solomon assembled the elders of Israel, and all the heads of the tribes, the chief of the fathers of the children of Israel, unto Jerusalem, *to bring up the ark of the covenant of the Lord* out of the city of David which is Zion. Wherefore all the men of Israel assembled themselves unto the king *in the feast which was in the seventh month"* (2 Chronicles 5:2-3).**

As they begin to praise God, **"having cymbals and psalteries and harps, stood at the east end of the altar, and with them an hundred and twenty priests sounding with** trumpets:...For He is good; for his mercy endureth for ever: that then the house was filled with a cloud, even the house of the Lord; So that the priests could not stand to minister by reason of the cloud: for the glory of the Lord had filled the house of God" (2 Chronicles 5:12-14).

"Then Solomon assembled the elders of Israel...that they might bring up the Ark of the Covenant of the Lord out of the city of David, which is Zion. And all the men of Israel assembled themselves unto king Solomon *at the feast* in the month Ethanim [Tishri], which is *the seventh month"* (I Kings 8:1-2).

THE FIFTEENTH DAY OF TISHRI
THE FEAST OF TABERNACLES

THEME: THE COMING OF THE PRESENCE OF GOD

1. THE DEDICATION OF SOLOMON'S TEMPLE

2. THE POSSIBLE BIRTHDAY OF JESUS CHRIST

3. THE POSSIBLE USHERING IN OF THE KINGDOM AGE AND THE LONG-AWAITED MESSIAH

Figure 3

2. The Possible Birthday of Jesus Christ

As described previously, the evidence from John 1:14 indicates that Jesus was born on the Feast of Tabernacles in the fall of the year, rather than the traditional date of December 25th. If this is correct, then the normal period of pregnancy would mean that Mary conceived Jesus forty weeks earlier, precisely on December 25th. This curious fact may account for the early Church's acceptance of the date of December 25th, in addition to transforming the existing Roman holiday into a Christmas celebration of Christ's incarnation.

3. The Beginning of the Kingdom Age—the Millennium

It is possible that this great Feast of Tabernacles will see its prophetic fulfillment in that glorious day when the Lord of hosts will usher in the long-awaited Millennium of peace.

"And *the Lord shall be king over all the earth: in that day shall there be one Lord, and his name one....*And it shall come to pass, that every one that is left of *all the nations* which came against Jerusalem *shall even go up from year to year to worship the King,* the Lord of hosts, and *to keep the feast of tabernacles"* (Zechariah 14:9,16).

The Lord says that His command for all nations and people to commemorate this Feast of Tabernacles forever is so important that if they disobey, God will punish them (Zechariah 14:16-21). What is the possible significance of this Feast of Tabernacles to Gentile nations? Today, most non-Jews are totally unaware of this feast day and its meaning. What event could happen on the Feast of Tabernacles that would be of such worldwide significance that all nations will commemorate its anniversary forever in Jerusalem?

The defeat of Satan's plan to destroy man, the judgment of the wicked nations and the commencement of the Millennium will surely be celebrated forever with thanksgiving on its anniversary date by all nations saved from the final holocaust by Christ's second coming.

On the Feast of Tabernacles, leaders in Jewish synagogues throughout the world read this passage in Zechariah 14:1-21 which promises in detail their final Messianic deliverance from their persecutors and the beginning of the prophesied Kingdom.

The Twenty-fourth Day of Chisleu – The Ninth Month

Chisleu, the ninth month in the Jewish calendar, corresponds to our months of November-December. On the twenty-fifth day of the month, the Jews celebrate the Feast of Hanukkah—which was not one of the **"appointed feasts,"** but which commemorates the cleansing and rededication of the Second Temple in 165 B.C.

On the day before the Feast of Hanukkah, on the twenty-fourth day of Chisleu, Israel has witnessed four major historical events. It is quite possible that we will also see the defeat of Gog and Magog (the Russian-Arab armies) when they attack Israel on this anniversary date *(figure 4.)*

THE TWENTY-FOURTH DAY OF CHISLEU

THEME: CLEANSING AND RE-DEDICATION

1. **THE FOUNDATION OF THE SECOND TEMPLE IS LAID – 520 B.C.**

2. **THE ABOLITION OF THE TEMPLE SACRIFICE BY ANTIOCHUS IV IN 168 B.C.**

3. **THE RECAPTURE OF THE TEMPLE AND THE CLEANSING OF THE TEMPLE SANCTUARY IN 165 B.C.**

4. **JERUSALEM IS FREED FROM TURKISH RULE IN 1917**

5. **THE POSSIBLE DATE FOR THE MIRACULOUS DEFEAT OF THE RUSSIAN INVASION OF ISRAEL – WAR OF GOG AND MAGOG**

Figure 4

1. The Foundation of the Second Temple – 520 B.C.

The Jewish exiles returned from Babylon in 536 B.C. After sixteen years of tedious rebuilding of their farms and homes, the Lord stated through His prophet, Haggai in 520 B.C., that He would bless their endeavors only if they would change their priorities and first rebuild the Temple which lay in ruins. Haggai 1:15 records that they began to clear the rubble which had accumulated during the seventy years of desolation. After three months of preliminary work, the prophet declares that **"from the four and twentieth day of the ninth month, even from** *the day that the foundation of the Lord's Temple was laid,* **consider it....From this day I will bless you."** (Haggai 2:18-19)

This day, the twenty fourth day of the ninth month, Chisleu, ended the seventy prophesied years of "desolations" to the exact day, seventy biblical years (70 years times 360 days equals 25200 days) after the Babylonians began the "desolations" of the land with the besieging of Jerusalem on the tenth day of the month Tebeth, 589 B.C. (2 Kings 25:1).

2. The Abolition of the Temple Sacrifice – 168 B.C.

After the Jews rebuilt the Temple in 520 B.C., as decreed by Cyrus and Darius, they continued the observance of all the feasts even after Alexander the Great conquered Persia and made Israel into a province of his Greek Empire in 332

B.C. His successors, the Greek Seleucid kings allowed the Jews to practice their religion until the Greek-Syrian king, Antiochus IV, known as "Epiphanes", entered the Temple in 168 B.C. and "took away the golden altar and the candlestick of light" and other Temple furnishings, broke them in pieces and carried them off to his own country.

Later, he proclaimed that all the people should follow pagan gods and leave their own laws; and he also forbade the Jews to offer "sacrifices and atonements" in the Temple of God. He also commanded that they "should prohibit the sabbath and festival days to be celebrated" (1 Maccabees 1). The last true daily sacrifice took place on the twenty-fourth of Chisleu. The pagan sacrifices began the next day on the "five and twentieth dayof the ninth month (Chisleu)" (1 Maccabees 4:54).

3. The Recapture of the Temple and Cleansing of the Sanctuary – 165 B.C.

The abominations demanded by Antiochus IV provoked a revolution by those Jews who resisted his pretensions to be worshiped as a "god." A Jewish rebellion, led by an old man named Mattathias and his five sons, resulted in a spectacular war of religious independence. The sons, led by Judas Maccabaeus ("the Hammer"), fought the Syrian army occupying Jerusalem and defeated them against impossible odds in 165 B.C. The Jews reconquered the Temple site on the twenty fourth day of the ninth month exactly three years to the day after the evil King Antiochus IV had forced the ending of the Daily Sacrifice.

The next day, after conquering the Temple Mount on the twenty-fourth day of Chisleu, the anniversary of the last true daily sacrifice," Early in the morning on the twenty-fifth day of the ninth month of Chisleu...they rose and offered sacrifice, as the law directs, on the altar of burnt offering which they had built. At the very season and on the very day that the Gentiles had profaned it, it was dedicated with songs and harps" (1 Maccabees 4:52-54). Although a nearby fortress held out for some time, the Jews immediately cleansed the Temple precisely three years to the day after it was defiled.

Jewish legend, as recounted in the Talmud, says that a one-day's supply of the sacred oil was found hidden away in a wall of the Temple by a priest. When this was brought out to be used to light the lamp, it miraculously lasted for the full eight days of the celebration, until new oil could be made.

Today, this Feast of Dedication is commemorated by the Hanukkah celebration or the "Feast of Lights" for eight days, commencing on the twenty-fifth day of Chisleu. This festival represents the inextinguishable nature of the Jewish faith in God and was celebrated by Jesus Christ (John 10:22-23).

4. Jerusalem Freed from Turkish rule – A.D. 1917

For almost two thousand years the land of Israel was occupied by one empire after another. The Turkish rule lasted for almost four hundred years until World War I demolished the Ottoman Empire. The Allied Expeditionary Force, under the command of General Allenby, approached Jerusalem on December 9, 1917, the twenty-fourth day of Chisleu. General Allenby was a Christian and was concerned that the city of Jerusalem would be destroyed by his artillery unless the Turks first surrendered. Its huge walls could have held out for a considerable period. Miraculously, the Turks "gave up the city without a shot being fired."

Allenby decided to use propaganda and flew planes over Jerusalem which dropped thousands of leaflets to the Turkish defenders. Isaiah 31:5 may well have foreseen this unusual event: **"As birds flying, so will the Lord of Hosts defend Jerusalem: defending also he will deliver it; and passing over he will preserve it."** The leaflets told them to flee Jerusalem and were signed by Lord Allenby. Interestingly, the Turks had an old prophecy that they would never lose the Holy City until "a man of Allah" came to deliver it. The name, Allenby, reminded the Turks of this prophecy, "Allen - Allah, Beh – man "and this encouraged them to flee the city.

General Allenby chose to enter the city on foot out of his recognition that only Christ had the right to enter Jerusalem as a conquering King. Israel was now governed by the British mandate under the Balfour Declaration, which promised them a Jewish homeland. Thus was the foundation of modern Israel laid on this anniversary, the twenty-fourth day of Chisleu, 1917.

These are the four major events that have already occurred on this date. God's words to Haggai, **"Consider now from this day and upward, from the four and twentieth day of the ninth month, even from the day that the foundation of the Lord's temple was laid, consider it...from this day will I bless you"** (Haggai 2:18-19), certainly has been fulfilled in the history of the Jewish people so far. Is it unreasonable to expect that God will fulfill yet another prophetically significant event on this day?

5. The Possible Date of the Defeat of Gog and Magog – the Russian Invasion of Israel

The prophet Ezekiel (38:19--39:8) describes the awesome destruction God will deliver upon those nations which Russia will lead in attacking Israel. If you carefully compare Ezekiel 38:19-22 with Haggai 2:18-22, I believe you will see the strong probability that the twenty-fourth day of Chisleu—the day before Hanukkah in our month of December—is probably the day for this prophetic fulfillment. The Bible does not reveal the year of this battle, but recent events indicate it may be fairly soon.

Ezekiel 38:19-20 and Haggai 2:6,7 state that the earthquake will be so catastrophic that the whole world will be affected.

Yet once, it is a little while, and *I will shake the heavens and the earth, and the sea and the dry land;* and I will shake all nations, and the desire of all nations shall come: and I will fill this house with glory, saith the Lord of hosts" (Haggai 2:6-7).

"And I will call for a sword against him throughout all my mountains, saith the Lord God: *every man's sword shall be against his brother.* And I will plead against him with pestilence and with blood; and I will rain upon him, and upon his bands, and upon the many people that are with him, an *overflowing rain, and great hailstones, fire, and brimstone.* Thus will I magnify myself, and sanctify myself; and I will be known in the eyes of many nations, and they shall know that I am the Lord" (Ezekiel 38:21-23).

Notice the similarity to the wording of the specific prophecy of Haggai to the words of Ezekiel's prophecy:

"Consider now from this day and upward, from the four and twentieth day of the ninth month, even from the

day that the foundations of the Lord's Temple was laid, consider it....*From this day I will bless you.* And again the word of the Lord came unto Haggai in *the four and twentieth day of the month* [ninth], saying,...*I will shake the heavens and the earth;* and I will overthrow the throne of kingdoms, *and I will destroy the strength of the kingdoms of the heathen,* and I will overthrow the chariots, and those that ride in them; and the horses and their riders shall come down, *every one by the sword of his brother"* (Haggai 2:18-22).

There are awesome days ahead for Israel and the nations as the Lord of hosts once more intervenes in history to reveal His sovereignty and power. Only time will reveal whether **"the day whereof I have spoken"** will occur on this anniversary of so many of Israel's past deliverances.

"Behold, it is come, and it is done, saith the Lord God; *this is the day whereof I have spoken"* (Ezekiel 39:8).

As it is Written

Long ago in Bethlehem,
Born of low degree –
God in man came to earth
To set the captives free.

Inspired of God, the prophets foretold
How the Messiah would come one day.
As it is written, it came to pass –
No matter what men might say.

Our Saviour foretold in prophecy, too
The things that were to be.
And now His Word is coming to pass –
For all the world to see.

He said nation would rise against nation,
And that iniquity would abound:
That there would be famine and earthquakes,
And false prophets with doctrines unsound.

As it was in the days of Noah,
When man thought himself all-wise –
He will come like a thief in the night,
And His bride, the church, shall rise.

Then tribulation will curse this earth
Like man has never known.
For with great travail and anguished cries,
Even loved ones will betray their own.

But such shall hail the **King of Kings,**
Who was born of low degree.
Every knee shall bow, each tongue confess
That Jesus Christ is He.

God is not man that he should lie,
So do not be deceived.
You, too, will confess that Jesus is Lord –
Even if you haven't believed.

For he shall appear to all mankind
From the greatest unto the least.
As lightning shining unto the west
That cometh out of the east.

So watch the eastern sky,
O race of modern men.
As it is written, it shall come to pass –
Jesus is Coming Again!

– Myra Eaves Bumgardner

CHAPTER 7

Russia's Day of Destruction on the Mountains of Israel

"And the word of the Lord came unto me, saying, Son of man, set thy face against Gog, the land of Magog, the chief prince of Meshech and Tubal and prophesy against him, and say, Thus saith the Lord God: Behold I am against thee, O Gog, the chief prince of Meshech and Tubal: and I will turn thee back, and put hooks into thy jaws, and I will bring thee forth, and all thine army, horses and horsemen, all of them clothed with all sorts of armor, even a great company with bucklers and shields, all of them handling swords: Persia, Ethiopia, and Libya with them; all of them with shield and helmet: Gomer, and all his bands; the house of Togarmah of the north quarters, and all his bands: and many people with thee"
(Ezekiel 38:1-6).

The Lord is in control of history. Some of the appointments with destiny have already been kept and some are still in the future. Russia and her allies—many of those nations that formed the Warsaw Pact in 1955: Bulgaria, Czechoslovakia, East Germany, Hungary, Poland, Romania, and the Soviet Union—still await their appointment with destiny.

Ezekiel is the prophet whom God chose to record the message directed to the nations of the "far north." Ezekiel was among those captives from Jerusalem who were taken to Babylon when Nebuchadnezzar conquered Israel. He was raised near the Temple in Jerusalem and had studied to be a priest. One day, while he was **"among the captives by the river of Chebar,...the heavens were opened, and I saw visions of God" (Ezekiel 1:1).** He wrote his prophecies from Babylon from about 593 B.C. to 570 B.C. God's words through His prophet, Ezekiel were directed to his fellow captives as well as to those Jews still living in Jerusalem and the generations that would follow him.

Ezekiel prophesied that the rebirth of the nation of Israel would take place in 1948 as detailed in chapter 3. He saw clearly that Israel would arise miraculously from the graveyard of the nations, where she was buried in A.D. 70 by the Roman army led by Titus, and would become "a mighty army" in her ancient homeland. In 1948, Israel triumphed against an invasion by six well armed Arab armies. Her military forces consisted of a small voluntary citizen army, totally inadequate weapons, some jeeps and two small airplanes. Israel's armored force consisted of a few vehicles captured from her enemies. Yet, like David against Goliath, God miraculously caused a weak Israel to survive and prosper against incredible odds.

The prophet Ezekiel saw an amazing vision which depicted Israel as a **"valley which was full of dry bones."** This certainly described the fate of Israel after it's destruction by Rome in 70 A.D. and the centuries of persecution that followed. Anyone who has seen the sickening scene of the huge pits full of the emaciated, skeletal remains of the victims of the Nazi death camps can imagine that this perhaps, was the vision that the prophet saw twenty-five centuries ago. The Lord asked Him, **"'Can these bones live?' and I answered, 'O Lord God, thou knowest'" (Ezekiel 37:3).** Yet God told Ezekiel to watch a miraculous resurrection of these **"dry bones."** **"So I prophesied as He commanded me, and the breath came into them, and they lived, and stood up upon their feet, _an exceeding great army" (Ezekiel 37:10)._**

Today, after only forty years, Israel has the world's third most powerful air force and possesses more tanks than any other nation, except for the United States or Russia. The Israeli Defense Forces have rewritten the military manuals of the world with their audacious and brilliant tactics. According to many military analysts, today Israel has the third or fourth most powerful armed forces on earth.

Geographically, Israel occupies an area of land the size of New Jersey and only one-half the size of tiny Switzerland. Yet, despite its insignificant size and a population of only four million, Israel has attained a position of prime importance in the struggle between nations. For the last several years, over half of all of the resolutions of the General Assembly of the United Nations have concerned Israel. This astonishing fact can be explained only by prophecy and the fanatical hatred of Israel by the Warsaw Pact, the Arab nations and many Third World nations.

The prophet Zechariah prophesied thousands of years ago **"Behold, I will make Jerusalem a cup of trembling unto all the people round about, when they shall be in the siege both against Judah and against Jerusalem. and in that day will I make Jerusalem a burdensome stone for all people: all that burden themselves with it shall be cut in pieces, though all the people of the earth be gathered together against it"** (Zechariah 12:2-3).

Curiously, the first nation to formally recognize the state of Israel was Russia. In 1948, Stalin hoped that Israel would become a socialist nation and help offset the growing influence that the Western powers exercised in the Middle East. However, as Stalin soon came to realize, Israel would not become a pawn of her interests, so Russia quickly turned to the Arabs and encouraged their hatred towards the Jewish state.

More than twenty-five centuries ago the prophet Ezekiel prophesied concerning Russia and her allies (called "Magog"). He said that after Israel was reborn as a nation, Russia and her allies would attack her in an attempt to destroy her completely. Naturally, Ezekiel did not name Russia, East Germany, Poland and Bulgaria by their modern names. Rather, he referred to them by the names of the ancient tribes that occupied their geographical territories in his days. Ezekiel, chapter 38 and 39, describe this massive future invasion of Israel.

Ezekiel warned: **"Be thou prepared, and prepare for thyself, thou, and all thy company that are assembled unto thee, and be thou a guard unto them. After many days thou shalt be visited: in the latter years thou shalt come into the land that is brought back from the sword, and is gathered out of many people, against the mountains of Israel, which have been always waste: but it is brought forth out of the nations, and they shall dwell safely all of them. Thou shalt ascend and come like a storm, thou shalt be like a cloud to cover the land, thou, and all thy bands, and many people with thee"** (Ezekiel 38:7-9).

After the flood in Noah's day, his sons and grandsons dispersed to various parts of Asia, Europe and Africa. Ancient historians, such as Herodotus and Flavius Josephus in his *Antiquities of the Jews* tell us where these tribes ultimately settled. There is general agreement by Jewish and Christians scholars that these are the nations referred to by Ezekiel. The following chart and Figure 1 show the ancient name of each tribe and the modern nation that now occupies that particular territory.

The Nations of Ezekiel 38 : 1 – 6

The Ancient Nations	The Modern Nations
Gog and Magog	Russia
Meshech and Tubal	Moscow and Tobolsk
Persia	Iran, Iraq, Afghanistan
Ethiopia	Ethiopia and Sudan
Libya	Libya
Ashkenaz	Austria, Germany
Gomer	Eastern Europe
Togarmah	Southeastern Europe
"Many nations with you"	Various other nations allied to Russia

Figure 1

Jewish commentaries such as Kesses HaSofer identify "Magog" with the Russians and state that the word Mongol for the Siberian-Russian peoples is in fact derived from "Magog". While I was standing with my guide on the Great Wall of China, he described the numerous times in history that the armies have attacked at that very spot. He pointed out that due to the geography this would also be the logical place for the next Russian-Mongol attack on China. Arab writers confirm that in the Arabic language their name for the Great Wall of China is "the wall of Al Magog" because the Great Wall was built to keep out the invading armies from Magog (Russia).

Rev. Barnhouse, the great Presbyterian Bible teacher, wrote a fascinating treatise on the coming war of Gog and Magog and drew a map, based on the prophecies of Daniel and Ezekiel which showed a division of Europe, Asia and Africa between the forces of Magog (Russian Allies) and the nations of the ancient Roman Empire. His map, published in 1932, showed Russia allied with all of the countries as indicated in my maps – Figure 2 and 3 and as proven by the reading of your daily newspaper. He drew a line down the center of Germany based on the extent of the Roman Empire's occupation which was within 10 miles of the exact dividing line of West and East Germany that was imposed 13 years later by the victorious allies of World War II. He applied the same principles of interpretation to his prophetic study as are applied in this book. This is just one more example from history verifying that the Bible's prophecies can be taken in a common literal sense when the language and context are clear.

THE NATIONS OF EZEKIEL 38:1-6
THE WAR OF GOG AND MAGOG

THE TRIBAL GROUPS ARE DESCENDED FROM THE SONS OF NOAH – GENESIS 10 : 1-32

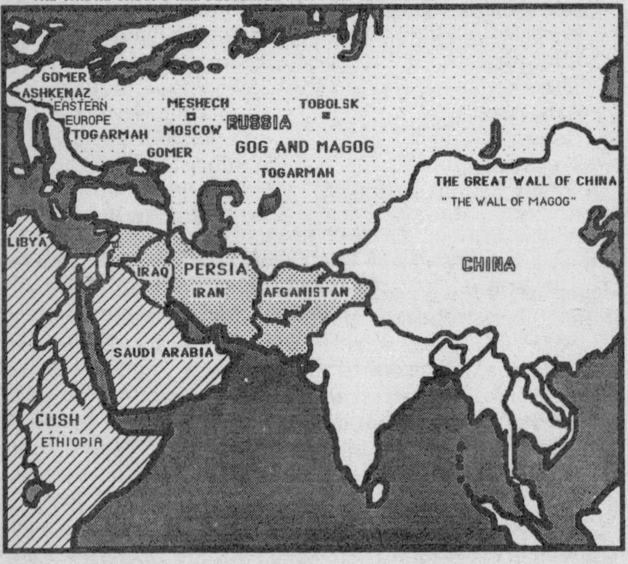

Figure 2

In Ezekiel 38:7 the prophet foretells that in this future conflict Russia (Magog) will also be the arm's supplier for all of these nations. God says, **"Be thou a guard [armorer] unto them"** It is fascinating to observe that the armories of each one of these nations, without exception, are filled with

AK-47 assault rifles, SAM missiles, RPG7 anti-tank weapons and various other Russian-manufactured arms, exactly as the Bible foretold thousands of years ago.

The prophet described an invasion that would come without warning in which the enemy invaded like a "storm" or "cloud to cover the land." It is possible that the prophet saw in vision an airborne invasion force, like D-day, and used the best words he had available to describe such an event.

Ezekiel refers to Russia attacking Israel at a time following her rebirth as a nation when she lived in a "land of unwalled villages" (38:11). It is interesting to note that, during the lifetime of Ezekiel and up until A.D. 1900, virtually all of the villages and cities in the Middle East had walls for defense. Ezekiel had never seen a village without walls. Yet, in our day, Israel is a "land of unwalled villages" for the simple reason that modern techniques of warfare (bombs and missiles) make city walls irrelevant for defense.

When the "Gog and Magog" invasion occurs, (see figure 2) it appears that the only response from the Western democracies is a diplomatic protest. **Ezekiel 38:13** says that **"Sheba and Dedan and the merchants of Tarshish" and "the young lions thereof, [probably the United Kingdom, the United States and the Commonwealth nations] shall say unto thee, "Art thou come to take a spoil?"** Tarshish, Sheba and Dedan were ancient trading nations and are believed by many Bible scholars to refer to Spain or Britain and their former colonies (**"the young lions thereof"**). It will not be the West which responds to this attack. The Superpower who intervenes to save Israel in its greatest hour of need will be their great defender, the God of Abraham.

God declares through His prophet Ezekiel that He will defeat Russia totally in the greatest military disaster in history. According to Ezekiel 39:2, five-sixth's of the Warsaw Pact armies (85 percent) will be annihilated upon the mountains of Israel. The Lord will trigger the greatest earthquake thus far in history, centered on the mountains of Israel, but affecting cities around the world. In addition, the destruction will be completed by **"pestilence, overflowing rain, great hailstones, fire, brimstone" (38:22)**. God will send such confusion and chaos that **"every man's sword** shall be against his brother" (verse 21). The devastation and loss of human life will be so great that "seven months shall the house of Israel be burying of them" (Ezekiel 39:12). The captured weapons will be used for fuel by the towns and villages of Israel for seven years (verse 9).

THE RUSSIAN INVASION OF ISRAEL
THE WAR OF GOG AND MAGOG

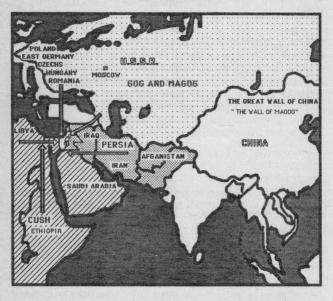

THE DIRECTION OF THE ARMIES ATTACKING ISRAEL —

Figure 3

Some Russian-produced weapons are manufactured with lignostone, a compressed wood product which was developed in Holland to be used as fuel. However, the Soviet weapon scientists found that this unique product was as strong as steel, light, pliable, and invisible to radar. These characteristics encouraged the Russians to use this product in many military vehicles and weapons. One of its characteristics is that it burns at very high temperatures and could be readily used as an alternative fuel.

It appears from Ezekiel 38:21 and 39:21-22 that God's purpose in this extraordinary intervention in history is to glorify and sanctify Himself in the sight of Israel and all other nations. The awesome destruction is not confined solely to the invading armies. God declares, **"And I will send a fire on Magog, and among them that dwell carelessly in the isles: and they shall know that I am the Lord"** (Ezekiel 39:6).

In June, 1982, Israel responded to a P.L.O. artillery bombardment of the villages of northern Galilee from a terrorist base in southern Lebanon. When the Israeli army entered Lebanon to destroy the P.L.O. bases, they expected to uncover substantial arms depots. However, they were astonished at the staggering number of weapons which Russia had stockpiled in tunnels carved out of the rock by an amazing tunneling machine developed in the U.S.S.R. Reports from Lebanon stated that there were tanks, anti-tank missiles, and thousands of shells. Huge underground supply dumps contained hundreds of thousands of uniforms, AK-47 assault rifles and millions of rounds of ammunition. These figures are so incredible that I would not have been able to report them without verification. An Israeli, Colonel (Reserve) Yehuda Levi, who was the Israeli Defense Forces media spokesman during the events in Lebanon was in a position to know firsthand about these captured Russian supplies. In a conversation I had with him in Vancouver, B.C., after those events, I asked him if the reports were correct. While, of course, he would not give additional details, he agreed that the reports were substantially correct.

For months, convoys of large covered trucks were seen in southern Lebanon heading toward Israel carrying these captured weapons. Few people realize that Israel now has a thriving arms business as a major supplier of mint condition Russian weapons.

The military reason for pre-positioning such enormous military supplies in Lebanon is that it is far easier and more efficient for Russia to airlift huge numbers of lightly armed men into Syria and Lebanon than to airlift supplies for them. The military equipment often weighs five to ten times the weight of the soldier who will use that equipment. The same logic forces the U.S.A. to pre-position enormous amounts of military logistics in Europe to be available for

American and Canadian troops who would be flown into West Germany in the event of a Russian invasion of Western Europe. The P.L.O., Iraq and Syria are themselves already so heavily armed that they had no practical use for this additional equipment.

The implications of these Soviet weapons in Lebanon are significant regarding the possible timing of this attack. The stored Russian military food rations (K rations) had a shelf life of only six months, which indicates that the massive attack on Israel was planned for the fall of 1982. Israel's "incursion" obviously set back the planned invasion somewhat, but it is clear that the political-military decision to attack Israel and risk a major war with the West has already been taken. In the years since 1982, Russia has had ample time to restore the weapons "lost" to Israel.

God set an appointment more than twenty-five hundred years ago to destroy Gog and Magog on the mountains of Israel **"Thus saith the Lord God; Art thou he of whom I have spoken in old time by my servants the prophets of Israel, which prophesied in those days many years that I would bring thee against them?" (Ezekiel 38:17).**

It is fascinating to read the Jewish commentaries on Ezekiel 38 and 39 which describe an oral tradition recorded from the Vilna Gaon that advises Jews to observe carefully when the Russian fleet (Magog) passes from the Black Sea through the Bosporus to the Mediterranean. "It is now the time to put on your Sabbath clothes because the Messiah is coming." For the first time in history, the Russian Navy has surpassed all other navies in the world in size, and has moved massive numbers of ships from the Black Sea into the Mediterranean Sea opposite Israel to challenge the former U.S. naval supremacy in that strategic area.

Although Scripture does not indicate the exact year in which this invasion and defeat will occur, the prophet Haggai give us a strong indication of the actual day of the year on the Jewish calendar when this prophecy will be fulfilled, as we discussed in the previous chapter. Haggai reveals that on the twenty-fourth day of the ninth month of the Jewish calendar (Chisleu), the day before Hanukkah, God will deliver Israel as He did twice before on this anniversary: (1) the defeat of the Syrian army and recapture of the Temple in 165 B.C. and (2) the capture of Jerusalem from the Turks in A.D. 1917.

The prophet Haggai declares: **"The Word of the Lord came unto Haggai in** *the four and twentieth day of the month* **[Chisleu], saying, Speak to Zerubbabel, governor of Judah, saying, I will shake the heavens and the earth; and I will overthrow the throne of kingdoms and I will destroy the strength of the kingdoms of the heathen; and I will overthrow the chariots, and those that ride in them; and the horses and their riders shall come down, every one by the sword of his brother"** (Haggai 2:20-22).

This description and the exact language is uncannily like that of Ezekiel 38 and 39 which describes Russia's defeat. The interesting point is that it names the exact day of the year on which this will occur. Since so many other prophecies have been so precisely fulfilled to the day, there is a strong likelihood that this event will also occur on its appointed day. **"Behold, it is come, and it is done, saith the Lord God;** *this is the day whereof I have spoken"* (Ezekiel 39:8).

God's appointment with Russia is set; it will be kept.

CHAPTER 8

The Ark of the Covenant and the Rebuilding of the Temple

"But in the last days it shall come to pass, that the mountain of the house of the Lord shall be established in the top of the mountains, and it shall be exalted above the hills; and people shall flow unto it" (Micah 4:1).

"In that day will I raise up the tabernacle of David that is fallen, and close up the breaches thereof; and I will raise up his ruins, and I will build it as in the days of old" (Amos 9:11).

One of the most interesting prophecies yet to be fulfilled involves the rebuilding of the Temple in Jerusalem. Various prophecies indicate that this Third Temple will be built before Satan's world dictator, the Antichrist, takes control and is finally destroyed by Jesus Christ when He returns to set up His Kingdom.

The prophet Daniel, in his vision of the Seventy Weeks (see Daniel 9:24-27) prophesied that this last great world dictator would make a peace treaty with Israel for seven years. After three and a half years he would break the treaty and enter their rebuilt Temple in Jerusalem and **"he shall cause the sacrifice and the oblation to cease" (Daniel 9:27).** Obviously, he cannot stop the Daily Sacrifice unless, previous to this, the Levitical sacrificial system has been reinstated. Since the Jewish Temple sacrifices have not been made since A.D. 70 when the Romans burned the Second Temple, at some point in the future the Jews will have to reinstate the Levitical sacrifice system on the Temple Mount.

Jesus Christ, in talking to His disciples about the last days and the Great Tribulation, warned the Jews that **"when** ye therefore shall see the abomination of desolation, spoken of by Daniel the prophet, stand in the holy place, (who so readeth, let him understand:) then let them which be in Judea flee into the mountains" (Matthew 24:15-16). The "abomination of desolation" is the ultimate defiling of the Holy Place in the last days by Satan demanding that he be worshiped as "God" in the Temple. This prophecy has not been fulfilled yet. Since the Temple with its Holy of Holies was destroyed almost two thousand years ago, Christ's prophecy requires that it be rebuilt in the future in order that the above prediction be fulfilled.

In his second letter to the church at Thessalonica, the Apostle Paul advised that the Lord will not return in glory to set up His kingdom until "that man of sin," the Antichrist, is revealed, "the son of perdition; who opposeth and exalteth himself above all that is called God, or that is worshipped; so that he as God sitteth in the temple of God, showing himself that he is God" (11 Thessalonians 2:3-4).

Obviously, in order for these events to occur, the Temple must be rebuilt by the Jews as a legitimate Temple of God. For almost two thousand years, Jews have dreamed of rebuilding the Temple. Since the stunningly victorious Six-Day War in June, 1967, Israel has possessed the city of Jerusalem. Despite United Nations' attempts to "internationalize" Jerusalem the attitude of Israel is best expressed in the words of General Moshe Dayan who said at the time, "No power on earth will remove us from this spot again." It should be noted that Israel still allows the Moslems to control and police the Temple Mount with its Muslim shrine, the Dome of the Rock. Religious Jews, of course, will not worship there, thereby fulfilling the prophecy of Luke 21:24 that "Jerusalem shall be trodden down of the Gentiles, until the times of the Gentiles be fulfilled."

"Should the Temple be Rebuilt?" ran the headline of an article in Time Magazine on June 20, 1967, following the recapture of the Temple Mount. The writer said, "Assuming that Israel keeps the Western Wall, which is one of the few remaining ruins of Judaism's Second Temple, has the time now come for the erection of the third Temple?" The article continues with this theme: "Such is Israel's euphoria today that some Jews see plausible theological grounds for discussing reconstruction. They base their argument on the contention that Israel has already entered its "Messianic Era."

In 1948, they note, Israel's Chief Rabbi ruled that, with the establishment of the Jewish state and the Ingathering of the Exiles, "the age of redemption" had begun. Today many of Israel's religious leaders are convinced that the Jews' victory over the Arabs has taken Judaism well beyond that point. Says historian Israel Eldad: "We are at the stage where David was when he liberated Jerusalem; from that time until the construction of the Temple of Solomon, only one generation passed, so will it be with us."[1]

The television show "60 Minutes" reported in March, 1985, that rabbinical students in Jerusalem are now studying the reintroduction of the ancient Jewish rites of sacrifice on the Temple Mount. The show was called "One Step in Heaven". Within five hundred yards to the northwest of the Western Wall of the ancient Temple, I took a photograph of this Yeshiva, or theological college, which is led by Rabbi Goren, the former Chief Rabbi of the Israel Defense Forces. This is the same Rabbi that blew the Shofar, the ram's horn, immediately after the recapture of the Western Wall of the Temple in June, 1967. This conquest returned the Temple site to Jewish control for the first time in almost two thousand years. In a Newsweek interview in November, 1981, Rabbi Goren declared that "the secret of the location of the Ark will be revealed just prior to building the Third Temple."

In Jerusalem today, religious Jews are forbidden by the Chief Rabbi to even walk on the Temple Mount lest they inadvertently walk on the Holy of Holies. Somehow in the near future a dramatic change must occur to allow the rebuilding of the Temple. Do the prophecies of the Bible give us a hint as to what this motivation will be? In my estimation, they do.

The Critical Importance of the Ark of the Covenant

The primary reason for the construction of both the Tabernacle in the wilderness and the Temple in Jerusalem was to provide a house for the Ark of the Covenant (see Exodus 25:22). The Shekinah glory of God dwelt above the mercy seat of the Ark in the Holy of Holies. The Ark was the most important object in Israel. Its sacredness and power was so overwhelming that improper handling of the Ark resulted in death (see 1 Chronicles 13:9-10). When the men of Bethshemesh violated God's rules about the Ark and looked inside to satisfy their curiosity, more than 50 thousand people died (see 1 Samuel 6:19). *(see figure 1.)*

THE ARK OF THE COVENANT

Figure 1

The army of Israel escorted the Ark of the Covenant around the walls of Jericho, and God's power caused the walls of Jericho to collapse miraculously (see Joshua 6). As the people of Israel ended their forty years of wandering in the wilderness, they finally stood before the Jordan River which had to be crossed before they could enter their Promised Land. God miraculously parted the waters of the Jordan River to show Israel that He would bring them into their Promised Land with the Ark of the Covenant leading them. **"And the priests that bare the ark of the covenant of the Lord stood firm on dry ground in the midst of Jordan, and all the Israelites passed over on dry ground, until all the people were passed clean over Jordan"** (Joshua 3:17).

Commentators, including David Lewis and Arthur Bloomfield, also see scriptural indications that the lost Ark will soon return to the Temple Mount and become the subject of newspaper headlines in our future. After being hidden for three thousand years, the Ark is once more ready to take it's place on the stage of human history. If the Ark of the Covenant once more appears, I believe that Israel will be compelled to rebuild the Temple with the Holy of Holies to house it. They would also have to institute a complete Levitical sacrifice system to complete the prophecy. Is this possible? What happened to the holy Ark in the first place? Where is it now? Does the Bible indicate that the Ark has a place in our future?

In Ezekiel 39:21-22 God declares that *"I will set my glory* among the heathen, and all the heathen shall see my judgment that I have executed; and my hand that I have laid upon them. So the house of Israel shall know that I am the Lord their God from that day and forward"*. These words, "I will set my glory among the heathen" may refer to the actual presence of the "Shikinah" glory of God above the Mercy Seat of the Ark.

In order that we might discover the truth about the Ark of the Covenant we will need to examine evidence from two different sources: (1) the secular history of ancient Ethiopia and (2), the prophecies and historical records of the Bible. These will enable us to come to a determination of the Ark's possible location and its possible role in our prophetic future.

The last time we read that the Ark of the Covenant was still <u>unquestionably</u> in the hands of Israel is the report of the Second Book of Chronicles 8:11 in which Solomon asked his wife, the pagan daughter of the Egyptian Pharaoh, to leave the area where the Ark of the Covenant was stored because she was not a believer. Shortly after this event the most important and powerful religious object in history disappears from the scene of Israel's national life. In all of the Bible's subsequent accounts of battles, rebellions, invasions and the looting of the Temple by various armies, there is not one single word about this most sacred and powerful object.

What could have happened to the Ark of the Covenant which would account for this amazing silence? There is one brief mention of an "ark" in 2 Chronicles 35:3 during the reign of King Josiah, when he ordered the priests to put this object back in the Temple, since it had been removed earlier by a wicked king to make room for his pagan idols. It is unlikely that this object referred to as an "ark" is, in fact, the true Ark of the Covenant because the Bible does not call it "the Ark of the Covenant".

Also, in light of the overwhelming divine punishment given to past defilers of the true Ark, it is difficult to believe that an evil king would have the audacity or the ability to remove the Ark and substitute false idols without divine retribution. However, if the Ethiopian history is correct and the "ark" referred to in 2 Chronicles 35:3 was a replica of the true Ark of the Covenant, then it is easy to understand how they could have removed this replica with impunity.

The Ethiopian Historical Records from their Royal Chronicles

During the reign of King Solomon, the famous Queen of Sheba visited Solomon in Jerusalem, several years after the Ark of the Covenant was placed in the Holy of Holies of the newly completed Temple.

Second Chronicles 9:12 tells us: **"And King Solomon gave to the Queen of Sheba all her desire, whatsoever she asked, beside that which she had brought unto the king. So she turned, and went away to her own land, she and her servants."** We know from the Bible that Solomon was not adverse to marrying foreign women and having children by them. According to Ethiopian history, the Queen of Sheba married King Solomon and they produced a son.

The Ethiopian Royal Chronicles record that Prince Menelik I of Ethiopia was the son of Solomon and the Queen of Sheba. He lived in the palace in Jerusalem and while being educated by the priests of the Temple he became a strong believer in Jehovah.

In a September, 1935, article in the National Geographic magazine, L. Roberts recorded his interviews with various priests in different parts of Ethiopia who consistently told the same story. They recounted that the Queen of Sheba had visited King Solomon and had "a child, Menelik I. Solomon educated the lad in Jerusalem until he was nineteen years old. The boy then returned to Ethiopia with a large group of

Jews, taking with him the true Ark of the Covenant. Many people believe that this Ark is now in some church along the northern boundary of present-day Ethiopia, near Aduwa (Adua) or Aksum; but, if it is here, it is so well guarded by the priests that no student from the Western world has been able to confirm or deny the legend." The Encyclopedia Britannica article confirms this tradition. "It [Aksum-Aduwa] contains the ancient church where, according to tradition, the Tabot, or Ark of the Covenant, brought from Jerusalem by the son of Solomon and the Queen of Sheba, was deposited and is still supposed to rest." *(see photo section)*

Menelik I, as a royal son of Solomon, was the founder of the longest-lived monarchy in history, with former Emperor Haile Selassie (who called himself the "Lion of Judah") claiming direct descent from King Solomon. In the 1974 takeover of Ethiopia by a Communist coup, the Emperor was imprisoned and died in jail under mysterious circumstances in 1975. The government buried him secretly in an unknown grave. Some of the descendants of Emperor Haile Selassie escaped and are now living in the West.

Prince Stephen Mengesha, the great-grandson of Emperor Haile Selassie, who now lives in Toronto, was kind enough to agree to several interviews in connection with this book. He confirmed my research about the importance of the Ark of the Covenant in Ethiopian history. Prince Mengesha's father, Prince Mengesha Sevoum was the Governor-General of the province of Tigre, which contains the ancient city of Aksum where tradition states the Ark was secretly hidden away by the custodians of the religious relics a long time ago.

Prince Stephen Mengesha spent several summers as a teenager exploring the region of Aksum, including the many ancient and almost inaccessible cave churches where early Christians held their services. He confirmed that the historic Church of Zion of Mary in Aksum is reported to be the repository of the Ark of the Covenant. A picture of Aksum and this Church of Zion of Mary is included in the center section of this book. The original ancient building was burnt in the sixteenth century. The present Church was rebuilt several hundred years ago over the original foundations and sub-basements of the ancient Repository. In 1965 Queen Elizabeth II visited this sacred building in a royal ceremony with the Emperor Haile Selassie. This area of Aksum is in the northern Tigre province which continues to fight successfully for its independence from the communist government of Ethiopia.

The Ethiopian official national epic known as the Glory of the Kings (Kebra-Nagast) contains an amazing story which offers an explanation of what happened to the Ark of the Covenant. In addition, there are several Ethiopian murals which tell how the Ark and the Tablets of the Law were taken to Ethiopia for safekeeping by Prince Menelik I. A photo of one of these murals is also included in the photo section. The Queen of Sheba, his mother, had died and the prince prepared to leave Jerusalem to return twenty-five hundred miles to his native country to become its king.

Prince Menelik bore an uncanny resemblance in beauty and regal bearing to his father. King Solomon wanted to give him a replica of the Ark to take with him to Ethiopia because the long distance would prevent him from ever again worshiping at the Temple in Jerusalem.

However, Prince Menelik was concerned with the growing apostasy of Israel and the fact that his father, Solomon was now allowing idols to be placed in the Temple to please his pagan wives. King Solomon gave the prince a going-away banquet and, after the priests were filled with wine, Menelik and his loyal associates switched arks and left the replica in its place in the Holy of Holies.

A group of priests with some representatives from several of the tribes of Israel reverently took the true Ark of the Covenant to Ethiopia for safekeeping until Israel should turn from idol worship and return to the pure worship of God. Unfortunately, Israel never wholly returned to following God exclusively and suffered a succession of mostly evil kings until both Israel and Judah were finally conquered four hundred years later. Thus, the Jewish descendants of Menelik I of Ethiopia, the royal son of Solomon, never returned the Ark of the Covenant to Jerusalem. The descendents of Menelik 1 and his Jewish priests, advisors and servants from the various tribes of Israel called themselves Beta-Israel and ultimately became a considerable part of their country's population, called today, "Falasha" Jews. (see figure 2.)

These descendants of Israel formed the ruling class during the greater part of Ethiopian history. The dynasty from Solomon and the Queen of Sheba ruled continuously until the twelfth century. The Abyssinian Royal Chronicles record that the Jewish Ethiopian kingdom was still being ruled by a Falasha Queen Judith about A.D. 950 and continued for two centuries. For several hundred years following a Muslim invasion in the twelfth century, the Muslims then ruled most of Ethiopia. Finally the original Solomonic dynasty was reestablished in A.D. 1558 by a Jewish king and continued until Emperor Haile Selassie.

Figure 2
THE ARK OF THE COVENANT
TAKEN TO ETHIOPIA

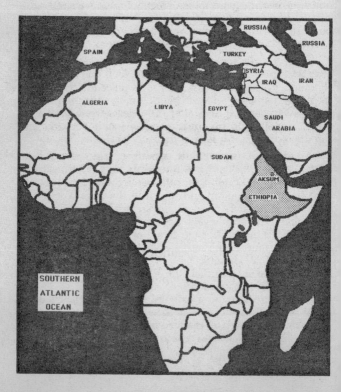

The Ethiopian language, Amharic, is of Semitic origin. The name "Falashas," which means "exiles," is given to Ethiopians descended from this group who still embrace the Jewish faith. Israel now officially admits these so-called "Black Jews" into Israel under their "Law of Return" and has mounted an extensive rescue effort during the last few years to bring thousands of these refugees home to the Promised Land. When word spread in May, 1948 that Israel had declared itself an independent nation many "Falashas" began converging to discuss plans to return to Israel and help with the rebuilding of the Temple.

Ethiopia also has a large Christian community. In Acts 8:26-39 we read that Philip, the evangelist, was led by God to Gaza where he met the Ethiopian eunuch, who was Treasurer to Candace, Queen of Ethiopia. The eunuch, as a member of the royal Jewish tribe, had come to Jerusalem to worship. On his return he was riding along a desert road in his carriage, reading from the scroll of Isaiah where the prophet describes Jesus (Isaiah 53:7-8). Philip led him to a knowledge of Jesus Christ as his personal Savior and baptized him. This conversion of this Ethiopian Jewish royal officer led to the beginning of the Ethiopian Coptic Church.

Visitors to Ethiopia have reported that the altars and communion tables of both ancient and modern Christian churches contain a wooden carving of the Ark of the Covenant, called the Tabot (the Holy Ark-Ge'ez), which recalls that the ancient Ark is still in their midst.

Prince Mengesha reported that an amazing underground explosion of Christian evangelism has occurred during the last few years, even among the revolutionary youth that originally supported the coup against Haile Selassie in 1974. Apparently the war, political repression and famine have caused many Ethiopians to turn to Christ despite the efforts of the government to suppress the Christian church.

It is fascinating to read the report in the Jewish magazine, B'nai B'rith Messenger in 1935 which stated: "The Tablets of the Law received by Moses on Mount Sinai and the Ark of the Covenant, both said to have been brought to Ethiopia from Jerusalem by Menelik, the son of King Solomon and the Queen of Sheba, who was the founder of the present Abyssinian dynasty, have been removed to the mountain strongholds of Abyssinia for safekeeping because of the impending Italian invasion, according to word received here from Addis Ababa, the capital of Ethiopia."

An article in the Toronto Star newspaper, dated July 19, 1981, states that "in July 1936, a news service reported from Paris that a Semitic syndicate had approached French underwriters about insuring the Ark – said by the dispatch to be in Ethiopia – against war damage. The report explained that 'the oblong, coffin-like chest of acacia wood, overlaid with gold within and without, was carried in ancient times as a protection against the enemy. It was believed that the Ethiopians, with their Semitic tradition and ancestry, might again bring it forth. This time it would be in the midst of tanks, airplanes and machine guns instead of spear-bearing bowman as recorded in the Old Testament.'"

The Ark of the Covenant According to the Bible

Do Bible prophecies reveal anything about the location and the future of the Ark?

As mentioned earlier, the last time Scripture clearly mentions the authentic Ark of the Covenant is in 2 Chronicles 8:11 during the reign of King Solomon. There is a final reference to an "ark" in the historical records of the Bible in 2 Chronicles 35:3 when, several hundred years later during the reign of King Josiah, a "holy ark" was returned to the Temple. If the Ethiopian history is correct then the true Ark of the Covenant was in Ethiopia at this time and the "ark" that had been removed earlier by one of the wicked kings and was now replaced by King Josiah was the replica which had been prepared in the time of King Solomon for his son, Menelik.

When we turn to the Old Testament prophets to discover any references to the Ark we find several intriguing references to a sacred object which may ultimately be revealed to be the "lost" Ark of the Covenant. In the verses that follow, the original word in each case is the Hebrew NES, but it has been translated in each verse by a different English word to fit the context as interpreted by the King James Version and New International Version translators.

The Hebrew word NES refers to an important object of respect, an object to awaken hope like a nation's flag. For example, the altar raised by Moses to celebrate God's defeat of the Amalekite forces, was called "Jehovah Nissi" (Jehovah my Banner). The word Nissi is derived from the root NES. It is possible that the word $\overline{NES}$ could be a symbol for the Art of the Covenant.

If the above suggestion is correct, then these prophecies seem to indicate that at the time Israel is invaded by Russia and her allies, God will bring forth the ancient Ark of the Covenant and miraculously defeat the enemies of Israel once more.

The prophet Jeremiah (4:6) states, **"Set up the standard [NES] toward Zion: retire [strengthen], stay not: for I will bring evil from the north, and a great destruction."**

In the great prophecy of Ezekiel (chapters: 38 and 39) about the coming war of Gog and Magog, he describes the supernatural defeat of the armies of the Russian and Warsaw Pact nations. The prophet then reports that God will set up an object of worship ("my Glory") that both the Gentile nations and Israel will recognize as proof that God has once more intervened in history to save his Chosen people.

"And *I will set my glory* among the heathen, and all the heathen shall see my judgment that I have executed, and my hand that I have laid upon them. So the house of Israel shall know that I am the Lord their God from that day and forward" (Ezekiel 39 : 21-22).

In Isaiah 18, we find the clearest indication that the Ark of the Covenant will be brought from Ethiopia at the time of the end. God addresses the people of Ethiopia in the first two verses and tells them of the part they will play in the unfolding events of the last days.

Isaiah's prophecy reads, **"Woe to the land shadowing with wings, which is beyond the rivers of *Ethiopia*:...All ye inhabitants of the world and dwellers on the earth, *see ye, when he lifteth up an ensign* [NES-ARK] *on the mountains:* and when he bloweth a trumpet, hear ye."** The closing verse declares: *"In that time shall the present* [NES-ARK] *be brought unto the Lord of hosts...*[from Ethiopia]*...to the place of the name of the Lord of hosts, the Mount Zion* "(Isaiah 18 : 1,3 & 7).

At the time of the miraculous defeat of Russia and the return of the Ark of the Covenant to Jerusalem, Isaiah appears to prophesy that God will intervene once again in history to affect the second great Exodus of the Jewish captives that are still held against their will in Russia and the communist block countries.

"**And it shall come to pass** *in that day,* **that the Lord shall set His hand again the second time to recover the remnant of His people, which shall be left, from Assyria, and from Egypt, and from Pathros, and** *from Cush* **[Ethiopia] and from Elam, and from Shinar, and from Hamath, and from the islands of the sea. And** *He shall set up an ensign [NES — ARK] for the nations,* **and shall assemble the outcasts of Israel, and gather together the dispersed of Judah from the four corners of the earth"** (Isaiah 11 : 11-12).

The prophet Ezekiel, after describing the miraculous defeat of Gog and Magog in Ezekiel 38 and 39, immediately prophesied, **"Now will I bring again [end] the captivity of Jacob, and have mercy upon the whole House of Israel... When I have brought them again from the people and gathered them out of their enemies' hands and am sanctified in the sight of many nations"** (Ezekiel 39:25-27).

A fascinating prophecy states that Israel will miraculously have its ancient pure language, Hebrew, restored to it, when God once again brings them back into their land. Even in the time of Christ, Hebrew was a "dying" language as it was used only by the scribes and priests for official religious purposes. Everyone else used the Greek language which had become the international "English" of its day. The revival of the ancient language of Hebrew in modern Israel, is another miraculous fulfillment of prophecy in our day. This recovery of a "dead" language and its revival after some two thousand years is a phenomenon without precedent in human history. It is interesting that God calls Hebrew a "pure" language. Several Israelis have stated that an unusual characteristic of Hebrew, is that one cannot use it to swear or take the name of the Lord in vain.

"For then will I turn to the people *a pure language,* **that they may all call upon the name of the Lord, to serve him with one consent.** *From beyond the rivers of Ethiopia my suppliants, even the daughter of my dispersed shall bring mine offering"* (Zephaniah 3:9-10).

Notice that the prophecy above connects the return of the "offering" from the dispersed of Ethiopia to the rebirth of Israel and the time of the revival of the pure Hebrew language. This "offering" could very well be the long lost Ark of the Covenant.

One final prophecy provides perhaps the strongest single evidence that the Ark will be recovered and have an important part to play in our future. The prophet Jeremiah describes a time when the Battle of Armageddon has been won and Israel is enjoying its Messianic kingdom.

"And it shall come to pass, when ye be multiplied and increased in the land, *in those days, saith the Lord, they shall say no more, the Ark of the Covenant of the Lord: neither shall it come to mind; neither shall they remember it; neither shall they visit it; neither shall that be done any more.*

"At that time they shall call Jerusalem the throne of the Lord; and all the nations shall be gathered unto it, to the name of the Lord, to Jerusalem:..." Jeremiah 3 : 16-17).

In other words, Jeremiah prophesied that, once the Battle of Armageddon is over and the Kingdom has commenced, then Israel will no longer talk about the Ark, they will no longer think about the Ark and they will no longer visit the Ark. The reason the Ark will no longer be important to Israel is that Jesus Christ will then be present to be worshiped directly as their Messiah-King.

Consider the fact that, as of today, no one has publicly talked about, thought about or visited the Ark of the Covenant in the almost three thousand years that have passed since it was last mentioned in the days of King Solomon, approximately 980 B.C. This prophecy of Jeremiah 3:16-17 does not make sense to me unless the lost Ark of the Covenant will first be rediscovered and, that in the years leading up to Israel's final great crisis, it will play a pivotal role in the spiritual life of the nation.

If the tentative suggestions of this chapter prove to be correct, then it becomes easy to see how the recovery of the lost Ark and its subsequent role in achieving a miraculous victory would encourage the Israelis to begin the rebuilding of their Temple. The placement of the Ark of the Covenant into the Holy of Holies of a rebuilt Temple would signal for Israel the final ushering in of the Messianic Era.

Some Christian and Jewish scholars believe that the true Ark of the Covenant is located somewhere else than Ethiopia. For example, there are Jewish traditional legends from the Apocrypha which relate that Jeremiah secretly hid the Ark and the altar of incense in a cave in Mount Pisgah in Jordan before the Babylonians burned the Temple (2 Maccabees 2:4-8). However, the story includes many elements which appear unlikely, including the fact that it contradicts the Bibles account of the Babylonian army capturing thousands of Temple artifacts and removing them to Babylon. Others have suggested it was taken to Massada in A.D. 70. This is contradicted by the fact that the Mishna commentary states clearly that the Ark was not the Second Temple.

Some believe that the Ark is located in one of the secret tunnels underneath the Temple Mount. A respected source told me in confidence that Jewish archeologists had in fact seen the Ark at a distance in one of these tunnels but were prevented from examining it because the Muslim authorities immediately sealed up the tunnel entrance. If this report is true, then I would presume that, in the light of the historical indications and prophetic scriptures already quoted, the Ark seen under the Temple Mount is, in fact, the replica that was made for Prince Menelik 1 by his father, King Solomon.

Only the fulfillment of the prophecies will prove conclusively precisely where the Ark is located and how it will be recovered and brought into the rebuilt Temple.

The question of the rebuilding of the Temple inevitably brings up the question as to how Israel could replace the existing structure known as the Dome of the Rock. This beautiful building was erected by Caliph Abdel Malik on the Temple Mount in A.D. 691. For almost thirteen centuries people have believed that this building was built directly over the site of the original Temple and Holy of Holies. If this was the case, it would be difficult to envision a situation in which Israel would be able to rebuild the Temple. Israel has been extremely protective of the religious and holy sites of both the Muslims and the Christians, despite the fact that historically both religions have often destroyed Jewish holy buildings. This sensitivity to Islamic veneration for the sacred Dome of the Rock led Moshe Dayan, as Defense Minister, to allow the Muslims to retain a guardianship role over the Temple Mount site, even after Israel had conquered East Jerusalem in 1967.

This act of generous toleration and sensitivity to Moslem feelings for the Dome of the Rock is seen by many Israelis today to have been a tremendous error in political judgment. However, even this decision was the fulfillment of a two-thousand- year-old prophecy made by the prophet John in the book of Revelation, chapter 11. In a vision of the final Tribulation period of three and one-half years leading up to the Battle of Armageddon he is told by the angel to:

"Rise and measure the temple of God, and the altar, and them that worship therein, *But the court which is without the temple, leave out, and measure it not, for it is given unto the Gentiles:* **and the holy city shall they tread under foot** *forty and two months."* **(Revelation 11:1-2).**

In other words, the prophet sees that there will be a period after the rebuilding of the Temple and the sacrificial altar, in which a part of the Temple Mount known as the Court of the Gentiles will still be given over to the Gentiles (the Arab Muslims) for forty-two months (three and one-half years) until Christ returns to set up His Kingdom.

The solution to this problem of the rebuilding of the Temple has awaited the completion of recent archeological research on the Temple Mount. Archeological work has enabled Israel to determine that the actual site of the original Solomon's Temple and hence, the location for the rebuilding of the Temple, is in the open area of the Temple Mount directly north of the Dome of the Rock.

In the months following the recapture of the Temple in June 1967, Israeli archeologists began to carefully dig a three-hundred-yard long tunnel in a northerly direction along the Western Wall from the area known as Wilson's Arch to the northwest corner of the ancient Temple Mount. This tunnel is almost sixty-five yards below the level of the streets of Jerusalem. It has become known as the Rabbi's Tunnel because, after 1967, the Rabbis used it to approach closely to the site of the Holy of Holies.

To the north of the Wailing Wall is an opening called Wilson's Arch. As I walked through the underground area where the orthodox Jews keep their sacred Torah Scrolls I was able to see where the scientists had dug deep down to expose the original massive Herodian foundation stones.

Some of these gigantic carved limestone foundation blocks were 46 feet by 10 feet by 10 feet. They weigh up to four hundred tons and are fitted so perfectly together that it is impossible to place even a razor blade between these stones. *(see figure 3.)*

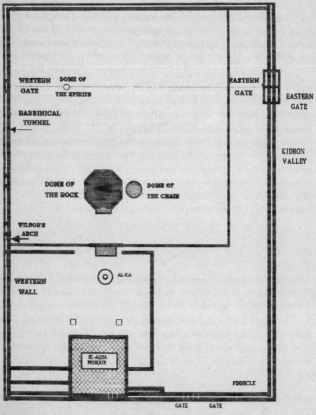

THE TEMPLE MOUNT
Figure 3

Further along the tunnel they have discovered the kind of thing archeologists only dream of finding. Several hundred feet north of Wilson's Arch they uncovered a gate that led into the Temple Mount which had been built in the time of the Second Temple. This Herodian gate was directly opposite the Eastern (Golden) Gate. The <u>Mishna</u> records that these Temple gates were precisely opposite each other and that the Eastern Gate led directly into the Beautiful Gate of the Second Temple. Now, after almost two thousand years, the Western Gate has been discovered. This proves beyond a shadow of a doubt that the location of the Temple, which lay precisely between these two gates, is north of the Dome of the Rock. An interesting photo I took from the Garden of Gethsemane, directly opposite the Eastern (Golden) Gate, shows clearly that the Dome of the Rock is built over one hundred and fifty feet to the south of the true site, directly west of the Eastern Gate.

This Western Gate was filled with the rocks and debris from the destruction of the Temple by the Roman army of Titus on the ninth of Av, A.D. 70. As the debris was cleared away, it was found that this gate led into a subterranean network of tunnels, some of which led directly eastward under the site of the Second Temple. Some of these tunnels led in different directions, confirming the legends that the whole area underneath the Temple Mount is honeycombed with secret passages and huge cisterns, as reported by Flavius Josephus. The Muslim authorities demanded that this Western Gate be sealed and the Israeli government agreed to limit the archeological diggings for the moment.

One of the underground cisterns that I saw could hold hundreds of thousands of gallons of water. These thirty-four cisterns were cut out of the natural limestone underlying the Temple Mount and can hold over twelve million gallons of water. This water storage was essential for the sanctuary services as well as for water reserves in the case of a siege.

Another confirmation of the true site of the ancient Temple and Holy of Holies is the location of a small Arabic cupola. It lies to the north of the Dome of the Rock and is exactly on an line drawn between the Eastern Gate and the newly discovered Western Gate in the archeologist's tunnel. This small Arab building, known as Qubbat el-Arwah, the Dome of the Spirits (or Winds), stands alone on the site of a raised flat foundation stone composed of the original bedrock of Mount Moriah. The Arabs also call this site Qubbat el-Alouah, the Dome of the Tablets, and these two names may well contain the ancient knowledge that this exact rock is, in fact, the ancient foundation stone that the Holy of Holies was built around. The Mishna records that there was a foundation stone in the Temple known to them as "Even Shetiyah" and that the Ark of the Covenant rested upon this foundation stone in Solomon's Temple. In the Second Temple, the Mishna records that the foundation stone stood alone in the Holy of Holies, because the Ark of the Covenant was missing.

In A.D. 1896 archeologists located a cistern, a short distance southeast of the Dome of the Spirits, which exactly conforms to its description in the Mishna. Its position was between the Temple porch and the Altar of Sacrifice. This pit was designed to contain the libation offerings connected with the Temple services. The existence of this cistern also tends to confirm the true location of the Holy of Holies.

As the diagrams of the Temple Mount (see figure 3 and 4) illustrate, the Third Temple can be rebuilt on the exact location of Solomon's Temple, with the Holy of Holies built around the ancient foundation stone, now occupied by the Dome of the Spirits. This means that Israel can rebuild the Temple without disturbing the site of the Muslim's Dome of the Rock. In addition the pictures of the model of the Second Temple clearly show that the Third Temple could be rebuilt on the original site and the Dome of the Rock could remain in the Court of the Gentiles over one hundred and fifty feet to the south of the rebuilt Temple.

Within Israel a group calling itself Ne'emanei Har Habayit, the Faithful of the Temple Mount, has built a model of the Temple and there is reliable information that a fund has already been set up to provide the money to rebuild the Temple.

The Temple Mount is in Israeli hands and the exact site for rebuilding is known and available. A fund has been created and a Temple priesthood is in training by Rabbi Goren's Yeshivat Torat Cohanin. In light of the evidence of the location of the Ark of the Covenant in Ethiopia, it seems that the stage is now set for the momentous events described by the ancient prophets of the Bible. Truly the echoes of the approaching footsteps of the Messiah can be heard in these exciting events.

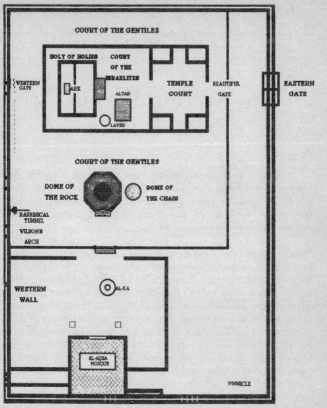

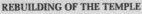

REBUILDING OF THE TEMPLE

Figure 4

CHAPTER 9

The Second Exodus –
From Russia

"Behold, I will bring them from the north country, and gather them from the coasts of the earth, and with them the blind and the lame, the woman with child and her that travaileth with child together: a great company shall return thither" (Jeremiah 31:8).

One of the most exciting events yet to occur in prophecy is the great outpouring of Jews from Russia. It will probably happen after the conclusion of Russia's disastrous attack on Israel. When God defeats their armies and delivers fire upon Magog (Russia), it is probable that, in the resulting chaos, many of the one hundred ethnic minorities and some of the twenty-seven different republics would try to separate from Russia. Many of the enslaved states of Eastern Europe would also undoubtedly seek their freedom. Over 40 percent of the population of the U.S.S.R. belongs to the Turkish-Mongol tribes, primarily Muslim, which are seeking greater autonomy. Even within Russia itself, over 90 percent of the people have never joined the Communist Party and may well seize any opportunity to throw off the yoke of 70 years of totalitarian oppression.

It is possible that this prophesied Jewish exodus from Russia will take place during the anarchy following this breakup of the Soviet Empire. The Jews have undergone persecution in Russia since the time of the Czars. During the rule of the czar in the nineteenth century they had to live under severe restrictions. Since the Communist Revolution in 1917, although officially free, these people have suffered continued repression. Despite the Russian agreement to the Helsinki Accord on Human Rights most Jews have been prevented from immigrating to the West or to Israel.

Hundreds of thousands of Jews have applied for exit visas, however, the number permitted to leave has dropped dramatically in recent years. There has been a slight lessening of restrictions under the "glasnost" policy of Soviet leader Mikhail Gorbachev, but the vast majority of Jews have experienced no end to their persecution. When a Russian Jew applies to leave the U.S.S.R., he often immediately loses his job, suffers tremendous harassment from the police and bureaucracy, and then can be arrested for not having a job (being a parasite). Despite this incredible "Catch 22" obstacle course, increasing numbers of Jews are applying to leave Russia.

As in the days of the Egyptian Pharaoh, God is saying, "Let my people go," and the Russian reply is identical to Pharaoh's, "NO!" However, Scripture declares that God will miraculously deliver His people from Russia just as He did from Egypt some thirty-five centuries ago.

The prophet Ezekiel, who prophesied of the Russian invasion of Israel in Ezekiel 38 and 39, goes on to say, **"Therefore thus saith the Lord God; Now will I bring again the captivity of Jacob, and have mercy upon the whole house of Israel, and will be jealous for my holy name;...When I have brought them again from the peoples, and** *gathered them out of their enemies' lands,* **and am sanctified in them in the sight of many nations"** (Ezekiel 39:25, 27).

The prophet Zechariah also spoke of the calling out of the Russian Jews when he wrote, **"Ho, ho, come forth, and flee from the land of the north, saith the Lord: for I have spread you abroad as the four winds of the heaven, saith the Lord"** (Zechariah 2:6).

When will this Second Exodus Occur?

Israel has celebrated the Exodus from Egypt each year on the night of Passover for more than thirty-five hundred years. This Exodus from Russia will be so miraculous that God Himself declares that Israel will celebrate this Russian Exodus in the future, rather than the ancient Exodus from Egypt.

"Therefore, behold, the days come, saith the Lord, that it shall no more be said, The Lord liveth, that brought up the children of Israel out of the land of Egypt; but, *The Lord* *liveth, that brought up the children of Israel from the land of the North,* **and from all the lands whither he had driven them: and I will bring them again into their land that I gave unto their fathers"** (Jeremiah 16:14-15).

It appears highly probable that this second Exodus will occur on the anniversary of the first Exodus, namely, on the Feast of Passover. The Bible records in Exodus 12:41-42 that God instructed Israel to celebrate Passover "forever" on the fourteenth of Nisan in remembrance of how God had saved them from the bondage of Egypt. However, in Jeremiah 16:14-15, after describing the Exodus from Russia, God tells Israel that, in the future, they will celebrate this "Russian" Exodus rather than the one from ancient Egypt. The probable reconciliation of these apparently contradictory scriptural statements is that the Jews will be freed from Russia on the same day, during Passover. Thus, the nation of Israel will continue to commemorate its ancient Passover Supper as commanded on the evening of fourteenth of Nisan, but will, from that point on, commemorate its second and more recent Exodus **"from of the land of the North."** If this prophesied second Exodus occurs on Passover, it will continue the pattern of biblical anniversaries discussed in previous chapters.

The Jews of Russia will be joined by Jews from many other countries as they are miraculously returned to the Promised Land:

"Behold, I will bring them from the north country, and gather them from the coasts of the earth, and with them the blind and the lame, the woman with child and her that travaileth with child together: a great company shall return thither" (Jeremiah 31:8).

When Israel has been saved by God, after being invaded by Russia and her allies, the nation will be transformed. Millions of Jews from Russia and other countries will return to the Promised Land. The presence of the Ark of the Covenant in Jerusalem will probably prompt the national religious leadership of Israel to rebuild the Temple. The political-military vacuum created by the destruction of Soviet military power (and the probable isolation of the United States) will set the political stage for the closing events of this age, leading us inexorably towards Armageddon and Christ's triumphant return to set up His Kingdom.

CHAPTER 10

The Rapture
The Hope of the Church

For what is our hope, or joy, or crown of rejoicing? Are not even ye in the presence of our Lord Jesus Christ at His coming?" (I Thessalonians 2:19).

In many different Scriptures, Christ has promised His Church that He will come to take her home to be with Him before the time known as the Great Tribulation of the "last days."

"For the Lord Himself shall descend from heaven with a shout, with voice of the archangel, and with the trump of God: and the dead in Christ shall rise first: then we which are alive and remain shall be caught up together with them in the clouds, to meet the Lord in the air: and so shall we ever be with the Lord. Wherefore comfort one another with these words" (1 Thessalonians 4:16-17).

During the last two hundred years, this belief in the imminent return of Christ for His Church has been a strong motivating factor to encourage Christian missions to **"Go ye therefore, and teach all nations, baptizing them in the name of the Father, and of the Son, and of the Holy Ghost" (Matthew 28:19).**

This hope and belief in the near return of Christ has prompted the creation of numerous missionary societies in Europe and North America which have brought the gospel to every nation on earth in this generation. As Christians read in the Scripture what God promises to the Church, they rejoice in the knowledge that our Lord has a unique future in store for them. However, along with the promises about His return to Rapture all believers, Jesus warned that the Rapture would be followed by the most terrible time of persecution known in the history of man, the Great Tribulation.

The Great Tribulation is a special period of God's judgment which is spoken of by Christ and the prophets. It commences three and one-half years after the future leader of the revived Roman Empire in Europe, the Antichrist, makes a seven year covenant or defense treaty with Israel. The Antichrist will break this treaty after the passage of three and one- half years by entering and seating Himself in the Holy of Holies in the rebuilt Temple in Jerusalem and claiming that he is God (see 2 Thessalonians 2:4).

Israel will rebel against this blasphemy causing the Antichrist to launch a reign of terror against all those who oppose his "worship." The Bible tells us clearly that this unparalleled time of tribulation, which begins when he enters the Temple, will last exactly 1260 days (see Daniel 12:7), which is 42 months of 30 days each (Revelation 13:5).

The event which will end this hell on earth will be the destruction of this Antichrist and the armies of the world at the Battle of Armageddon: **"He gathered them together into a place called in the Hebrew tongue Armageddon" (Revelation 16:16).** Jesus Christ will descend from heaven with His army of saints—the Church (Jude 14) and will destroy the Antichrist and his False Prophet with **"the brightness of his coming" (2 Thessalonians 2:8).**

The book of Revelation calls this period of three-and-a-half years "the Great Tribulation" (7:14) and describes the enormous destruction in which over half of the planet's population will die in **"the great winepress of the wrath of God" (Revelation 14:19).** However, praise God! The Lord has promised us that He has not appointed His Church to wrath but rather to salvation.

The Apostle Paul said, **"For yourselves know perfectly that the day of the Lord so cometh as a thief in the night....Ye are all the children of light, and the children of the day: we are not of the night, nor of darkness. Therefore let us not sleep, as do others; but let us watch and be sober . . . But let us, who are of the day, be sober, putting on the breastplate of faith and love; and for an helmet, the hope of salvation" (1 Thessalonians 5:2,5-6,8).**

Before looking at the many additional Scriptures which prove conclusively that the Church will be in Heaven with

Christ during the Great Tribulation, it may be instructive to examine the unfortunate teaching that has recently resurfaced which attempts to prove that the Church will go through the Great Tribulation and experience "the wrath of God" as described in chapters 4 through 19 of Revelation.

Why do Some Teach that the Church will go through the Tribulation?

Even those who believe that the Church must experience the Great Tribulation generally admit that there are many clear Scriptures which seem to teach that the Church will be in Heaven during this period. However, they have two problems or premises which force them to reject the teaching of this book (known as the pre-tribulation Rapture) and adopt the position called the "post-tribulation Rapture"

Those who teach against the pre-tribulation rapture usually hold these two premises. The first is an emotional one which contends that, since the Church has known persecution and tribulation throughout its two-thousand-year history, and many believers in totalitarian countries are in persecution today, it would somehow be unfair for the Church of the Western world to "escape to Heaven scot-free." While it is easy to understand such an emotion, it is wrong to build a doctrine on such flimsy material.

The reality is that many Christians in other countries in past centuries and today are undergoing tremendous persecutions and "tribulations." Of course, it is also true that those Christians who lived and died in peace throughout the last two thousand years have escaped the Great Tribulation.

The sad effect of the post-tribulation rapture position is that it can rob the Church of their blessed hope **"I also will keep thee from the hour of temptation, which shall come upon all the world, to try them that dwell upon the earth" (Revelation 3:10)**. Besides, if the Lord tarries much longer, it is entirely possible that the rising tide of sin, sensuality and anti-Christian laws, plus the drift toward "Big Brother" government, will inexorably lead to tremendous persecution for the Church in the Western world also. However, such persecution and tribulation of churches will not constitute the Great Tribulation.

The second and more important reason why some are teaching that the Church will be present during this terrible time is the failure to distinguish between God's plan for Israel and the Church, especially in that prophecy revealed by Christ in Matthew 24. They often acknowledge that there are many strong promises of a pre-tribulation rapture, such as this author cites. However, they inevitably come back to their interpretation of Matthew 24, which in their minds overrides these Scriptures and seems to indicate that the Rapture follows the events of the Great Tribulation.

In the passage in Matthew 24, Christ is explaining to His Jewish disciples (on the Temple mount) those events that will occur in Israel and other nations which lead up to the return of Christ as their Jewish Messiah. Please note that, at this point, before the crucifixion of our Lord and the coming of the Holy Spirit at Pentecost, there was no such thing as a Christian Church. The disciples' question concerns the coming of Israel's long-promised Kingdom; not the coming of Christ for His Church (which they did not even know about). If you had told one of the disciples during the week before Christ's crucifixion that there would someday be an organization called the Church, based on Christ's teachings, that would not follow Jewish Law or the Temple Sacrifices and would contain 99 percent uncircumcised Gentiles; he would probably have fallen off his chair in disbelief. One of the classic mistakes in interpretation is to take this conversation between Christ and His Jewish disciples concerning the Messianic Kingdom and read back into it the reality of the Christian Church which would not even come into existence until the Jews rejected Christ and God created the Church on the day of Pentecost.

Therefore, because of the context you would expect Christ's answer to concern the questioned coming of the kingdom for Israel, unless He specifically revealed that He was talking about the future Church. Christ does not mention the Church to His disciples in this conversation; thus we find that Israel is primarily in view here in the prophecy of Matthew 24.

Matthew 24 speaks of the Great Tribulation, beginning at verse 15 where Christ states that the Antichrist will set up the "abomination of desolation" (a supernatural statue of the Antichrist) to be worshiped in the Temple. In verses 40 and 41, Jesus says: **"Then shall two be in the field; the one** shall be taken, and the other left. Two women shall be grinding at the mill; the one shall be taken, and the other left."

This chapter tells us that at the end of the Great Tribulation, God will send His angels and **"they shall gather together <u>his elect</u> from the four winds, from one end of heaven to the other"** (verse 31). These "elect" are the people who become believers during the Great Tribulation of three and a half years. This gathering together is not the Rapture. This gathering of tribulation believers takes place at the end of the Tribulation, whereas the Rapture of the Church occurs sometime prior to the beginning of the Great Tribulation when Antichrist sets himself up as "God" in the Temple. Notice that the angels **"gather the elect"** (verse 31), whereas, at the time of the Rapture, **"The Lord himself shall descend from heaven with a shout, with the voice of the archangel, and with the trump of God: and the dead in Christ shall rise first" (1 Thessalonians 4:16-17).** This gathering of the "elect" Tribulation saints will occur at the conclusion of three and a half years of the most detailed prophetic events ever predicted.

Therefore: this gathering of the elect cannot occur immediately. The Bible describes many Tribulation events which must occur prior to the "gathering" of the Tribulation saints and thus, it cannot be correctly described as "imminent." These facts have caused many scholars to believe that this "gathering" is therefore, a different event than the "Rapture" of the Church. However, when we turn our attention to the coming of Christ for His Church, we find that there are no warnings or signals given of the timing of the Rapture. The Rapture can literally occur at any time.

Scriptural Indications of a Pre-Tribulation Rapture

Scripture presents five definite indications supporting the pre-tribulation Rapture:

First, in the first three chapters of Revelation the Church is mentioned nineteen times as being on earth. However, from Revelation chapters 4 to 19, which begins to describe in great detail the Great Tribulation, there is not one mention of the Church on the earth.

The Church is described during this period as participating in the Marriage Supper of the Lamb and at the "bema" judgement seat before Christ in Heaven. An interesting point is that Revelation 6:17 and 7:1-8 prophesies that before the great day of God's wrath comes the angels are told to hold back their judgement **"till we have sealed the servants of our God on their foreheads"** (verse 3). The prophet then describes that the angels **"sealed an hundred and forty and four thousand of all the tribes of the children of Israel"** (verse 4). The passage then describes that 12,000 from each of the named tribes of Israel are sealed for divine protection. This description of the sealing of the servants of God exclusively from the 12 tribes of Israel, before the wrath of God is unleashed in the Great Tribulation, would strongly indicate that the Church is not mentioned because it is already safely in Heaven at this time.

Second, Revelation 4 tells us that when John was **"in the Spirit"** and was "raptured" up to Heaven to stand before the throne of Heaven, he saw twenty-four elders with crowns on their heads. But Paul, in 2 Timothy 4:8, says that **"henceforth there is laid up for me a crown of righteousness, which the Lord, the righteous judge, shall give me at that day: and not to me only, but unto all them also that love his appearing."** Second Corinthians 5:10 tells of that day when **"we must all appear before the judgment seat of Christ; that every one may receive the things done in his body, according to that he hath done, whether it be good or bad."**

Therefore, as the twenty-four elders represent the Church and already have their crowns in his prophetic vision, then John has been taken to a time just after the Rapture and sees the rewarding of crowns to the raptured Christians at the judgment seat. After he witnesses the Rapture to Heaven, he then sees the sequential series of judgments of the Great Tribulation occurring upon the earth.

Third, as mentioned earlier, Matthew 24 describes the events of the Tribulation and focuses on Israel, not the Church. Jesus says that those in Judea (not North America) should flee to the hills (verse 16). Matthew records that the Jews should pray that it does not occur on the Sabbath (verse 20). The reason for this is that, after the Temple is rebuilt, the rabbinical restriction of a "sabbath day's journey" will again be in effect.

This rabbinical requirement (an interpretation of God's instruction in Exodus 16:29 forbidding "work" on the Sabbath) prohibited a Jew from walking (or fleeing) more than two thousand cubits from where he finds himself at the beginning of the Sabbath day. Obviously, these Jewish restrictions have no meaning for a Christian who is not under law. Jesus was referring to the Jews during the Tribulation, not the Church.

Fourth, Paul tells the Thessalonians that **"God hath not appointed us to wrath, but to obtain salvation by our Lord Jesus Christ" (1 Thessalonians 5:9).** Then verse 11 advises us to **"comfort yourselves together, and edify one another, even as also ye do"** because of this fact. In what manner would we comfort each other if our only hope is to endure through three and a half years of the wrath of God? Notice that Paul contrasts two separate and opposite destinies. He reminds the Church that its destiny is the Lord's salvation and that the Church has not been appointed by God to the wrath of the Great Tribulation.

Fifth, one of the strongest proofs that the Rapture will precede the revealing of the man of lawlessness, the Antichrist, is found in 2 Thessalonians 2:1-9. The church at Thessalonica was confused and they felt apprehensive that the great Day of the Lord could occur at any moment. Paul appeals to their memory of his teaching about **"the coming of our Lord Jesus Christ, and by our gathering together unto him"** (verse 1), and tells them not to be troubled by the incorrect teaching that Armageddon awaits the Church. He very specifically points out: *"That day shall not come,* except there come a falling away first, and *that man of sin be revealed,* the son of perdition" (verse 3).

This "revealing" of the Antichrist does not occur when he is born, nor probably even when he makes a seven-year treaty with Israel (see Daniel 9:27). He will be "revealed" in his satanic nature when he seats himself in the rebuilt Temple in Jerusalem, claiming to be God and demanding worship as God. It is this act which reveals his satanic character as Antichrist and confirms that he has been totally possessed by Satan.

Paul also says that the man of sin (or lawlessness) will only be revealed **"in his [apppointed] time"** (verse 6). He clearly indicates that there is an individual who, by his supernatural power, hinders or restrains the Antichrist **"until he be taken out of the way"** (verse 7) **"And then shall that Wicked be revealed,...even him, whose coming is after the working of Satan with all power and signs and lying wonders"** (verse 8).

Several suggestions have been offered by scholars as to the identity of the supernatural power of whom Paul says, **"The one who now holds it back will continue to do so till he is taken out of the way" (2 Thessalonians 2:7, NIV).** Some have thought the restrainer of Antichrist is human government, but that suggestion is disproved by the fact that governments or kingdoms will continue after Antichrist is revealed (see Revelation 13:7), and the fact that the singular personal pronoun "he" is used. Others have suggested that the Church is the "he"; however, nowhere else is the Church addressed as "he", nor does the Church have any power except that which God manifests through it. The "He" whom Paul says is holding back "the man of sin" is none other than the Holy Spirit.

Prior to Christ ascending to Heaven, He promised His disciples that the Holy Spirit would come to empower the Church and He would never leave it. In John 14:16-17, Jesus promised that the Holy Spirit would abide in His Church forever in His role as the Counselor. He even said that the Counselor could not come until He had ascended (John 16:7). However, unless the Holy Spirit is taken out of the way in His office as Counselor, Antichrist will not be able to be revealed. John 16:8-11 makes it clear that the Holy Spirit is He that restrains the Antichrist: **"And when he is come, he will reprove the world of sin, and of righteousness, and of judgment: of sin, because they believe not on me; of righteousness, because I go to my Father, and ye see me no more; of judgment, because the prince of this world is judged".**

Since we have been assured by Jesus that the father **"shall give you another Comforter, that he may abide with you for ever" (John 14:16),** it is probable that when the Holy Spirit removes Himself as the restrainer of the Antichrist; it is because the time has come when the Church (the Bride of Christ) has already been raptured and is now in heaven at the Marriage Supper of the Lamb.

It is worthwhile to remember that the Holy Spirit, as part of the Trinity, will continue to act throughout earth and heaven as He acted in Old Testament times prior to His coming at Pentecost in A.D.32. It is only in His role or office as the Comforter of the Church and the restrainer of the Antichrist that He will remove Himself. The third Person of the Trinity was, is now, and always will be omnipresent.

The day is coming, though it is known only to God Himself, when he will call every Christian, living and dead, to meet Him in the air and return home to Heaven to the great Marriage Supper of the Lamb. Since it is imminent, it could happen without warning at any moment. All we know about its timing is that it has not occurred yet, and that it will occur before the three and one-half year Great Tribulation begins.

The Father tells the Church **"to wait for his Son from heaven, whom he raised from the dead, even Jesus, which delivered us from the wrath to come"** (I Thessalonians 1:10).

CHAPTER 11

The Antichrist and the Revival of the Roman Empire

"Thou, O king, sawest, and behold a great image. This great image, whose brightness was excellent, stood before thee; and the form thereof was terrible. This image's head was of fine gold, his breast and his arms of silver, his belly and his thighs of brass, his legs of iron, his feet part of iron and part of clay. Thou sawest till that a stone was cut out without hands, which smote the image upon his feet that were of iron and clay, and brake them to pieces" (Daniel 2: 31-34).

Daniel's Vision of a Revived Roman Empire

One of the reasons Daniel rose from exile to become the prime minister of the greatest empire of the ancient world was his God-given ability to interpret the dreams and visions of King Nebuchadnezzar of Babylon. One of the king's dreams was of a great statue composed of different metals. Daniel revealed that this image symbolized the future course of world empires until the end of this age. One of the most significant revelations was that there would be only four world empires from Babylon in 606 B.C., until the Second Coming of Christ when He would introduce His heavenly and eternal "Stone" kingdom with Himself as Messiah King.

This vision of the great image revealed that each stage of these four empires would decrease in value (head of gold, chest of silver, thighs of bronze, legs of iron and feet of both iron and clay), but would increase in strength. As Daniel 2 indicates, the first empire was Babylon (Daniel 2:37-38); historians and Bible scholars agree that the second was Media-Persia; the third, Greece; and the fourth empire was the Roman Empire. The iron legs represent Rome in its empire stage. And the empire that is still to come, the feet with ten toes, represent the revived Roman Empire in its final form during the period leading up to the Battle of Armageddon.

One of the most amazing aspects of this prophecy is that it predicted that no matter what ambitious men would attempt; no world empire would ever successfully replace the Roman Empire. Mohammed, Charlemagne, Genghis Khan, Frederich Barbarossa, Napoleon, the British Empire, Adolf Hitler, and the Russians have all attempted to build a fifth world empire, but each in turn has failed. The future is in the hands of God (2:45) and He has decreed that this last world power will be a revival of the ancient Roman Empire within a confederacy of ten nations, based upon the territory of the old Roman Empire.

The Antichrist-Leader of the Revived Roman Empire

Several years later, Daniel himself had a parallel vision of this final stage of the revived Roman Empire: **"After this I saw in the night visions, and behold a fourth beast, dreadful and terrible, and strong exceedingly; and it had great iron teeth: it devoured and brake in pieces, and stamped the residue with the feet of it: and it was diverse from all the beasts that were before it; and it had ten horns. I considered the horns, and, behold, there came up among them another little horn, before whom there were three of the first horns plucked up by the roots" (Daniel 7:7-8).**

The interpretation of this vision indicates that after these ten nations have formed a ten-nation "Roman confederacy", then the "little horn," the new leader of Western Europe (the Antichrist), will seize three of the nations by force. Then the other seven nations apparently will submit and join him. Although he will rule for seven years (9:27), his absolute power over all of the nations of the earth and over the new believers, the "tribulation saints," will last only for 1260 days from his sacrilegious entrance into the new Temple in Jerusalem (Daniel 7:25) until the final Battle of Armageddon when he will be destroyed by Christ.

This revived Roman Empire of ten nations will probably closely follow the geographical outlines of the ancient one. The map (figure 1.) illustrates the extent of ancient Rome. Notice the old boundary line which represents the deepest penetration of the Roman legions into Germany. It is startling to realize that this ancient boundary is almost exactly the division that exists today between East and West Germany. Rome never conquered Ireland, and it is significant that Great Britain has lost the southern Republic of Ireland and it is not improbable that Britain will eventually withdraw from Northern Ireland. Scotland was never conquered by Rome and Emperor Hadrian. In A.D. 121, his legions built Hadrian's Wall to separate Roman England from free Scotland and kept out the invaders for almost two hundred years. In this light, it is fascinating to follow the negotiations of the Scottish nationalists who are seeking devolution, or actual independence for Scotland since the development of the incredibly valuable North Sea oil off the northern shores of Scotland.

THE FOURTH KINGDOM OF DANIEL – THE ROMAN EMPIRE
THE REVIVAL OF THE ROMAN EMPIRE

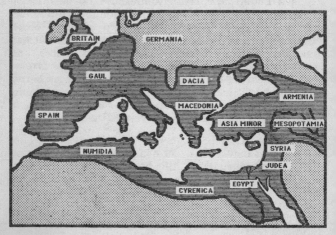

Figure 1

The tremendous upheaval that would follow the breakup of the Soviet Empire (as a consequence of the defeat

142

of Russia when she attacks Israel) could create an opportunity for a dynamic European leader to seize control of the three Eastern European nations which will have broken free in the chaos of Russia's military defeat. These three nations (Bulgaria, Romania and Yugoslavia) were once part of the ancient Roman Empire and have been, like three rib bones, caught in the jaws of the Russian bear since 1945. These three nations could escape Russian domination when God defeats Russia and its allies when they attack Israel (see Daniel 7:5) and represent the first successful conquest of the Antichrist on his road to world power.

In June, 1979, Europe held its first election for the European Parliament, the first directly elected, multinational assembly in history, which was set up to deal with European community problems. This is a natural development of a process which began in 1958 with the founding of the European Common Market (officially known as the European Economic Community or E.E.C.) and the North Atlantic Treaty Organization. Europe, unknowingly, began its first tentative steps toward the long-prophesied ten-nation confederacy based on the ancient Roman Empire. Interestingly, the E.E.C. is based on the Treaty of Rome, which was signed in Rome on March 25, 1967. Jean Monnet was one of the inspirers of this union and declared the ultimate objective when he said, "Once a common market interest has been created, then political union will come naturally."

A report from Brussels in January, 1985, told of a poll which showed that 52 percent of Europeans supported the idea of transforming the present, ten-nation Common Market into a true confederacy to be known as the United States of Europe. This proposed confederation would go well beyond the current economic, customs union, and involve defense as well as political union similar to Canada's provinces or the United States of America. All of these actions are the embryonic stages of the final Revival of the Roman Empire foreseen by the prophet Daniel.

The Last Seven Years - Daniel's 70th Week

In an earlier chapter we saw the absolute precision of the fulfillment of Daniel's vision of the seventy "weeks" of years. Jesus Christ was "cut-off" (9:26) on Palm Sunday, A.D. 32, exactly to the day that the sixty-nine "weeks" of years terminated. That left one remaining "week" of years (seven years) to be fulfilled at the end of this age, just before Christ returns at the Battle of Armageddon to set up the kingdom that has been postponed almost two thousand years because Israel rejected her Messiah.

The diagram (figure 2.) illustrates this seventieth "week" of seven years that will commence with a seven-year treaty made with Israel by the Antichrist, the leader of the ten-nation revived Roman Empire. This treaty will guarantee Israel's security. After more than forty years in a state of war with her Arab neighbors, Israeli citizens bear the highest taxes for defense of any nation in the world. It is easy to see why Israel will be tempted to make a defense treaty and covenant with the Antichrist and his empire to finally be able to rest from eternal vigilance. As indicated in chapter 6 ("The Feast of Tabernacles"), it is possible that this treaty will be signed in the fall of the year, on Israel's Feast of Tabernacles, the fifteenth day of the month Tishri. **"And he shall confirm the covenant with many for one week: and in the midst of the week he shall cause the sacrifice and the oblation to cease, and for the overspreading of abominations he shall make it desolate, even until the consummation, and that determined shall be poured upon the desolate" (Daniel 9:27).** This prophecy is focused on Israel, not the Church. The vision is given to a Hebrew prophet in answer to his question as to what will happen to his people Israel in the future.

In other words the Antichrist, the world dictator, will force the Jews to stop the sacrifices in the rebuilt Temple, and then he will set up an idol of himself (the abomination) in the Temple to be worshiped as "God" until he is destroyed at the end of the seven years when Christ returns. This period, from his entering the Temple until his destruction, will last exactly 1260 days (Daniel 7:25; 12:6-7; Revelation 13:5), or forty-two months of thirty days each. Revelation 13:3,14-18 tells us that the Antichrist will be killed and miraculously rise from the dead through Satan's power exactly at the midpoint of the last seven years.

It is probable that this will occur on Passover, with his resurrection occurring on the Feast of Firstfruits (the seventeenth of Nisan, in the spring) in order that he can imitate Christ as "Messiah" and pretend to fulfill the biblical prophecies about Christ's first coming.

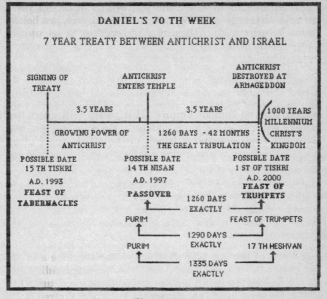

Figure 2

Interestingly, this would fit the pattern of biblically significant events occurring on Jewish feast days. As predicted in the Bible, his time of total power lasts only 1260 days or 42 months of 30 days each (Revelation 13:5). This period of 1260 days would bring us to the first day of Tishri, the Feast of Trumpets, upon which we can expect the Antichrist's destruction at the prophesied Battle of Armageddon (Joel 2:1-2, 15). It is fascinating to consider the curious details that the prophet Daniel supplies to supplement this future history. After Daniel describes the Antichrist's power over the Holy People for three and one half years (a time and times and the dividing of time – 360 days plus 2 times 360 days plus one half of 360 days = 1260 days) in Daniel 7:25. However, Daniel is told in his last vision that the conclusion would be <u>1290 days</u> **"from the time that the daily sacrifice is taken away"** and also that **"Blessed is he that waiteth, and cometh to the thousand three hundred and five and thirty days (1335 days – Daniel 12:11-12).**

In all the commentaries in my library I have never seen an adequate explanation of how these three different figures could be reconciled in the career and death of the Antichrist at the Battle of Armageddon.

Let me offer a possible scenario which might fit these prophetic scriptural indications of the exact timing of the Great Tribulation *(see Figure 2 – bottom of diagram)*. In keeping with the pattern of biblical anniversaries, it is possible that the Antichrist will stop the Daily Sacrifice in the Temple on the Feast of Purim, which occurs 30 days before the Feast of Passover in A.D. 1997. Some thirty days later on Passover, someone, possibly a Jewish believer will kill this tyrant; but he will rise from the dead due to the supernatural power of Satan (Revelation 13:3-8, 15-18). He would be possessed by Satan on Passover in exactly the same manner as Judas Iscariot (Luke 22:1-3). This is the true "revealing" of "the Man of Sin" in his Satanic-possessed nature as the Antichrist.

Thus, these two periods end on the same day, the Feast of Trumpets, the Battle of Armageddon. However, the first event, the stopping of the Daily Sacrifice would occur thirty days before the Passover on the Feast of Purim, the anniversary of that day recorded in the book of Esther 3:13 when the ancient enemy of the Jews sought to destroy the entire Jewish race. If this interpretation is correct then 1335 days from the Feast of Purim in A.D. 1997 would bring up to a day known in the biblical calendar as the 17th day of Heshvan (45 days after the Battle of Armageddon and the death of Antichrist at the Second Coming of Christ). It seems more than coincidental that this day of blessing, according to the prophet Daniel in chapter 12:12, should be the exact anniversary of the day that God destroyed all life on Earth in the Flood in the days of Noah. The 17th day of Heshvan is the day that the 40 days of rain began and the fountains of the deep opened to destroy man's sinful rebellion. Another key anniversary connected with the 17th day of Heshvan was the great day of blessing brought about when Lord Balfour made the famous Balfour Declaration in November 2, 1917 to declare that Palestine would become a Jewish National Homeland for the first time in almost two thousand years. It would certainly be consistent for God to commemorate this anniversary by ushering in the final blessings of the promised Millennial Kingdom on that day.

Only time will tell whether or not this is the correct interpretation.

The Final Battle of Armageddon

This final great Battle of Armageddon will occur in northern Israel and extend down the great Valley of Jezreel, below the mountain of Megiddo. The name Armageddon comes from Har for "mountain" and the ancient city of Megiddo which overlooks this enormous plain. It is also known as the Valley of Jehoshaphat (the valley of God's judgement) and according to Revelation 16:16, this ancient battle ground will be the scene of the most devastating military confrontation in human history.

The battles will rage over a 200 mile long zone down towards the city of Jerusalem and the battle carnage will be so terrible that horses will sink into the resulting mire of blood, bodies and mud until the blood reaches "to the horses' bridles" (Revelation 14:19-20). If you have ever seen some of the awful war photos of the quagmire of blood and mud produced by artillery and modern conventional weapons, you can imagine that this whole fertile valley will turn into a bloodbath under the assault of the massive 200 million man army of the "Kings of the East" against the combined armies of the Western nations, led by the Antichrist.

With Russia already destroyed in the earlier battle of Magog and America probably somewhat isolationist, the political vacuum will have been filled by a resurgent Europe under the leadership of the Antichrist. The other major political-military power will be a combination of the vast populations of China, Southeast Asia, and India together with the technological and economic leadership of a re-militarized Japan. Already, China and Japan have signed a 30 year treaty of cooperation In this new situation, the Antichrist and the Revived Roman Empire will have guaranteed Israel's security and her probable control of the oil supplies of the Middle East. From a geopolitical standpoint, Israel's strategic position at the meeting point of Europe, Africa and Asia has always made the control of this land essential for a world empire. The power, whether East or West, that controls Israel and the Middle Eastern oil will control the world.

The prophet Daniel describes that while the Antichrist is at his headquarters in Jerusalem, he will be attacked by African and Arab nations led by a "King of the South" and another group of nations led by a "King of the North" (probably Syria). When his forces quickly defeat these attacks, he will conquer Egypt, Libya and Ethiopia (Daniel 11:40-43). However, the nations of the world that resent his totalitarian dictatorship will finally decide that this is the time to attack the Antichrist in Israel and win world power. As these nations to the East (China, India, Japan, etc.) and the North (the remaining parts of Russia), begin to mobilize their vast armies for this final decisive battle, the Antichrist will gather all the remaining nations of the West still under his control and will bring them to Israel to face the approaching armies of the "Kings of the East" (Daniel 11:44-45). The prophet John tells us that God will miraculously dry up the great river Euphrates to allow this enormous 200 million man army to cross over the river to approach northern Israel (Revelation 16:12-16).

The Angel's prophecy that the army of the Eastern nations would contain 200 million men shocked the prophet John (Revelation 9:13-16). The entire population of the Roman Empire in the first century was only about 200 million men, woman and children. Naturally, it was hard for John and indeed, for many Bible commentators over the years, to believe that the angel "literally" meant that one side alone of this Battle of Armageddon would contain that enormous number of soldiers. Until World War 11, only 12 battles in human history have apparently been fought with more than 50,000 soldiers on both sides. It is only in this century that we have seen the complete mobilization of a nation's resources for war. According to *The War Atlas* the worldwide arms buildup in 1988 has created armies which can field 570 million soldiers when all reserves are called up.

When my wife Kaye and I were visiting China in 1986, as we stood on Tian'An Men Square in Bejing, the largest square in the world, we were shocked to see that the reports about the results of the One Child Policy in China were true. Before us on the square, out of the hundreds of thousands of families out for a Sunday stroll, there were almost no young Chinese girls in evidence. There were at least nine young boys for every girl. In my research I had discovered that the result of the rigorously enforced One Child Policy in China since 1978 has been that out of all live births, nine boys were being born for every female child. When we questioned Chinese officials about these reports and our own eyewitness impressions, they confirmed that the 9 to 1 ratio of boys to girls is a fact. The Chinese have developed several reliable methods to determine the sex of the fetus early in the pregnancy. Since they can only have one child, most Chinese couples choose to abort the female fetus and keep trying until they conceive a male fetus. If a woman has a second pregnancy she is forced to abort it. If she becomes pregnant a third time she is forced to undergo sterilization.

Whenever a Chinese couple successfully avoids the authorities and has a second child, a fine is levied of one year's income. The Chinese naturally would like their family name to continue and to have a male child return from school at age 18 to help contribute to the family income. A girl will naturally not continue the family name and she will go to live in her husband's home and help support his parents, not her own. For all these reasons, most Chinese couples abort female fetuses and try to only bear a male child. For thousands of years the male-female balance of human populations has remained close to 50-50. For the first time in history, human political decisions, biological testing techniques and self interest have combined to produce a massive sexual imbalance in the population of the largest nation on earth (one quarter of the world's population). The social, political and military ramifications of an excess 125 million young men without hope of ever being married and finding stability in a home are already giving nightmares to the political planners in China.

They went on to say that although the one child policy was essential to stop famine in China, this unexpected disproportion of boys to girls was already being discussed in party meetings as the greatest potential social problem that China would face in the next decade. With a base population of 1 billion, 100 million people today, this imbalance of boys to girls will produce an unprecedented situation in human history. In the late 1990's China will have an excess of 125 million Chinese boys of military age with no girls for them to marry and no prospects of their every having a family of their own. This same phenomenon is now being reported in India, Korea and other Asian

149

countries. When this group of 125 million military age young men is added to the armies that these huge countries already possess, it is possible to see that the biblical prophecy of a 200 million man army from the "Kings of the East" is not only literally possible; it is a terrible reality facing our world in the late 1990's. Two thousand years ago God described the consequences of such events in telling John that the "Kings of the East" would have an army of 200 million.

During this incredible Battle of Armageddon, Christ will return from Heaven with His heavenly army (the millions of saints described in Jude, verse 14,15) and destroy the nations of the world that have joined in battle to destroy Israel and each other. Christ will destroy the Antichrist and the False Prophet and their armies. He will defend Jerusalem and all who call upon His Name for protection (Zechariah 12:8-9). Jesus Christ will visibly return in glory as the "King of Kings and Lord of Lords" to set up His kingdom forever (Revelation 19:11-16).

All of Israel's past events have occurred on anniversaries of their feast and fast days on the Jewish liturgical calendar. It would be consistent if this same pattern held and these final climatic events which usher in the Millennium were to occur on the last three significant feast days of the year including the Feast of Trumpets, the Day of Atonement and the final Feast of Tabernacles.

Only the events themselves, of course, will prove whether or not these patterns of biblical anniversaries will continue to be prophetically fulfilled during Israel's final crisis, the Battle of Armageddon.

CHAPTER 12

God's Prophetic
Time Cycles

"Remember the former things of old: for I am God, and there is none else; I am God, and there is none like me, declaring the end from the beginning, and from ancient times the things that are not yet done, saying, My counsel shall stand, and I will do all my pleasure" (Isaiah 46:9-10).

One cannot study the Bible for long without being struck forcibly by the strange phenomenon that a great number of historical and prophetic events concerning the Jews which have occurred according to precise time cycles. If you were to discover, while studying the history of any other nation, that many significant events occurred according to precise time cycles, you would be justified in concluding that some supernatural power was intervening in the affairs of that nation. The fact is that whenever we examine the historical dates and events of any other nation's history we discover that events occur at random, with no discernable pattern of anniversaries. It is only when we turn to the history of Israel that a different phenomenon appears. God has revealed His sovereignty and prophetic foreknowledge through His appointment of events for Israel according to precise cycles of time.

Scripture records several significant biblical time cycles. The most important periods consist of 40 days, 40 years, 50 years, 70 years, 430 years, 490 years and 2,520 years.

Some of the cycles are well-known to us. Some, unless you are a student of prophecy, may not be as familiar.

The Forty-Year Cycle

Probably the best known cycle is the forty-year cycle. This period appears repeatedly throughout Israel's history in connection with a time of testing and probation. The Scriptures record twelve of these forty year cycles:

Moses in Egypt	Acts 7:23
Moses in Madian	Acts 7:30
Israel in the Wilderness	Deuteronomy 8:2
Israel under the Judge Othniel	Judges 3:11
Israel under the Judge Barak	Judges 5:31
Israel under Gideon	Judges 8:28
Israel enslaved by the Philistines	Judges 13:1
Israel under the Judge Eli	1 Samuel 4:18
Israel under King Saul	Acts 13:21
Israel under King David	2 Samuel 5:4
Israel under King Solomon	1 Kings 11:42
Israel under King Joash	2 Chronicles 24:1

The Forty-Day Cycle

In addition, there are thirteen periods of forty days recorded in the Old and New Testament that are significant times of probation and testing.

The length of rainfall during Noah's Flood	Genesis 7:4, 12
Israel mourns for Jacob	Genesis 50:3
Moses on Mount Sinai	Exodus 24:18
Moses intercedes for Israel	Deuteronomy 9:25
Moses' second time on Mount Sinai	Exodus 34:28
Moses' second fasting period	Deuteronomy 9:18
The 12 spies search Canaan	Numbers 13:25
Goliath challenges Israel	1 Samuel 17:16
Jonah's forty days and Nineveh	Jonah 3:4
Elijah's fasting journey	1 Kings 19:8
Ezekiel lies forty days on right side	Ezekiel 4:5

| Jesus fasts and is tempted by Satan | Matthew 4:2 |
| From Jesus' Resurrection to His Ascension | Acts 1:2 |

In respect of some of these events, Christians today celebrate the forty days of Lent as a time of self-denial and spiritual preparation.

The Seventy-Year Cycle

The Bible speaks of three historically significant events in Israel's history that each spanned seventy years.

1. The Babylonian Captivity   606 B.C. to 536 B.C.

This seventy year captivity began with Nebuchadnezzar invading Judea (Daniel 1:1-2) and ended with the decree issued by Cyrus in 536 B.C. which authorized the Jews to return to Jerusalem.

God has always been precise in His dealing with Israel in terms of it's stewardship of the land. When Israel crossed the Jordan River to enter the Promised Land, they entered a special covenant relationship with God that was expressed by the Law of the Sabbath of the Land. According to this Law, every seven years Israel was to let the land lie fallow and not harvest the crops. God promised that He would provide a bumper crop in the sixth year to carry them over the "Sabbath year" of rest for the land and provide enough seed to plant again in the eighth year of the cycle.

This act of obedience would show Israel's total trust and obedience to God. When the seventh cycle, the forty-ninth year occurred, God would supply enough to feed them during both the forty-ninth and the fiftieth years. Then the cycle would resume (Leviticus 25:1-13,18-22.). This fiftieth year was to be known as the Year of Jubilee in which the land would lie at rest, all debts were to be cancelled and all slaves were to be set free. This Jubilee Year became a symbol and promise of the Great Jubilee when true liberty would be realized as the Messiah came to set up His Kingdom.

There is no Scriptural evidence that Israel has ever faithfully kept the Law of the Sabbath of the Land, letting the land lie fallow for a whole year.

Once Israel had adopted a monarchy under King Saul in 1096 B.C., for the first time, the Law of the Sabbath of the Land could have been enforced by decree. However, Israel did not obey God in this matter and 490 years later, in 606 B.C., she had missed keeping this Sabbath a total of seventy times. Moses had prophesied more than 850 years earlier that Israel would disobey this Law and would go into captivity for their disobedience.

"Then shall the land enjoy her sabbaths, as long as it lieth desolate, and ye be in your enemies land; even then shall the land rest;...*because it did not rest in your sabbaths, when ye dwelt upon it* (Leviticus 26:34,35).

The year 606 B.C. was a Year of Jubilee and therefore it was also a Sabbath rest year for the land. The prophet Jeremiah records that in one last weak attempt at partial obedience, **"King Zedekiah had made a *covenant* with all the people which were at Jerusalem, *to proclaim liberty unto them."* (Jeremiah 34:8).** However after freeing their Hebrew slaves, the princes and the aristocracy broke their solemn covenant of liberty that they had made before God and enslaved their servants again. In anger God declared: *"Ye have not hearkened unto me, in proclaiming liberty,* **every one to his brother, and every man to his neighbor: behold, I proclaim a liberty for you, saith the Lord, to the sword, to the pestilence, and to the famine;** *and I will make you to be removed into all the kingdoms of the earth"* **(Jeremiah 34:8,17).**

The record of 2 Chronicles 36:17-21 declares that God specifically took Israel into captivity in Babylon in 606 B.C. **"to fulfill the word of the Lord by the mouth of Jeremiah, until the land had enjoyed her sabbaths;** *for as long as she lay desolate she kept sabbath, to fulfill threescore and ten years"* **(verse 21).**

In other words, God decided to force Israel to keep the Sabbath of the Land and catch up the missed seventy years of letting the land rest (Jeremiah 25:11). After the completion of this seventy year period God fulfilled His word: **"That after *seventy years* be accomplished at Babylon I will visit you, and perform my good word toward you, in causing you to return to this place" (Jeremiah 29:10).**

2. The Babylonian Desolations   589 B.C. to 520 B.C.

This seventy-year period of "desolations" began with the conquering of the land and besieging of Jerusalem by Nebuchadnezzar on the tenth day of the tenth month, Tebeth, 589 B.C., and ended seventy biblical years later (biblical years of 360 days each) to the exact day in 520 B.C., the twenty-fourth day of Chisleu, when the foundation of the second Temple was laid (see Haggai 2:18). The interval between these dates is exactly 70 biblical-prophetic years, which equals 25,200 days (70 times 360 days equals 25,200 days precisely). This precision of fulfillment using this 360 day year is one of the strong proofs that God still uses the ancient 360 day biblical year in calculating the interval or duration for prophetic periods.

3. The Restoration Period   515 B.C. to 445 B.C.

This period began with the dedication of the Second Temple on Passover, 515 B.C. (Ezra 6:15-22), and ended exactly seventy years later with the decree by the Persian King Artaxerxes authorizing Nehemiah to rebuild the walls of Jerusalem in the month of Nisan, 445 B.C. (Nehemiah 2:1, 7).

The Four-Hundred-and-Thirty Year Cycle

Two significant periods of 430 years are indicated in the scriptural records.

1. The Period from the Abrahamic Covenant to the Exodus from Egypt   430 years

Abraham received God's Covenant that his descendants would inherit the land on Passover, the fourteenth of Nisan (Genesis 15:18). The Exodus occurred on Passover. **"It came to pass at the end of *the four hundred and thirty years,* even the selfsame day it came to pass, that all the hosts of the Lord went out from the land of Egypt"** (Exodus 12:41; (see also Galatians 3:17). On the same day, the fourteenth of Nisan, God later told the Israelites to observe the Passover annually forever.

2. The Period from the Closing of the Old Testament to the Public Ministry of Christ   430 Years

Malachi wrote the last book of the Old Testament in 396 B.C. and the canon of the Old Testament was closed by the Great Synagogue. In Malachi 3:1 he prophesied: **"Behold, I** will send my messenger, and he shall prepare the way before me: and the Lord, whom ye seek, shall suddenly come to his temple". Jesus commenced His public teaching, which forms the beginning of the New Testament period, 430 biblical years later. The period from 396 B.C. to the fall of A.D. 28 equals 430 biblical years (Note- only one year between 1B.C. and A.D. 1). This period is equal to 423.8 calendar years.

The Four-Hundred and Ninety Year Cycle

The entire chronology of God's dealing with Israel (from the birth of Abraham to the final setting up of Christ's kingdom on earth) is marked with five startlingly precise periods of 490 years. In several of these periods an unusual principle is revealed: While Israel is in total disobedience, God's hand is removed and prophetic time is suspended. It is, in a sense, not counted.

When God set forth the regulations for a Nazirite – a person who made a vow of separation to the Lord, He said that if the person broke any of the regulations for Nazirites, **"The previous days do not count, because he became defiled during his separation" (Numbers 6:12 NIV).** Israel is, by analogy, a "Nazirite" nation set apart for God. When they were "defiled," it appears that God treated these periods of disobedience as though they were a blank and not to be counted in the divine chronology.

1. From the Birth of Abraham to the Exodus   490 Years

Abraham was seventy-five years old when he left for Canaan. From the giving of the Covenant to the Exodus was 430 years (Exodus 12:40). However, we need to subtract the fifteen years of rebellion when Abraham disobeyed God and had a son by Hagar. Abraham had lost faith in God's promise of a natural son and had disobeyed God and tried to create an heir his own way with Hagar. Ishmael was in Abraham's house fifteen years until Abraham trusted God to miraculously produce Isaac, the promised seed. The total period from the birth of Abraham till the Exodus is 490 years as God counts the time. (75 plus 430 equals 505 years; minus the 15 years of disobedience, equals 490 years).

2. The Period from the Coronation of King Saul in 1096 B.C. until the Babylonian Captivity in 606 B.C.   490 Years

This period is discussed in detail in the section on the Seventy Year Cycles.

3. The Dedication of the First Temple in 1005 B.C.
to the Decree of Artaxerxes to rebuild
Jerusalem in 445 B.C.   **490 Years**

This is a period of 560 years. When we subtract the seventy years of Babylonian captivity, as time not counted, the remaining total is 490 years.

4. From the Dedication of the First Temple in
1005 B.C. under Solomon to the Dedication
of the Second Temple in 515 B.C.   **490 Years**

It is a remarkable fact that the First Temple under Solomon was dedicated on the Feast of Tabernacles, the fifteenth day of Tishri, and the Second Temple was dedicated to God by Ezra, the scribe on the same Feast of Tabernacles 490 years later to the exact day (see 1 Kings 8:2,65 and Nehemiah 8:14-18).

5. Daniel's Vision of the Seventy Weeks   490 Years

Daniel's seventy weeks was discussed fully in chapter 2. The period from 445 B.C. (March 14) to A.D. 32 (April 6) is 483 biblical years to the day. The "final week" of seven years will be fulfilled in our generation to seal up the vision (see Daniel 9:24-27). This will complete the 490 years.

As we review these remarkable periods of 490 years in God's dealings with Israel, we are reminded of God's sovereignty in precisely controlling Israel's history. **"My counsel shall stand, and I will do all my pleasure" (Isaiah 46:10).** Truly, it is God that is unfolding His will in human history.

The Twenty-Five Hundred and Twenty Year Cycle

The 2,520 cycle is the largest and most unique of all prophetic periods. Over the centuries many students of prophecy have interpreted the **"times of the Gentiles,"** referred to by Christ in Luke 21:22-24 and by Paul in Romans 11:25-27, as being a period of 2,520 years.

"For these be the days of vengeance, that all things which are written may be fulfilled....And they shall fall by the edge of the sword, and shall be led away captive into

157

all nations: and *Jerusalem shall be trodden down of the Gentiles, until the times of the Gentiles be fulfilled"* (Luke 21:22,24).

"For I would not, brethren, that ye should be ignorant of this mystery, lest ye should be wise in your own conceits; that *blindness in part is happened to Israel, until the fullness of the Gentiles be come in"* (Romans 11:25).

There are four time cycles of 2,520 years indicated in the Scriptures. Three of these periods find their fulfillment in the last days leading to the setting up of the Millennial kingdom; explanation will be fully explored in chapter 13.

The first of these 2,520 year prophetic time cycles are described in detail in chapter 3 dealing with Ezekiel's prophecy of the birth of Israel on May 15, 1948.

1. The Babylonian Captivity to Israel's Rebirth in 1948   2520 Years

This cycle of 2520 years has already been fulfilled by the ending of the worldwide captivity and return of Israel exactly as prophesied by the prophet Ezekiel (chapter 4:4-6)

From the ending of the Babylonian captivity in 536 B.C. to the rebirth of Israel on May 15, 1948, is a period of exactly 2,520 biblical years. See chapter 3 for a full discussion.

2. The Times of the Gentiles   2520 Years

This period began with the Babylonian Captivity and continues through 2520 biblical years till our generation. This is fully discussed in chapter 13.

3. The Times of Israel in the Land   2520 Years

This cycle of 2520 years began with the entry of Israel into the Promised Land in 1451 B.C. and continued until A.D. 70 when it was interrupted by the destruction of their national existence. After almost two thousand years Christ will return to set up their Millennium Kingdom of 1000 years. The 1520 years from 1451 B.C. to A.D.70; plus the 1000 years of the promised kingdom give us a total of 2520 Years.

4. The Jerusalem Temple Period.   2520 Years

This period extends from the building of the Second Temple in 520 B.C. to the final cleansing of the rebuilt Temple in our immediate future. (See chapter 13 for a complete discussion).

Can any reasonable person believe that all of this has occurred simply by chance? It seems far more logical to this writer that we are observing an incredible display of God's sovereignty and that this phenomenon proves beyond a shadow of a doubt that God truly has His hands on His Chosen People.

CHAPTER 13

Does Prophecy Reveal the Time of Israel's Final Crisis?

"Behold, I will make thee know what shall be in the last end of the indignation [the Great Tribulation]; for at the time appointed the end shall be" (Daniel 8:19).

The angel was sent to Daniel to answer his question as to how long it would be until God would finally set up His eternal Kingdom on earth. The answer given was that the appointed time was set and it would occur a long time after the life of Daniel. However, Daniel was not left in darkness concerning his question, but was given many interesting time indications of when that final appointment with destiny would finally come. In this chapter we will examine some of these prophecies as they relate to Israel and her final crisis, the Battle of Armageddon, and the coming of her Messiah King.

Man's Appointment in the Valley of Decision

Over twenty-five centuries ago God set an appointment for Israel and the nations which will not be postponed, no matter what man wishes. God described through His prophets "The Great Day of the Lord" on which mankind will finally see Jesus Christ, not as a suffering servant, but rather as the conquering "King of Kings and Lord of Hosts".

"And I heard, but I understood not: then said I, O my Lord, what shall be the end of these things? And he said, Go thy way, Daniel: for the words are closed up and sealed till the time of the end. Many shall be purified, and made white, and tried; but the wicked shall do wickedly: and none of the wicked shall understand; but the wise shall understand....But go thou thy way till the end be: for thou

shalt rest, and stand in thy lot at the end of the days"
(Daniel 12:8-10,13).

One of the most misunderstood subjects in the study of prophecy is the determination of the time of Israel's final crisis. The reason for this misunderstanding is that we often confuse God's prophecies concerning Israel with those prophecies concerning the Rapture of the Church. No one, including this author, will ever know the day of the promised Rapture, the translation of the saints, until that day arrives. There are no preconditions to the Rapture. There are no events that must occur prior to Christ calling His Church home to heaven. In fact, if Christ had raptured the Church in the first century, the end-time events would still have occurred on schedule in this generation without contradicting a single prophecy about the final crisis for Israel in this generation.

Therefore, this chapter is not about the Rapture of the Church but about "the last days" for the nation of Israel before Her Messiah returns in glory.

In the book of Joel, the prophet declares that God, first, will end the long captivity of Judah and Jerusalem, and then He, **"will also gather all nations, and will bring them down into the valley of Jehoshaphat, and will plead with them there for my people and for my heritage Israel, whom they have scattered among the nations"**...(Joel 3:2)

"Let the heathen be wakened, and come up to the valley of Jehoshaphat: for there will I sit to judge all the heathen round about" (verse 12); **"Multitudes, multitudes in the valley of decision: for the Day of the Lord is near in the valley of decision"** (verse 14).

Can We Know Anything About the Time of Israel's Final Crisis?

For many years sincere and prudent Christians have been warned against looking into the prophecies of the Bible for indications of God's timing and specific signs leading up to the "last days."

Usually these well intentioned warnings have hinged on two factors: one is based on an interpretation of certain Scriptures which we will examine, and the other is based on the history of prophetic interpretation.

The Scriptural Interpretations

The scriptural passage, which is usually quoted out of context, is the following: **"But of the times and seasons, brethren, ye have no need that I write unto you. For you yourselves know perfectly that the Day of the Lord so cometh as a thief in the night." (1 Thessalonians 5:1-2)**

At first glance, this verse would seem to state that we, the Church, should be as ignorant as to the timing of the Day of the Lord, as a householder is unaware of the time that a thief will choose to break into his house at night. If this were the correct interpretation, we would willingly join those who ignore prophecy about the last days as useless speculation. However, when we wish to clearly understand a scriptural passage, we must look at the whole context and not just examine a few verses out of context. When we examine fully 1 Thessalonians 5:1-10, we will see that precisely the opposite message is conveyed to the Church by Paul, namely, that we are not to be ignorant of the time of the Day of the Lord as it relates to Israel and the nations.

Earlier in his letter to the Church, Paul exhorted them to remain faithful and sanctified until **"the coming of our Lord Jesus Christ with all His saints" (1 Thessalonians 3:13)**. He comforted them with the knowledge that **"we which are alive and remain shall be caught up together with them [those who have already died in the faith] in the clouds to meet the Lord in the air" (1 Thessalonians 4:17)**.

The phrase "caught up" is translated from the Latin word rapere, which connotes "to snatch away." This is the source of the word "Rapture" which most Christians use to describe the resurrection of the believers in the Church and their transformation into immortal spiritual bodies to be with Christ.

Paul then continues his instructions in 1 Thessalonians 5:1-11, by informing the Church that, the children **"of the night"** and **"of darkness"** (the unbelievers) will be overtaken by surprise by **"the Day of the Lord"** as **"a thief in the night;"**..."**and they shall not escape.**" He then states that it should be totally different for the Christians, **"the children of the light, and the children of the day"**.

Paul says, **"But ye, brethren, are not in darkness that that day should overtake you as a thief. Ye are all the** children of light, and the children of the day: we are not of the night, nor of darkness. Therefore let us not sleep, as do others [the children of the night – unbelievers]; but let us watch and be sober."

"For God hath not appointed us to wrath, but to obtain salvation by our Lord Jesus Christ....Wherefore [because of these facts] comfort yourselves together, and edify one another, even as also ye do" (1 Thessalonians 5:1-11). Far from telling us to ignore prophecy and the signs of the last days, Paul specifically warns us to be watchful, hopeful and joyful as we see the beginning signs of "the last days" because it means the Rapture is close at hand.

Moses, in Deuteronomy 29:29, told us that, "the secret things belong unto the Lord our God: but those things which are revealed belong unto us and to our children for ever, that we may do all the works of this Law." God has revealed many of the details of our immediate future through His precise prophecies as discussed in the preceding pages.

If we choose to ignore the warning signs that the last days are fast approaching, then we will be like the church at Sardis which Christ warned by saying, "Be watchful, and strengthen the things which remain...If therefore thou shalt not watch, I will come on thee as a thief, and thou shalt not know what hour I will come upon thee" (Revelation 3:2-3).

For many Christians, the one real objection to inquiring into the time of the "last days" is their understanding of the statement of Jesus to His disciples given in Mark 13:32. Jesus said, "But of that day and that hour knoweth no man, no, not the angels which are in heaven, neither the Son, but the Father."

Many Christians have understood this verse to be an absolute universal statement regarding prophetic interpretation which applies, not only to Christ's disciples in A.D. 32, but also to the Christians of every generation, including this generation that is witnessing the signs leading up to His Second Coming. It is important to study this verse in its context. Jesus had just finished prophesying that the generation that is alive when Israel becomes a nation will live to see the fulfillment of all of the prophecies of the "last days."

163

The whole passage reads: **"But of that day and that hour knoweth no man, no, not the angels which are in heaven, neither the Son, but the Father.** *Take ye heed, watch and pray; for ye know not when the time is.* **For the Son of man is as a man taking a far journey, who left his house, and gave authority to his servants, and to every man his work, and commanded the porter to watch.** *Watch ye therefore:* **for ye know not when the master of the house cometh, at even, or at midnight, or at the cockcrowing, or in the morning: lest coming suddenly he find you sleeping.** *And what I say unto you, I say unto all, Watch"* (Mark 13:32-37).

Please note that even in this passage where He declares that, at that time, no one knew the "day nor the hour;" Christ goes on to command that the response to the uncertainty of the exact time of His coming must be eternal watchfulness; not sleep or lack of interest in His return.

Two Key Questions

The two key questions to be answered in any fair inquiry into the appropriateness of this study are simply these: (1) Is the statement of Christ in Mark 13:32 a universal statement for all time, thereby prohibiting careful, prudent consideration as we see the signs of the approach of the last days ? or (2) Is Christ's statement a description of the lack of knowledge of His disciples about this subject during the generation before the Church or the New Testament existed?

It is important to remember that Christ made this statement to His Jewish disciples prior to His crucifixion, before the existence of the Church had been announced and before the further revelations of all of the New Testament prophecies, especially the book of Revelation. Obviously, like all other statements, it must be studied in its context. Before His death and resurrection, much of the truth about His second coming was veiled from His followers. The very fact that there would be a Church was unknown to all but God at the time of Jesus' remark to His disciples.

Consider the fact that during the Great Tribulation anyone who has access to a Bible will be able to calculate the 1260 days (see Revelation 11:2; 11:3; 12:6; 13:5; and Daniel 7:25) from the time Antichrist enters the rebuilt Temple and can know to the exact day when the Battle of

Armageddon will occur. God has given such a specific time prophecy to encourage those who become believers during the Great Tribulation. The persecution of the Mark of the Beast during those terrible three and one-half years will be so horrible that God felt it was essential that they be assured that it would not go on forever, but would end 1260 days after it began.

These facts indicate that Christ's statement, **"But of that day and hour knoweth no man,"** is not an universal, unlimited pronouncement for all time, but rather, it is a description of the limited knowledge of the time of the "last days" which would prevail from the first century until the final generation of which Christ prophesied, **"This generation shall not pass away, till all be fulfilled" (Luke 21:32).**

The closing chapter of the book of Daniel reveals that it will only be in that time period just before the end that believers will understand the things he prophesied.

"Daniel, *close up and seal the words of the scroll until the time of the end.* Many will go here and there to increase knowledge [of these prophecies]....**Go your way, Daniel, because the words are closed up and** *sealed until the time of the end.*...**None of the wicked will understand, but those who are wise will understand" (Daniel 12:4, 9-10, NIV).** Daniel was told to seal the vision "until the time of the end." The clear implication is that, as "the time of the end" approached. the visions and their meaning would be unsealed. While unbelievers would never understand; believers would begin to" understand" as the crisis approached.

After Christ ascended to glory, He gave an additional revelation to His Church through the prophet John. This book of Revelation removes some of the veil about future events and reveals new information, including some precise prophetic time periods which throw new light on some Old Testament prophecies about **"the time appointed"** when **"the end shall be" (Daniel 8:19).**

The Historical Problem

The second reason many Christians have been warned against looking into prophecy is the historical fact that many commentators have incorrectly interpreted the time of the end in the past. Subsequent events have sometimes proved that their deductions were incorrect. The truth is that in any area of study, scholars will often make errors which will seem obvious enough to those who come after them.

Unfortunately, the area of Bible prophecy seems to be the only area where such early mistakes have led to the suggestion that the whole area of study be abandoned. In any other area of study, we learn from the mistakes of the pioneers and, using the knowledge we have gained, we move on to develop more sound conclusions. Almost all previous commentators on prophecy have ignored the true length of the biblical year (360 days) which the prophets used and have thus miscalculated the time periods involved in many of the prophecies. In addition, the "Historical" school of interpretation has unfortunately insisted that the prophecies of Daniel and Revelation, which refer clearly to the 1260 literal days of the reign of Antichrist, must be interpreted as a period of 1260 years (on the Day-Year Theory – the idea that whenever a prophecy says a day, it automatically must mean a year).

Some great scholars, including Rev. John Cummings, Dr. Grattan Guinness in his Approaching End of the Age and Bishop Newton's Dissertations on the Prophecies have tried in vain to force this interpretation to somehow indicate the period of the Roman Catholic Papacy, etc. and have set dozens of commencement and termination points for such a 1260 day-year period; all without success.

However, we would be mistaken if we failed to heed the direct command of Christ to "watch and pray," simply out of a disappointment with the mistakes of past commentators.

The Time of the Rapture is Unknowable

One paramount point which we must keep in mind is that the time of the Rapture of the Church is not indicated in the Scriptures. No one will know when this event is to take place until the moment it happens and Christians are Raptured to meet Christ in the air and return with Him to the Marriage Supper of the Lamb in Heaven. The reason is that, while there are many specific time indications for

Israel's "last days;" there are no time predictions for the Church.

I am not a prophet, nor have I received a revelation from God about the time of the end. I am simply a student of Scripture and I would like to share with others the results of my research for their consideration. These time cycles are simply logical deductions and calculations based on the same principles as developed in the earlier time cycles which the history of Israel proves have already been fulfilled precisely. There are many Scriptures which indicate that the Lord has set His appointment with destiny for Israel from the beginning of time. However, we must always recognize that God is sovereign and may choose to delay His appointed judgment of the world.

The apostle Peter told us that **"the Lord is not slack concerning His promise, as some men count slackness; but is *long-suffering toward us, not willing that any should perish,* but that all should come to repentance. But the day of the Lord will come as a thief in the night"** (2 Peter 3:9-10).

In the days of Jonah, God responded to the national repentance of Nineveh by cancelling the prophesied judgment that was to have begun in forty days. He alone is sovereign and will choose the time.

Nevertheless, if these prophetic time cycles continue to run their course, mankind is approaching the most awesome and significant crisis in history. Only time and the passage of events will reveal whether the Lord will continue these appointed cycles and bring them to their conclusion in our generation.

Part of the reason for our increased understanding of these Scriptures is that we enjoy the privilege of viewing biblical prophecies from the vantage point of this final generation, with many prophecies already partially fulfilled. The analysis of fulfilled prophecies allows us to confirm the correct principles of interpretation, such as the biblical-prophetic 360-day year, and come to a more accurate understanding of how these end-time prophecies may be fulfilled.

In my library I have more than fifteen hundred volumes on prophecy, some of them published as early as A.D.1650. It is interesting to note that during the first two centuries of the Christian Era, early writers, such as Julias Africanus, Cyprian and Hippotylus show a far greater understanding of prophecy than most medieval Christian commentators until the time of the Reformation. Unfortunately, with all of the other theological concerns of that time, the Reformers seldom wrote on prophecy. In fact, John Calvin's commentary on the Bible includes every single book except the prophetic book of Revelation. Most of the Reformers had personally suffered under the persecution of the medieval Catholic Church and its Inquisition. When they did address prophetic subjects, quite understandably, they focussed primarily on the Antichrist and his Babylonian mystery religious system as described in the book of the Revelation.

It is only during the last two-hundred years that the focus has finally returned to the one-quarter of Scripture that is composed of prophetic themes. That is one reason why a clearer understanding of the Rapture and the First Resurrection is only found in the writings of commentators of the last two centuries. If current students of prophecy can see further, it is simply because, as Sir Isaac Newton quoted Bernard of Clairvaux in his fascinating treatise called Observations on Daniel and the Revelation, we "stand on the shoulders of those giants who went before us."

In the next chapter we will consider some possible answers to Daniel's question, **"How long shall it be to the end of these wonders?"** (Daniel 12:6). This is no longer a question of idle prophetic speculation but, rather, it is a question whose answer will vitally affect every person alive. For the Christian believer, the approach of the" last days" promises the imminent return of Jesus Christ when **"we which are alive and remain shall be caught up together with them in the clouds to meet the Lord in the air; and so shall we ever be with the Lord"** (1 Thessalonians 4:17), before the Great Tribulation commences.

For the Jew; the coming tragic "time of Jacob's trouble" threatens to be the greatest of all persecutions but it will mercifully climax in the triumphant victory of their long-awaited Messiah who will lead them into their promised Kingdom. For the unbeliever; the impending cataclysmic events will push them into making their eternal choice as to whether they will follow Christ or Satan.

As we have seen in previous chapters, the Lord has fulfilled many of Israel's prophecies with incredible precision as to time. Since God says, **"I am the Lord, I change not" (see Malachi 3:6),** we can expect that those same amazing time cycles and biblical anniversaries which are evident in Israel's past will repeat themselves now that Israel is once again an independent nation on the world stage. The same Director who guided Israel's actions in the early scenes of world history has already set the stage for the final act. That act commenced on May 15, 1948, when Israel rose from the valley of "dry bones" to become a mighty nation.

A healthy degree of caution is certainly in order as we examine these possible interpretations of future time cycles. Many sincere students of prophecy have previously calculated dates for the fulfilling of these events, only to see the date come and go, disproving their calculations. The result, of course, is that the world and most Christians tend to ridicule or ignore all prophecy completely. However, this attitude is unjustified. What other area of study, biblical or otherwise, is abandoned because earlier efforts failed to arrive at a complete understanding of the subject? If scholars had abandoned the study of sciences such as geology or physics simply because they found that their early theories were proven inaccurate, there would be few scientists or advanced scientific knowledge today.

We must learn from the failures as well as the successes of early biblical scholars. We must never be dogmatic in our setting dates but should carefully interpret and prayerfully consider the data; time alone will reveal whether or not we have correctly understood a specific prophecy.

Several factors influence our ability to accurately interpret the specific times of unfulfilled prophecy. First, some prophecies are written in such a way that they can only be fully understood when they have already been fulfilled. Then, we can look back and see the incredible precision of their fulfillment. Second, there is at present some uncertainty which exists regarding the precise dating of some of the very early historical events (before 606 B.C.) in the life of Israel. This factor hinders us from determining with absolute assurance the exact commencement dates of a few of the prophetic time cycles.

However, despite these problems, Jesus in His day condemned the spiritual leaders of Israel for not recognizing the signs of the Messiah's coming, as they had been extensively prophesied through the Old Testament. In light of the tremendous amount of prophecies regarding "this generation" and Christ's command to "Watch" we should prudently inquire into what Scripture reveals about the timing of these important future events.

In the next chapter, we will consider these prophetic time cycles and examine the Scriptural indications of the signs that we are approaching the final days for Israel's last crisis and the coming of the Messiah.

CHAPTER 14

Prophetic Time Indications for the Final Battle of Armageddon

"But now [God] commandeth all men every where to repent: because he hath appointed a day, in which He will judge the world in righteousness by that man [Jesus] whom He hath ordained" (Acts 17:30-31).

"Behold, I will make thee know what shall be in the last end on the indignation; for at the appointed time the end shall be" (Daniel 8:19).

Eight Major Prophetic Time Cycles

When one considers the astonishing precision with which the Lord has prophesied the past events in the history of Israel, it is more than likely that within the Scriptures, there are indications of the time He has set for these appointed future events, for Israel's final crisis.

As the pattern of God's precise historical timetables for Israel unfolded in my studies, I began to wonder if these precise time cycles and biblical anniversaries would continue to operate now that Israel was back in the Promised Land. Several years ago in my study of the prophecy of Ezekiel 4:4-6, I discovered that his unusual vision of the ending of the worldwide captivity of Israel had been fulfilled precisely on May 14, 1948. It seemed possible that God's system of prophetic time cycles for Israel and the nations might still be in effect. In the light of this understanding, I would like to prayerfully share with you the results of many years of careful Bible study. There are eight major prophetic time cycles which terminate in our generation. The fact that each of them independently arrive at the same "appointed time" in the next decade is, to me, more than mildly intriguing.

1. "One Day is With The Lord as a Thousand Years"

The Apostle Peter was taught by Jesus for three years before His crucifixion and for another forty days following His resurrection. During this time Christ opened the Scriptures to His disciples concerning the prophecies about Himself (see Luke 24:25-27, 45). As a result of this time of intensive training, when Peter wrote his epistles, he discussed the Lord's Second Coming. He knew that this event was far into the future and so he wrote, **"Knowing this first, that there shall come in the last days scoffers, walking after their own lusts, And saying, *Where is the promise of his coming?* for since the fathers fell asleep, all things continue as they were from the beginning of the creation"** (2 Peter 3:3-4).

Peter then explained to the Church that there was one particular fact regarding this apparent delay of the "last days" of which they should be aware:

"But, *beloved, be not ignorant of this one thing*, that *one day is with the Lord as a thousand years, and a thousand years as one day*. The Lord is not slack concerning his promise, as some men count slackness; but is long-suffering toward us, not willing that any should perish, but that all should come to repentance" (2 Peter:8-9). The "day" he spoke about referred to the "week" of creation (see Genesis 1 and 2), as being a microcosm of the Great Sabbath Week of God's dealing with His creation, mankind. *(see Figure 1.)*

Just as the creation and the replenishing of the earth took six days and then God rested on the seventh day, so there would be six thousand years and then the great Sabbath rest of one thousand years (the Millennium) as described in Hebrews 4:4,7-9 and Revelation chapter 20.

A number of evangelical scholars believe that evidence exists which indicates a much longer duration for man's existence than the 6000 or so years which are indicated by a normal reading of the chronological account given in the Book of Genesis. However, for purposes of this discussion I will take the position of virtually all earlier commentators, Jewish and Christian, from the first century until the mid 1800's. As will be evident from the foregoing chapters, I take the scriptural account in its common sense meaning and interpretation. Jesus Christ Himself and the apostles often referred to Adam, Enoch and Noah as historical characters and none of the inspired writers of the New Testament indicate that either the historical accounts of Genesis or its chronological details are to be understood in a symbolic, mythical or non-literal manner. Since the Bible was given as a God inspired revelation of truth to all men and women of all the generations since it was written, it seems odd and unlikely in the extreme to me to think that God allowed the writers to include chronological data which clearly indicates a 6000 year duration from Adam, if in fact, man was created millions of years ago. Early Christian writers including Lactantius dealt with this controversy 1700 years ago, because even then, theories were prevalent from Plato, Cicero and the Chaldeans that man has existed on this planet for "many thousands of ages." Lactantius in his <u>Divine Institutes,</u> chapter 14 states, "But we, whom the Holy Scriptures instruct to the knowledge of the truth, know the beginning and the end of the world (age), respecting which we will now speak in the end of our work,...Therefore let the philosophers, who enumerate thousands of ages from the beginning of the world, know that the six thousandth year is not yet completed, and that when this number is completed the consummation must take place."

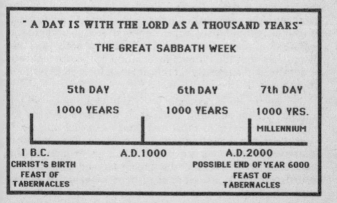

Figure 1

The Scriptures do not give any date for determining when the universe was originally created. However, the chronology of the Old Testament suggest that the time of the creation of Adam and Eve occurred approximately 4000 B.C. The Bible precisely listed the age of each patriarch (i.e. Lamech-182 years) when the next patriarch (i.e. Noah) is born. Even if the next patriarch in the recorded genealogy was a great-grandson, rather than a son; this method of listing their age when the next patriarch was born provides an exact continuous chronology of this period.

The time interval between Adam and Abraham is thus clearly indicated and the possibility of missing gaps in the recorded genealogy would not alter the duration of this period. The long overlapping lifespans of Adam, Lamech, Shem, and Abraham indicates how easily the accurate history of this time period could have been passed down intact. The oral history of these events could have been passed from Adam to Lamech to Shem and he could have told Abraham. Quite aside from this, the inspiration of the Holy Scriptures by God assures us that the facts recorded are accurate and reliable.

The Genesis account clearly indicates that there are two distinct processes and stages of creation which are involved in the Genesis account. The original creation of the universe is described in Genesis 1:1, **"In the beginning God created the Heaven and the Earth."** No date is indicated for this event and it is possible that it took place in the dateless past. Recent scientific discoveries concerning the background radiation of the universe tend to confirm both the "Big Bang" theory of the immediate creation of the universe out of nothing and suggests that this creation took place billions of years ago

However, there are many dating techniques which suggest that the earth and moon are far younger than the 4.6 billion years given in most text books. As just one small example of the mounting scientific evidence for a younger solar system; consider the recent landings of man on the moon's surface. Because the moon has no atmosphere, scientists had calculated that billions of years of falling meteoritic space dust would have accumulated a thick layer up to two thousand feet in depth. There was concern that our spacecraft would sink deeply into this light dust. If you remember, the lunar landing module had very long legs and huge landing pads to prevent it from sinking out of sight. Much to the surprise of the scientists, it turned out that there was <u>less than two inches of moon dust</u>. Recent measurements of the influx of meteoritic dust confirm that the layer should be two thousand feet thick if the moon is in fact 4.6 billion years old. The existence of only two inches of dust is just one more evidence that the solar system may in fact be less that ten thousand years old.[1]

Genesis 1:2 states that, at some time after the original creation, the world became **"without form and void"** ("tohu va bohu" – Hebrew for waste, destruction and emptiness). The books of Isaiah, Jeremiah and Ezekiel seem to refer to the destruction of the original creation, apparently in connection with the rebellion of Satan and his demonic angels in the dateless past. Genesis 1:3 takes up the second part of the creation story which describes the re-creation of life on this planet and continues in verse 28 to record God's command to **"be fruitful and multiply and *replenish* the earth"**.

Early Jewish and Christian writers believed that this "re-creation" of the earth and the beginning of man's history from Adam occurred approximately four thousand years prior to the time the New Testament was written. Archbishop Ussher in A.D. 1650 calculated back from the birth of Christ, based on the dates and chronological data given in the Scriptures, and arrived at the date of 4004 B.C. for Adam's creation.

King David, in Psalm 90:4 referred to the same symbolic time scale when he said, **"For a thousand years in thy sight are but as yesterday when it is past, and as a watch in the night."**

There is a document known as the <u>Epistle of Barnabas</u> which was written to the early churches. Many early church leaders, including Origen and Jerome, believed this document to be genuine. Even though it has never been part of the Bible and may not be written by the Barnabas we are familiar with, it is valuable as extra-biblical information concerning history and the early teachings of the Church, just as the works of early historians such as Josephus add to our knowledge of the Scriptures. As you know, Barnabas was the first partner of the Apostle Paul when he began his missionary journeys. In this Epistle, Barnabas speaks of the creation account in Genesis: "And God made in six days the works of His hands; and He finished them on the seventh day, and He rested on the seventh day and sanctified it. Consider, my children, what that signifies, He finished them in six days. The meaning of it is this: **that in six thousand years the Lord God will bring all things to an end. For with him, one day is a thousand years; as Himself testifieth, saying, behold this day shall be as a thousand years.** Therefore children, in six days, that is, in six thousand years, shall all things be accomplished. And what is it that He saith, and He rested the seventh day; He meaneth this; that when His Son shall come, and abolish the season of the wicked one [the Antichrist], and judge the ungodly; and shall change the sun and the moon, and the stars, then He shall gloriously rest in that seventh day." [2]

Early Church commentators, including Methodius, Bishop of Tyre, point out that the reason Adam died at the age of 930 years (Genesis 5:5) and did not live past one thousand years, was because God had prophesied that, **"In the day that thou eatest thereof (the forbidden fruit) thou shalt surely die" (Genesis 2:17).** Since a day was equal to a thousand years in God's sight, Adam had to die before the day (1000 years) was completed.

Irenaeus, another church father writing in A.D. 150 about Genesis in his book <u>Against Heresies</u> states as a belief of the early church the following:

"This is an account of the things formerly created, as also it is a prophecy of what is to come. For the day of the Lord is as a thousand years; and in six days created things were completed; it is evident, therefore, that they will come to an end at the sixth thousand years."[3]

Therefore, if we were to take these calculations according to Barnabas and Irenaeus, our time line would look like that in figure 1. The two-thousand-year period preceding the beginning of the "seventh day" is calculated from the fifteenth of Tishri, the Feast of the Tabernacles, in the year 1 B.C. when Jesus was born. In the Gospel of John, the apostle says, **"The word became flesh , and tabernacled [dwelt] among us" (John 1:14 RSV margin).** It is possible that John is referring to the fact that Jesus was born on the anniversary of the Feast of Tabernacles, the fifteenth of Tishri, 1 B.C.. (the anniversary of the Dedication of both

Temples and the coming of the Shekinah Glory). The clearly stated chronological data provided by Luke 3:1-3, confirms that Christ was born in 1 B.C. and this was the unanimous view of the Church in the first centuries. (See "The Date of the Nativity of Christ" – Appendix.)

If these calculations are correct, and Christ was born at the beginning of the fifth day (1 B.C), then the fifth and sixth days (two thousand years) have nearly elapsed. We could look for the beginning of the seventh day (the Millennium— a thousand years of peace, Revelation 20:2-6) to commence in the fall of the year A.D. 2000 on the fifteenth of Tishri, the first day of the Feast of Tabernacles--exactly two thousand years from Christ's birth.

In the writings of Methodius, in A.D. 300, we find the following reference to the Feast of Tabernacles: "For since in six days God made the heaven and earth, and finished the whole world...and blessed the seventh day and sanctified it, so by a figure in the seventh month, when the fruits of the earth have been gathered in, we are commanded to keep the feast [of Tabernacles] to the Lord, which signifies that, when this world shall be terminated at the seventh thousand years, when God shall have completed the world, He shall rejoice in us....Then, when the appointed times shall have been accomplished, and God shall have ceased to form this creation, in the seventh month, the great resurrection-day, it is commanded that the Feast of our Tabernacles shall be celebrated to the Lord."[4]

2. "After Two Days He will Revive Us: In the Third Day He will Raise Us Up"

The Jews also have taught that God's dealing with His people would be encompassed within a "Great Sabbath Week" of seven thousand years. The prophet Hosea, in his messianic prophecy, referred to this prophetic time cycle in telling of the final restoration of Israel.

"Come, and let us return unto the Lord: for he hath torn, and he will heal us; he hath smitten, and he will bind us up. And *after two days will he revive us: in the third day he will raise us up,* and we shall live in his sight. Then shall we know, if we follow on to know the Lord: *his going forth is prepared as the morning; and he shall come unto*

177

us as the rain, as the latter and former rain unto the earth" (Hosea 6:1-3).

In interpreting the meaning of these **"two days,"** we must remember that the biblical year in history and prophecy has only 360 days. Therefore, one thousand prophetic years would contain only 360 thousand days (1,000 x 360) and this is equal to 985.626 years according to our present calendar. Both Jewish and Christian authorities interpret the "Great Sabbath" as the final seventh day of one thousand years, following the six thousand years (6 x 1000 years) starting from Adam.

Rabbi Ketina said in Gemara, a commentary on the Talmud, "The world endures six thousand years and one thousand it shall be laid waste [that is, the enemies of God shall be destroyed], whereof it is said, ' The Lord alone shall be exalted in that day.' As out of seven years every seventh [is a] year of remission, so out of the seven thousand years of the world, the seventh millennium shall be the millennial [1000 years] years of remission, that God alone may be exalted in that day."[5] In A.D. 1552, Bishop Latimer wrote the following words regarding his understanding of this one thousand year period which will start around A.D. 2000: "The world was ordained to endure, as all learned men affirm, 6000 years. Now of that number, there be passed 5,552 years [as of A.D. 1552], so that there is no more left but 448 years [ending in A.D. 2000]" *(See figure 2.)*

" AFTER TWO DAYS, HE WILL REVIVE US "

"ONE DAY IS WITH THE LORD AS A THOUSAND YEARS "

ONE THOUSAND BIBLICAL YEARS = 360 X 1000 = 360,000 DAYS

EQUALS : 985.626 CALENDAR YEARS

5th DAY	6th DAY
985.626 YRS	985.626 YRS

A.D. 28.8 (FALL)
COMMENCEMENT OF
CHRIST'S MINISTRY

A.D. 2000
" HE WILL
REVIVE US"

Figure 2

178

Even during the Reformation, there were Christian scholars who understood that the sabbatical week of seven thousand years indicated that the time of the "last days" would occur towards the year A.D. 2000.

One of the oldest books in my library is The Chronology on the Old and New Testament, written by Archbishop Ussher in A.D. 1650. In this Latin volume, Ussher, who had access to many ancient church manuscripts which were tragically lost in the burning of early Irish churches during the savage Irish wars, also calculated that the Millennium would begin in A.D. 1997. His whole chronological system was adjusted to his assumption that Christ was born in 4 B.C. If he had calculated from 1 B.C., his calculation would have placed the start of the Millennium in the year A.D. 2000 (See "The Date of the Nativity of Christ" in the appendix).[6]

Rabbi Elias, who lived two hundred years before Christ, said, "The world endures six thousand years: two thousand before the law, two thousand under the law, and two thousand under Messiah."[7]

Lactantius, a Christian scholar who lived around A.D. 300, wrote in his seventh Book of Divine Institutions: "Because all the works of God were finished in six days, it is necessary that the world should remain in this state six ages, that is six thousand years. Because having finished the works He rested on the seventh day and blessed it; it is necessary that at the end of the sixth thousandth year all wickedness should be abolished out of the earth and justice should reign for a thousand years."[8]

Writings could be produced in great numbers from other early church fathers including Victorinus, Bishop of Petau, Hippotylus, Justin Martyr and Methodius to illustrate this belief that the Millennium would commence upon the completion of six thousand years from Adam. This widespread evidence, together with 2 Peter 3:8, is a strong argument that this belief was, in fact, the genuine teaching of the apostles and the early Church.

3. The Cleansing of the Sanctuary

In another of Daniel's visions he writes: **"Yea, he magnified himself even to the prince of the host, and by him** the daily sacrifice was taken away, and the place of his sanctuary was cast down. And an host was given him against the daily sacrifice by reason of transgression, and it cast down the truth to the ground; and it practised, and prospered. Then I heard one saint speaking, and another saint said unto that certain saint which spake, *How long shall be the vision concerning the daily sacrifice, and the transgression of desolation, to give both the sanctuary and the host to be trodden under foot?"* (Daniel 8:11-13).

This prophecy has been one of the most difficult for commentators to explain. Most writers agree that the commencement of this vision is clearly the desecration of the Temple in Jerusalem when the Syrian king, Antiochus Epiphanes, invaded Israel in June, 168 B.C., and sacrificed a pig on the Temple altar to insult the Jewish faith. After Daniel had witnessed this vision of the horrible sacrilege he records, **"And I Daniel fainted, and was sick certain days; afterward I rose up, and did the king's business; and I was astonished at the vision, but none understood it"** (Daniel 8:27).

The first **"saint"** referred to in verse 13 (rendered "that certain one" in the Masoretic Text, which means "Palmoni – the numberer of secrets" in Hebrew), responded to the question of **"how long"** as follows: **"And he said unto me, Unto two thousand and three hundred days; then shall the sanctuary be cleansed"** (Verse 14). This answer is very important because it is the most specific time prophecy about the length of time until the end of the last days.

Curiously, this is one of the few numbers in the Bible where there is a discrepancy in early manuscripts of the Old Testament. The manuscript versions from which our modern versions (including the King James and New International Version) translated this passage record the number as 2,300 days; the Greek Septuagint, which was used by the Jews in Christ's day, says 2,400 days. Bishop Thomas Newton, in his excellent book Dissertations on the Prophecies, written in 1754, confirmed that there was a third set of manuscript copies of the book of Daniel, to which the early church father, Jerome, refers in his commentary on Daniel. In this set of manuscripts the number was given as 2,200 days.[9] Due to these discrepancies between manuscript copies we must proceed with caution. Only when this prophecy is fulfilled, when the sanctuary is finally cleansed by Christ, will we know with absolute certainty which number, 2300, 2400 or 2200, is the correct one. With this caution in mind, please consider the following possibilities.

First, most commentators have interpreted this period as 2,300 normal days and have tried, without success, to make them fit the historical time frame of the three years between the time when Antiochus Epiphanes desecrated the Temple in 168 B.C.and when the Jews won the battle of Jerusalem and cleansed the Temple. in 165 B.C.

However, according to the historical book of Maccabees, the Temple was cleansed exactly 1,080 days (three biblical years of 360 days each) from the day the daily sacrifice was forbidden by Antiochus. (Some writers have interpreted the 2,300 mornings and evenings as 1,150 days; but even this misses the mark by 70 days.)

Second, let us consider the possibility that the correct number is 2,200 days and that the context demands that in this case the days stand for years in a similar manner as recorded in Numbers 14:33-34 and Ezekiel 4:4-6. The angel told Daniel that, **"The vision of the evenings and mornings that has been given you is true, but seal up the vision, for** *it concerns the distant future"* **(Daniel 8:26 NIV).** That would mean that, in this particular prophecy (as in Ezekiel 4:4-6), the 2,200 days duration of the vision would represent 2,200 biblical years.

In the book of Numbers we read that Israel was sentenced to 40 years in the wilderness because they rejected the Promised Land after the ten spies gave a fearful report on their spy mission of 40 days. Numbers 14:34 says, **"After the number of the days in which ye searched the land,** *even forty days, each day for a year, shall ye bear your iniquities, even forty years,* **and ye shall know my breach of promise".** The prophet Ezekiel used the same "year for a day" symbolism in 4:4-5. Jerome's manuscript version of Daniel 8:14 reads: "And he said unto me, *Unto two thousand and two hundred days; then shall the sanctuary be cleansed."*

In Daniel 8:13, "another saint" asked the question, **"How long shall be the vision concerning the daily sacrifice?"** The angel Gabriel replied: **"Understand, O son of man: for at the time of the end shall be the vision....Behold, I will make** thee know what shall be in the last end of the indignation: *for at the appointed time the end shall be....* And the vision of the evening and the morning which was told is true: wherefore shut thou up the vision; for it shall be many days" (Daniel 8:17,19,26).

The vision commenced on the twenty-fourth day of the ninth month, in the fall of 168 B.C., when the Temple was profaned and the Daily Sacrifices were halted. Its termination, in the distant future, will occur when the rebuilt Temple is finally cleansed by the coming of Messiah, according to Jerome's version, after 2,200 "days" or years. Twenty-two hundred prophetic years of 360 days each, equals 792,000 days. Divide this by our calendar year of 365.25 days, and we arrive at a duration for the vision of 2,168.4 calendar years. Therefore, if we start with the commencement of the vision, the desecration of the Temple, which took place in 168.9 B.C. (late fall), and we then add 2,168.4 years (2200 day-years), then the conclusion of the prophecy, the time for the Messianic cleansing of the sanctuary would take place in the fall of A.D. 2000. *(See figure 3.)*

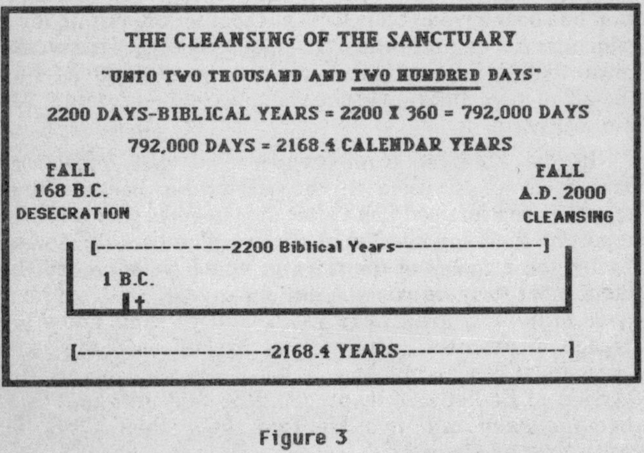

THE CLEANSING OF THE SANCTUARY

"UNTO TWO THOUSAND AND TWO HUNDRED DAYS"

2200 DAYS–BIBLICAL YEARS = 2200 X 360 = 792,000 DAYS

792,000 DAYS = 2168.4 CALENDAR YEARS

FALL
168 B.C.
DESECRATION

FALL
A.D. 2000
CLEANSING

[-----------------2200 Biblical Years-----------------]

1 B.C.

[-----------------------2168.4 YEARS-----------------]

Figure 3

However, since various manuscripts disagree concerning the number of day-years during which the desecration of the sanctuary will last, time alone will prove whether or not this tentative interpretation is valid, but it is certainly intriguing.

4. The Times of the Gentiles

When Jesus was telling his disciples about the times of the end, He said, **"Jerusalem shall be trodden down of the Gentiles, until the times of the Gentiles be fulfilled" (Luke 21:24)**. The phrase **"the times of the Gentiles"** refers to the prophetic period beginning with the time when Israel lost its preeminent world position in 606 B.C. and continuing until the Gentile world kingdoms run their course and the promised Messianic Kingdom is established forever.

God originally set Israel **"in praise, and in name, and in honor; and that thou mayest be an holy people unto the Lord thy God, as he hath spoken" (Deuteronomy 26:19)**. God placed Israel central to the hierarchy of the nations. But, due to her disobedience, she lost her exalted position when God allowed the Babylonian Empire to conquer Jerusalem in 606 B.C. Before that, during the reign of Zedekiah, king of Judah, the Lord commanded the prophet Jeremiah to put a yoke on his neck as a symbol of bondage and present himself before the ambassadors of all the nations who were gathered in Jerusalem. He was to tell them that all their countries would now be under submission to the new Gentile world order under Nebuchadnezzar, the king of Babylon (see Jeremiah 27:1-11). By this act, God illustrated that the sovereignty of the world was now passing from Israel to a succession of Gentile world empires.

So the "times of the Gentiles" which Jesus spoke about began at that point in 606 B.C. and will continue until the promised Messiah brings in the Kingdom Age.

While Daniel was in Babylon he was called on to interpret a vision which God had given to Nebuchadnezzar, the proud king. The dream was fulfilled when the king was made insane for a period of seven years. During this period of 2,520 days (7 x 360 days), he displayed a violent madness which symbolized the terrible wars and insane turbulence of nations which was to last for some twenty five centuries. Finally at the end of the prophesied 2520 days, God restored his sanity and he became humble before God as he recognized that God alone truly reigns.

Over the years many students of prophecy have felt that this period of 2,520 days symbolizes the "times of the Gentiles." In the last century, some calculated this period of 2,520 days to be 2,520 modern calendar years, so they added 2,520 years from 606 B.C. and calculated that some tremendous end-time event would occur in A.D. 1914. It is intriguing that on the ninth of Av, 1914, the first World War, which was the beginning of truly global war, was launched, thus fulfilling Jesus' prophecy that **"nation shall rise against nation, and kingdom against kingdom" (Matthew 24:7).** Jesus goes on to say that **"all these things are the beginning of sorrows" (verse 8).**

This tragic war ended a century of peace and produced consequences that still influence our world, from the fall of empires and the rise of communism to the Balfour Declaration which promised a Jewish homeland in British mandated Palestine.

The only thing wrong with the calculations of these students of prophecy is that the duration of the "seven times" (the duration of Nebuchadnezzar's insanity) should be interpreted as 2,520 biblical years of 360 days each. This works out to 907,200 days, or 2,483.8 of our calendar years. Since the "times of the Gentiles" began when the Babylonians captured Jerusalem in 606 B.C., the 2483.8 year duration of the prophetic period would have terminated in the fall of A.D. 1878.

History tells us that many people expected the Lord to come during that year. In fact, a great explosion of books on prophecy, written by sincere Christians who looked for the Second Coming, appeared during that decade. I have hundreds of them in my library.

The Lord did not return at that time; but that brings us back to Peter's interesting statement in 2 Peter 3:1-9 concerning the attitude of people prior to the return of Christ. Peter told us that unbelievers will scoff at Christ's return, saying that **"there shall come in the last days scoffers, walking after their own lusts, And saying, *Where is the promise of his coming?* for since the fathers fell asleep, all things continue as they were from the beginning of the creation. For this they willingly are ignorant of, that by the word of God the heavens were of old, and the earth standing out of the water and in the water: *whereby the*** *world that then was, being overflowed with water, perished:"* (2 Peter 3:3-6). Peter likened this delay to the postponement of the worldwide flood in Noah's day, when God waited 120 years because *"The Lord is not slack concerning his promise, as some men count slackness; but is long-suffering toward us, not willing that any should perish, but that all should come to repentance"* (2 Peter 3:9). Jesus told His disciples, *"But as the days of Noah were, so shall also the coming of the Son of man be."* (Matthew 24:37).

This parallel with Noah's flood could indicate that God would delay His long-promised judgment for an additional 120 biblical years of 360 days each, which is equal to 118.3 of our calendar years.

"The Lord said, My Spirit shall not always strive with man, for that he also is flesh: yet his days shall be *an hundred and twenty years"* (Genesis 6:3) During this 120-year delay God encouraged Noah to preach repentance and build an Ark to save his family and enable the human race to survive the coming flood of judgment.

If I am correct in my interpretation, then the "times of the Gentiles" were initially completed in the fall of A.D. 1878, and God, once again delayed His appointed judgment, **"As in the days of Noah,"** and has given mankind an additional 120 biblical years of warning (118.3 calendar years). When we add the "delay" of 118.3 years to the fall of 1878, the termination point for "the times of the Gentiles" would occur in A.D. 1997. God's prophesied judgment of mankind throughout the three and one-half years of the Great Tribulation would then bring us again to the year 2000. *(See figure 4.)*

5. The Times of Israel

From the date of Israel's possession of the Promised Land in the year 1451 B.C. until they lost their land in A.D. 70 to the Romans is a period of 1,520 years. When we take this historical period of 1,520 years and add to it the prophesied Millennium of 1,000 years (Revelation 20:6), we arrive at a parallel period of 2,520 years for Israel's association with the Promised Land of the Covenant. It is interesting that this period of 2,520 years of "the times of

Israel" is a perfect counterpart to the 2,520 years of the "times of the Gentiles" (*See figure 5.*)

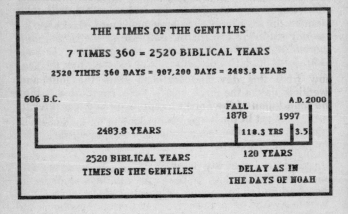

Figure 4

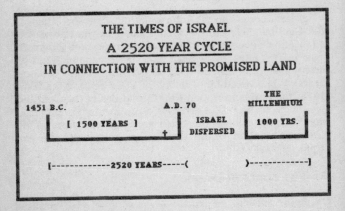

Figure 5

6. The Jerusalem Temple Cycle

The Jews had returned to Jerusalem from the Babylonian Captivity in 536 B.C. Now after sixteen years it was time to rebuild the Temple. God sent word to His prophet Haggai and said: "Is it time for you, O ye, to dwell in your ceiled houses, and this house lie waste?...Go up to the mountain, and bring wood, and build the house; and I will take pleasure in it, and I will be glorified, saith the Lord" (Haggai 1:4,8). The people received this word from the Lord and prepared to rebuild the Temple in 520 B.C.

Then God spoke again to Haggai and said: "Consider now from this day and upward, from the four and twentieth day of the ninth month, *even from the day that the foundation of the Lord's temple was laid, consider it. Is the seed yet in the barn? yea, as yet the vine, and the fig tree, and the pomegranate, and the olive tree, hath not brought forth: from this day will I bless you"* (Haggai 2:18-19). "The glory of this latter house shall be greater than of the former, saith the Lord of hosts: and in this place will I give peace, saith the Lord of hosts" (2:9).

This cycle of 2,520 years began with the laying of the foundation of the Second Temple on the twenty-fourth day of the ninth month (Chisleu—our December) in 520 B.C. It will end with the final cleansing of the Temple-Sanctuary by Christ in the year A.D. 2000. This completes a perfect parallel with the termination of the 2,200 years of Daniel 8:14, and the cleansing of the sanctuary cycle discussed previously, which also ends in the year 2000 A.D. *(See figure 6.)*

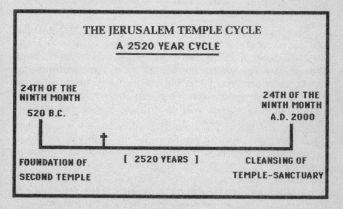

THE JERUSALEM TEMPLE CYCLE

A 2520 YEAR CYCLE

24TH OF THE
NINTH MONTH
520 B.C.

24TH OF THE
NINTH MONTH
A.D. 2000

FOUNDATION OF
SECOND TEMPLE

[2520 YEARS]

CLEANSING OF
TEMPLE-SANCTUARY

Figure 6

7. The Great 490 Year Cycle for Israel

The prophet Daniel, who was given the most precise of all the time prophecies in the Scriptures, revealed that God had established a prophetic period of "seventy weeks" or 490 years which would govern His divine dealings with the history and future of His chosen people: *Seventy weeks are determined upon thy people and upon thy holy city, to finish the transgression,* **and to make an end of sins, and to make reconciliation for iniquity, and to bring in everlasting righteousness, and** *to seal up the vision and prophecy, and to anoint the most Holy."* **(Daniel 9:24).**

As we discussed in an earlier chapter about God's time cycles, this 490-year cycle has marked the life of Israel, from the birth of Abraham, to the glorious dawn of their Kingdom Age, the Millennium, **"To bring in everlasting righteousness, and to seal up the vision and prophecy."**

Six periods of 490 years each have already been fulfilled in Israel's history. The last of the six cycles of 490 years, the period of Daniel's seventy weeks of years, is discussed in detail in chapter 2 . In the analysis it was demonstrated that this seventy-week period was divided into two portions: the first composed of sixty-nine "weeks" of years (483 biblical years) — which were fulfilled to the exact day when the Messiah was "cut off" on Palm Sunday, April 3, A.D. 32; the second portion is composed of a future "week" of years (seven biblical years).

The second period of seven years will be fulfilled in the last seven years of this age. The signing of a seven-year treaty between the Antichrist and Israel will begin this last "week" of seven years, and the Battle of Armageddon and the commencement of the Millennium will mark its close exactly seven years later. We can expect that this last "week" of seven years will be fulfilled just as precisely as the first sixty-nine "week" portion.

If the first six prophetic time indications we have examined are accurate, then the Millennium would begin in the Fall of A.D. 2000. The seven-year treaty between the Antichrist and Israel, the last "week" of Daniel's vision, would then have to be signed in the Fall of the year 1993. A long interval occurs between the ending of the sixty-ninth "week" in A.D. 32 and the recommencement of the prophetic time clock for Israel in A.D. 1993.

In light of the phenomenon of the many earlier 490-year cycles in the history of Israel, It is impossible to ignore the fact that this great interval between the two parts of Daniel's vision of seventy weeks is also composed of a fourfold cycle of 490 years, totaling 1,960 calendar years (4 x 490 years = 1,960 calendar years). *(See figure 7.)*

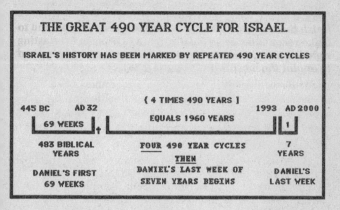

THE GREAT 490 YEAR CYCLE FOR ISRAEL

ISRAEL'S HISTORY HAS BEEN MARKED BY REPEATED 490 YEAR CYCLES

445 BC   AD 32   { 4 TIMES 490 YEARS }   1993   AD 2000

69 WEEKS   EQUALS 1960 YEARS

483 BIBLICAL YEARS   FOUR 490 YEAR CYCLES   7 YEARS

THEN

DANIEL'S FIRST 69 WEEKS   DANIEL'S LAST WEEK OF SEVEN YEARS BEGINS   DANIEL'S LAST WEEK

Figure 7

8. The Great Jubilee Period

God told Moses to set forth two tremendous principles for Israel once they entered the Promised Land (on the tenth day of Nisan, 1451 B.C.). Leviticus 25:2-10 records those principals. The first involved the Law of the Sabbath of the Land:

"When ye come into the land which I give you, then shall the land keep a sabbath unto the Lord. Six years thou shalt sow thy field, and six years thou shalt prune thy vineyard, and gather in the fruit thereof; But in the seventh year shall be a sabbath of rest unto the land, a sabbath for the Lord" (Leviticus 25:2-5).

The second principle had to do with the Year of Jubilee: **"And thou shalt number seven sabbaths of years unto thee, seven times seven years; and the space of the seven sabbaths of years shall be unto thee forty and nine years.**

Then shalt thou cause the trumpet of the jubilee to sound on the tenth day of the seventh month, in the day of atonement shall ye make the trumpet sound throughout all your land. And ye shall hallow the fiftieth year, and *proclaim liberty* throughout all the land unto all the inhabitants thereof: it shall be a jubilee unto you; and ye shall return every man unto his possession, and ye shall return every man unto his family. *A jubilee shall that fiftieth year be unto you:* ye shall not sow, neither reap that which groweth of itself in it, nor gather the grapes in it of thy vine undressed. For it is the jubilee, it shall be holy unto you: ye shall eat the increase thereof out of the field" (Leviticus 25: 8-12).

Therefore, every fiftieth year was a Year of Jubilee. All debts were to be cancelled, the land was to be returned to the original family owner and liberty was to be declared to all slaves.

Leviticus 16 describes the ceremony which the High Priest would lead on the solemn Day of Atonement. He would enter the Holy of Holies in the Temple on the tenth day of Tishri (the months of September/October on our calendar) and, after sprinkling the blood, he would announce the cancellation of all debts, proclaim liberty to all captives, and the restoration of all things (Leviticus 16:1-34 and 25: 9-10). Unfortunately, in its thirty-five hundred year history, there is no evidence that Israel has ever kept the Sabbath Year of the land or the sacred Jubilee Year by letting the land rest completely throughout Israel in obedience to God's command.

As outlined in chapter 12, it is worthwhile to note that from the coronation of King Saul in 1096 B.C. until 606 B.C., Israel missed seventy Sabbath years during this 490-year period. They failed to obey God and trust Him to let the land rest. God intervened in judgment and caused the land to lie fallow all the while His people were held captive in Babylon for a period of seventy years, just as he promised He would do if they neglected to keep the Sabbath years (Leviticus 26:34-35,43).

The Jubilee system will be fulfilled when Jesus Christ, our "high priest whom we confess" (Hebrews 3:1) returns and the Millennium Kingdom begins. This Jubilee Cycle of sabbatical years and Jubilee Years began when the Israelites crossed the Jordan River in 1451 B.C. (Joshua 4:19) and should end with the Day of Atonement, tenth Tishri, in the fall of the year, completing seventy Jubilee Years—3,500 biblical years; 3,500 years of 360 days (3500 times 360 equals 1,260,000 days divided by 365.25 days equals 3449.7 calendar years). This gives us a duration for the seventy Jubilee Cycles of a total of 3,450 calendar years. If this interpretation is correct, then the Seventieth Jubilee – after the 3450 calendar year period which began in 1451 B.C. – will begin on the Day of Atonement in the Fall of the year A.D. 2000. (See figure 8.) This Grand Jubilee would be celebrated on the Day of Atonement, the tenth day of Tishri, or the ninth of October, in the year A.D. 2000.

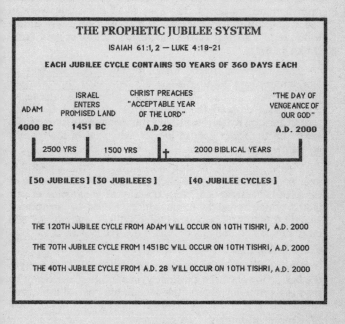

Figure 8

Further confirmation that God will fulfill these prophecies on the basis of the Jewish Sabbatical Year and Jubilee Year system is given in Luke 4:18-21. After Jesus was

191

baptized and went through the forty-day trial and temptation by Satan in the wilderness, He came to the synagogue in His hometown of Nazareth where He began His public ministry in the autumn of A.D. 28.

It is no accident that He began by reading from the prophecy of Isaiah 61:1: **"When He had opened the book, he found the place where it was written, ' The spirit of the Lord is upon me; because He hath anointed me to preach the gospel to the poor; he hath sent me to heal the brokenhearted, to preach deliverance to the captives, and the recovering of sight to the blind,** *to set at liberty* **them that are bruised,** *To preach the acceptable year of the Lord.* **And he closed the book, and he gave it again to the minister and sat down. The eyes of all them that were in the synagogue were fastened on him, and he began to say unto them,** *'This day is this scripture fulfilled in your ears'* **(Luke 4:18-21.**

The year when this occurred, the fall of A.D. 28, was, in fact, not only a Jubilee Year, but was also the thirtieth Jubilee since the Sabbatical-Jubilee system of years began when Israel crossed the Jordan River in 1451 B.C. Thus, Jesus Christ precisely fulfilled **"the acceptable year of the Lord"** on the exact year of Jubilee—the year of liberty and release.

Please note that He stopped reading at **"the acceptable year of the Lord"** because He knew that the next phrase of the prophet's sentence, **"and the day of vengeance of our God,"** which refers to Armageddon, would be postponed exactly 2,000 biblical years (2000 biblical years times 360 days equals 720,000 days divided by 365.25 equals 1971.25 calendar years).

If we add 2000 biblical years (1971.25 calendar years) to the beginning of Christ's ministry on a Jubilee Year when He read the prophecy about **"the acceptable year of the Lord"** in the fall of A.D. 28; we arrive at the year A.D. 2000, forty Jubilee Cycles later.

The next Jubilee Year will occur in A.D. 2000, completing the Sabbatical-Jubilee system of years—the seventieth Great Jubilee. (See figure 8.)

In the thirtieth Jubilee Year, Christ commenced His ministry in A.D. 28. In the seventieth Jubilee Year, Christ may commence His Kingdom in A.D.2000. It is also interesting that both the First and Second Temple were dedicated to the Lord on the Feast of Tabernacles in a Year of Jubilee.

The great Jubilee Year will truly be "a year of release," a proclamation of liberty and "a restitution of all things" as God truly transforms the kingdoms of this world into the Kingdom of God. Luke appeals to fulfilled prophecy as a proof that Christ will finally come again to fulfill the promise implied in the Year of Jubilee.

"But those things, which God before had showed by the mouth of all his prophets, that Christ should suffer, he hath so fulfilled. Repent ye therefore, and be converted, that your sins may be blotted out, *when the times of refreshing shall come* from the presence of the Lord; and he shall send Jesus Christ, which before was preached unto you: *Whom the heaven must receive until the times of restitution of all things*, which God hath spoken by the mouth of all his holy prophets since the world began" (Acts 3:18-21).

Dr. Edersheim in his excellent book, The Temple, records that the following words are spoken in the Jewish synagogue liturgy for the Day of Atonement: "Raise up for us a right intercessor, I have found a ransom [Atonement] Bring us back in Jubilee to Zion. Thy city and in joy as of old to Jerusalem, the House of the Holiness! Then shall we bring before thy face the sacrifices that are due."[10]

In my research into biblical prophecies I have discovered several other indications which suggest that the year A.D. 2000 is a probable termination point for the "last days." A possible confirmation that these prophecies are about to be fulfilled may be found in the thousands of pastors and believers around the world that are receiving a quiet assurance in their own spirit that the Second Coming of the Lord is quickly approaching. This quiet acceptance that "the times of refreshing" are now at hand is not leading to any fanaticism. Rather, this appreciation of the nearness of the return of the Lord is leading to a renewed commitment and love for Christ. An obedience to His command to care for our brothers and to go into all the world and preach the gospel is a natural consequence to this expectation that our Lord is coming soon.

Three Important Cautions

In regard to the foregoing interpretations, it is vital that we remind ourselves of three important factors:

First, these are only interpretations and not prophetic revelations. Although I believe these interpretations are valid, only time itself will prove whether or not they are accurate.

Second, even if these interpretations are valid conclusions as to the correct time of the conclusion of these appointed prophetic time cycles, God is sovereign and may accelerate or postpone "the time appointed."

Thirdly, even if these interpretations are correct regarding the time of the Great Tribulation and the beginning of the Millennium, there is no possibility for us to determine the time of the Rapture of the Church. The time of the Rapture is known only by God. It is possible that the Rapture is not even set to occur on a certain day. It may well be that, in His sovereignty, God has set a certain number of souls which He will gather into that "peculiar people," the Church, before His return.

Second Peter 3:12 suggests that Christians should be **"looking for and hasting unto the coming of the day of God,"** by evangelizing a lost world to find faith in Jesus Christ. It is possible that once the last person accepts Christ, and joins the Body of Christ, Christ will call His Church home to heaven at the Rapture.

Many students of prophecy believe that the Rapture of believers will be followed immediately either by Daniel's Seventieth Week (the seven-year treaty which Antichrist will make with Israel), or the "revealing" of the Antichrist when he sets himself up as "god" in the rebuilt Temple. There is no biblical proof or requirement that the Rapture occur on either of these occasions.

The time of the Rapture is known only to God and it could occur at any time, from today until the day when the Holy Spirit is removed as the hinderer so that the Antichrist can "reveal" himself in the Temple. Once the Antichrist reveals his nature, the focus of God's program for man will be centered upon Israel, the Two Witnesses and the 144 thousand Jewish witnesses. The revelation of the Antichrist is the last possible moment that the Rapture could occur, if our interpretation of the many Scriptures regarding the Rapture is correct.

From the Rapture until the return of Christ with His saints at the Battle of Armageddon, the Church is described by the book of Revelation (chapter 4 through 19) as participating in the Marriage Supper of the Lamb and enjoying Heaven. While the Lord has revealed His sovereignty in incredibly precise time prophecies for Israel and the nations, times are never given for the Church nor for the Rapture.

Notes:

1. Stuart Ross Taylor, *Lunar Science: A Post-Appolo View,*
   (New York: Pregamon Press, Inc., 1975) pp. 84, 92

2. Barnabus, *The Epistle of Barnabus – The Ante-Nicene Fathers,*
   (Grand Rapids: Eerdmans Publishing Co., 1987) Vol. 1, pp. 146-147

3. Irenaeus, *Against Heresies – The Anti-Nicene Fathers,*
   (Grand Rapids: Eerdmans Publishing Co., 1987) Vol. 1, p. 557

4. Methodius, *The Banquet Of The Ten Virgins – The Anti-Nicene Fathers,*
   (Grand Rapids: Eerdmans Publishing Co., 1987) Vol. VI, p. 344

5. Bishop Thomas Newton, *Dissertations On The Prophecies,*
   (London: 1817) Vol. 2, p. 373

6. Archbishop Jacob Usher, *Chronology Of The Old and New Testaments,*
   (Verona: 1750)

7. Bishop Burnett, *The Sacred Theory Of The Earth,*
   (London: 1816) p. 408

8. Lactantitius, *The Divine Institutes – The Anti-Nicene Fathers,*
   (Grand Rapids: Eerdmans Publishing Co., 1987) Vol. VII, p. 211

9. Bishop Thomas Newton, *Dissertations On The Prophecies,*
   (London 1817) Vol. I, p. 317

10. Dr. A. Edersheim, *The Temple,*
    (London: The Religious Tract Society, 1880) p. 121

CHAPTER 15

The Second Coming of Christ

"For the Lord himself shall descend from heaven with a shout, with the voice of the archangel, and with the trump of God: and the dead in Christ shall rise first: then we which are alive and remain shall be caught up together with them in the clouds, to meet the Lord in the air: and so shall we ever be with the Lord. Wherefore comfort one another with these words" (1 Thessalonians 4:16-18).

Mankind stands today, not merely at the crossroads of his historical destiny, but rather at the edge of a cliff, overlooking a bottomless pit. Before him lies an abyss filled with the worst horrors of all our nightmares: nuclear annihilation, famine of unimaginable proportions, chemical and biological warfare, unleashed international terrorism. Men's hearts "fail them for fear" as they contemplate the death of democracy in country after country, the rise of dictatorship, anarchy and violence, drug dependence, unprecedented natural disasters; a drastic decline of those family values and love that make life worthwhile. All of these horrors – and more – are just one small step away.

It is not surprising that thoughtful men and women should lose hope as they contemplate the sobering truth that our race has shown a much greater ability to endure approaching disasters than to avoid them. History is full of examples, from World War I, to the present, of leaders who were totally aware of impending disasters and yet seemed incapable of changing their course of actions which led inevitably to the very thing they feared.

Many knowledgeable scientists, military specialists and political commentators can see no way out, humanly speaking, of our present dilemma. World leaders have a desperate sense that we are approaching a final conflict of the nations. Newspapers and magazines continually remind us that we live in an increasingly dangerous world where terrorist actions, superpower miscalculation or even an accidental missile launch could plunge us into a nuclear Armageddon.

More than 65 percent of school children, according to recent surveys, believe that a nuclear war will occur before they have a chance to build a career or start a family. This unprecedented fear of the future is no doubt a factor in the explosion of pleasure-seeking that we see manifested in drug abuse, crime and sexual promiscuity.

However, there is a hope for mankind. It lies in the sure fulfillment of the prophecies of the Bible. They clearly tell us that Jesus Christ will return in the hour of man's greatest crisis to deliver him from the destruction of the Great Tribulation and the Battle of Armageddon.

During the first centuries after Christ ascended into heaven, believers often greeted one another by saying, "Maranatha," which means "the Lord cometh." Despite persecution and hardship they rejoiced in the certain knowledge that Jesus Christ, who rose from the dead and appeared to more than five hundred witnesses, would someday return to set up an eternal kingdom of peace.

The Second Coming is the greatest single theme in Scripture. While there are more than three hundred prophecies in the Old Testatment regarding His first coming, there are more than eight times as many verses devoted to His Second Coming. Obviously, if God feels that the return of the Messiah is of such vital importance; we dare not ignore the signs.

The first prediction that the seed of woman (Christ) would bruise the head of the seed of Satan (Antichrist) was given by God immediately after the fall of Adam and Eve as reported in Genesis 3:15:

"I will put enmity between thee [Satan] and the woman, and between thy seed [Antichrist] and her seed [Jesus]; it shall bruise thy head, and thou shall bruise his heel." The New Testament book of Jude recalls the prophecy of Enoch, who lived before the Flood and was himself "raptured" to heaven. **"Enoch, also, the seventh from Adam, prophesied**

of these, saying: 'Behold, the Lord cometh with ten thousands of his saints, to execute judgment upon all "(Jude verse 14-15).

In the book of Revelation, John records the last message of our Lord: "And, behold, I come quickly; and my reward is with me, to give every man according as his work shall be" (22:12). John ends his revelation with, "He which testifieth these things saith, Surely, I come quickly. Amen. Even so, come, Lord Jesus" (22:20).

The Signs of the Approaching Holocaust

Shortly before Jesus was crucified, His disciples asked Him, "Tell us, when shall these things be? and what shall be the sign of thy coming, and of the end of the world?" (Matthew 24:3). The Master's answer describes the signs that will lead up to the Great Tribulation and the ultimate Battle of Armageddon. The Church has been promised that she will escape the coming Tribulation. Thus, these promised signs leading to the Great Tribulation become indications of how close we are to the approach of that great day when the trumpet will blow and "all them also that love His appearing" shall rise to meet Him in the air. Each of these prophesied signs show the nearness of His coming.

"Jesus answered and said unto them, Take heed that no man deceive you. For *many shall come in my name, saying I am Christ*; and shall deceive many. And *ye shall hear of wars and rumors of wars:* see that ye be not troubled: for all these things must come to pass, but the end is not yet. For *nation shall rise against nation, and kingdom against kingdom* and there shall be *famines* and *pestilences*, and *earthquakes, in divers places.* All these are the beginning of sorrows. Then shall they deliver you up to be afflicted. and shall kill you: and *ye shall be hated of all nations for my name's sake.* And then shall many be offended, and shall betray one another, and shall hate one another. And many false prophets shall rise, and shall deceive many. And because iniquity shall abound, *the love of many shall wax cold.* But he that shall endure unto the end, the same shall be saved. And *this gospel of the kingdom shall be preached in all the world for a witness unto all nations; and then shall the end come.*" (Matthew 24:4-14).

1. The Rise of False Christs

"Take heed that no man deceive you for many shall come in my name, saying, I am the Christ; and shall deceive many" (Matthew 24:4-5).

In A.D. 132, Simon Bar Kochba, "The Star of the East," led the Jews in a furious revolt against their Roman conquerors. This was the kind of Messiah the Jews were looking for. The great Rabbinical scholar Akiba acknowledged him as the "Messiah." However, the Emperor Hadrian brought his legions against the Jewish army, in A.D. 135, on the ninth day of Av (August), destroying 580 thousand men in a desperate battle southwest of Jerusalem. More than three million Jews died throughout the Middle East, leading to a dispersion which lasted almost eighteen centuries.

People are still looking for a Messiah that will lead them to a transcendent experience. Today we have had Guru Maharhaj Ji, Sun Myung Moon, Charles Manson, Jim Jones, Ron L. Hubbard, and many others. The almost cultic worship of entertainers and sports personalities prepares the way for the worship of the Antichrist. In the increasing despair of modern man, we see the beginning of that attitude which will one day manifest itself in the worship of the Antichrist in the Temple in Jerusalem.

2. Wars and Rumors of Wars

Christ said, "And ye shall hear of wars and rumors of wars: see that ye be not troubled: for all these things must come to pass, but the end is not yet. For nation shall rise against nation, and kingdom against kingdom" (Matthew 24:6-7).

In all of recorded history the world has suffered thirteen years of war for every single year of peace; but since 1945 the pace has increased tremendously, with more than three hundred wars being fought in the past forty-one years. In fact, a military study, The War Atlas, records that since 1945, not one single day has passed without the waging of some sort of war or conflict somewhere in the world. This is truly a century of death, wars and worldwide military alliances in which only the stars are neutral.

Far more sobering than the increasing frequency of wars is the fact that science and unlimited military budgets have combined to produce the means for massive worldwide destruction: nuclear, chemical, biological weapons, and an astronomical amount of conventional weapons. Consider some of the following facts and ask yourself where this is all heading.

Twenty-five centuries ago, the prophet Joel foresaw our day and prophesied the following message: **"Proclaim ye this among the Gentiles; Prepare war, wake up the mighty men, let all the men of war draw near; let them come up: Beat your plowshares into swords, and your pruning hooks into spears" (Joel 3:9-10).**

The standing armies of the world today contain 32 million soldiers. With complete war mobilization, these nations could field armies of 570 million troops. According to a report by the Club of Rome, called Reshaping The International Order, close to 50 percent (some 500,000) of all scientists work on weapons research, while over 40 percent of all funds spent on scientific research are focused on arms. The annual international arms trade has grown in 1988 to almost one trillion dollars . If only a small fraction of this investment was redirected "from swords into plowshares" it would permanently solve the Third World's hunger and health problems.

The Middle East is a ticking time bomb which could easily set off an thermonuclear war. The Arab nations surrounding Israel now have three times the artillery and tanks and possess 500 thousand more soldiers than the combined armies of N.A.T.O. In other words, tiny Israel, smaller than Switzerland is confronted with a military threat from the Arab nations alone, which is stronger than the combined military strength of the armed forces of the North Atlantic Treaty Organization. In light of the repeated Arab threats to destroy Israel, it is understandable that she refuses to give up the West Bank. If Arab armies had possession of the West Bank, they could easily attack across the narrow band of land connecting northern and southern Israel. At certain points it is only 9 miles from the West Bank area to the Mediterranean Sea. Israel could be cut in two within hours with modern armored forces because she would lack the strategic depth of the West Bank to absorb and hold against an attacking army. The U.N. Security

Resolution 242 guaranteed Israel "recognized and secure borders". Without the West Bank, Israel is militarily indefensible.

The World Military Expenditures and Arms Transfers, 1987 reports that of the top ten arms importing nations in the world, five of them are in the Middle East. Even the poorest of the Third World countries borrow hundreds of millions of dollars annually to buy huge supplies of weapons. As soon as the developed nations have designed a new version of a weapon, their arms salesmen find some poor country that will acquire the old version and thus the cycle of death continues. This overkill has continued to such an absurd degree that there is now one military weapon and the equivalent of four thousand pounds of explosives for every man, woman and child alive.

The Trident submarine is just one small part of the superpower's nuclear forces. Consider the unbelievable destructive power represented by the eighteen submarines already built and twelve more that are on order. According to the April 26, 1987 issue of the Toronto Star, the newest Trident, the U.S.S. Pennsylvania costs 2.7 Billion dollars. Each submarine has twenty-four missiles with a minimum of fourteen individually targeted warheads per missile. The new improved D5 super, accurate warheads can deliver their lethal explosives to within 100 yards of the target while staying submerged under the ocean some 10,000 miles away. Since each Trident warhead is five times more powerful than the bomb which devastated Hiroshima and each submarine can destroy over 408 cities or military bases, we have now progressed to the point that this one ship can deliver more destruction than all of the weapons of World War II.

Nuclear and political scientists from the Massachusetts Institute of Technology and Harvard University met in November of 1975 to discuss the probability of nuclear war in light of the present geopolitical situation and the fact that historically, nations that have armed for war have inevitably used such weapons in wars to further their political aims. They concluded that a thermonuclear war would certainly occur before the year 2000.

The only way to prevent such a terrible war would be a decision by all nation-states to surrender their sovereignty to an authoritarian world government. In fact, biblical prophecy predicts that precisely this outcome will result in the last days of this generation when nations turn over all power to the Antichrist in the hope that he will provide world peace.

An item in the May 16, 1982, issue of the Toronto Star revealed that Israel had developed two hundred nuclear weapons. In the fall of 1986, there was a major media uproar when an Israeli nuclear technician publicly confirmed this fact. An embattled Israel finds itself surrounded by enormously well armed Arab nations with virtually unlimited military support from Russia. It is no wonder that she prefers to rely on some nuclear arms of her own, rather than trust that the United States would risk her own survival if an ultimate confrontation developed in the Mideast between Russia and Israel.

According to the Center for Defense Information, so far there have been ninety-six serious nuclear accidents, each one bringing us one small step closer to nuclear Armageddon.

For thousands of years mankind has engaged in warfare, but in all that time, most battles involved only several thousand participants and lacked the means of totally destroying the enemy. Our century has seen the perfection of mass warfare in which all elements of society unite to either annihilate the opponent or obtain unconditional surrender. Around the world approximately eighty million people work in or for the armed forces of their countries. In 1987, global military spending topped nine hundred and thirty billion dollars according to the United States Arms Control and Disarmament Agency report.

These numbers are so large that it is hard to comprehend the true magnitude of the dollars mankind invests in warfare preparation. The cost of a single Exocet air-to-ship missile would equal the annual income of more than ten thousand people in most Third World countries. Military spending has totally distorted our priorities. As an example, developed countries spend on international aid less than one-half of one percent of their annual military budgets.[1]

Over 140 million people have died in this century due to war and its aftermath. Seven nations, including Israel, now possess more than sixty thousand nuclear warheads. In his sobering book *The Fate of the Earth*, author Jonathan Schell pointed out that the Soviets have enough weapons to totally wipe out all United States military targets several times over and still have eight thousand nuclear warheads left. If they then targeted every American city and town, in order of population size, every community with a population of fifteen hundred people or more could be hit by a one megaton bomb (eighty times the power of the Hiroshima bomb). Obviously, the Soviets would run out of targets long before they ran out of bombs. The same overkill capacity exists for U.S. forces.[2]

Jesus Christ, in the book of Revelation, said that, in the final three-and-one-half years of the Great Tribulation, the red horse of the Apocalypse (representing war) would go forth to destroy and take peace from the earth (see Revelation 6:3-4). Surely, even now, we can hear his approaching hoofbeats.

Jesus also said: **"For then shall be great tribulation, such as was not since the beginning of the world to this time, no, nor ever shall be. And except those days should be shortened, there should no flesh be saved: but for the elect's sake those days shall be shortened"** (Matthew 24: 21-22).

When you contemplate the enormous problems facing mankind – disease, starvation, ecological disasters and homelessness – you recognize that there must be a terrible moral vacuum at the core of our civilization as you see the vast expenditures which we have wasted on the tools of annihilation.

The words of President Eisenhower, reported in the New York Times on April 17, 1953, still challenge us a quarter century later:

A life of perpetual fear and tension; a burden of arms draining the wealth and the labor of all peoples; a wasting of strength that defies the American system or the Soviet system or any system to achieve the true abundance and happiness for the people of this earth.. Every gun that is made, every warship launched, every rocket fired signifies, in the final sense, a theft from those who hunger and are not fed, those who are cold and are not clothed. This world in arms is not spending money alone. It is spending the sweat of its laborers, the genius of its scientists, the hopes of its children. We pay for a single fighter plane with a half million bushels of wheat. We pay for a single destroyer with new homes that could have housed more than 8000 people...This is not a way of life at all, in any true sense. Under the cloud of threatening war, it is humanity, hanging from a cross of iron. [3]

When you consider the number of nuclear, chemical and biological weapons in the hands of today's political leaders, you can understand the viewpoint of one nuclear scientist. He was asked by a reporter to predict what weapons would be used in World War III. After a long pause he said, "I'm not sure. But I'll tell you what will be used in World War IV. Rocks!"

Fortunately for Christians, we know that no man can do anything unless God allows it, and we have the sure promise that Christ will take all believers to be with Him before the worst war in history begins. For those who are not believers in Christ, the question regarding World War III is not "if" but "when?"

People cry out for peace, but no rational nation dares to disarm before it's potential enemy agrees to do the same. We are trapped in a complex game in which one wrong move will result in the mutual suicide of all players. As the popular movie Wargames so clearly showed, "the only winning strategy is not to play." While this may be emotionally satisfying in fiction, we must survive in the real world where other nations are as committed to their national goals as we are to ours.

In the final surrender ceremonies of World War II, General Douglas MacArthur summed up the lessons of this horrendous war that claimed over 60 million lives. His words still stand as a warning to our generation: "We have had our last chance. If we do not now devise some greater and more equitable system, Armageddon will be at the door. The problem is basically theological and involves a spiritual recrudescence and improvement of human character. It must be of the spirit if we are to save the flesh."[4]

Humanly speaking, with the hindsight of thousands of years of our violent history, it is difficult to develop a credible scenario of some way that man can escape from this awesome holocaust. Jesus Christ described this situation to His disciples as follows:

"Upon the earth distress of nations, with perplexity;... men's hearts failing them for fear, and for looking after those things which are coming on the earth: for the powers of heaven shall be shaken" (Luke 21: 25-26).

Since General Secretary Michael Gorbachev and President Reagan have begun their series of disarmament discussions, a wave of euphoria has sweep over many in the forlorn hope that real peace and disarmament is at hand. Sadly, few people have read the small print of this treaty which specifies that only a small number of obsolete missiles will be eliminated. Even if this treaty is approved, not one nuclear bomb will actually be destroyed; they will simply be recycled into new weapons.

Sir William Stephenson, (Intrepid) the head of Combined intelligence Operations during World War II, made a speech to the American Bar Association in May, 1988 regarding Soviet capabilities and intentions. According to Stephenson, in November, 1987 Gorbachev made a secret speech to the top leadership of Russia on the anniversary of the Communist coup of 1917. The thrust of Gorbachev's speech was that Russia must adopt policies "that stops the U.S. Strategic Defense Initiative (S.D.I.) and puts the Americans to sleep." Stephenson went on to conclude that the West would accept the proclamations of peace and democracy at their utmost peril. In the same way that Adolf Hitler promised Neville Chamberlain "Peace in our Time", the Soviets are talking peace while rapidly continuing the most massive buildup of armaments in the history of the world. Acccording to the historical research of Sidney Lens, since 1945 there have been a total of six thousand disarmament negotiating sessions. Not one single thermonuclear warhead has been destroyed to date as a consequence of these forty-three years of disarmament agreements.

Since 1947, the Bulletin of the Atomic Scientists has displayed a clock on its cover which symbolizes how close these specialists feel we are to a nuclear Armageddon. Their clock now shows that it is only three minutes to that final midnight. If you are unconcerned about this impending nuclear conflict, you are probably either a Christian who trusts that Christ will save His church or you simply do not understand the situation. The second horse of the Apocalypse the red horse, represents war and is even now preparing to ride.

"**And when he had opened the second seal, I heard the second beast say, Come and see. And there went out another horse that was red; and power was given to him that sat thereon to take peace from the earth, and that they should kill one another; and there was given unto him a great sword**" (Revelation 6: 3-4).

3. Famines

Another warning sign which Christ gave us is that **"there shall be famines"** which would be widespread and devastating, leading up to the final conflict (Matthew 24:7). Only ten years ago the "Green Revolution" seemed to promise the end of hunger in our generation.

Now we are faced with drought and appalling famine throughout Africa, India and Southeast Asia. Over forty million may starve during the next four years in the sub-Sahara region of Africa. Russia and China are still unable to feed themselves. It is staggering to realize that even in the worst of the last several years of famine in Ethiopia, there were reliable reports that food was being "exported" from Ethiopia to Russia to pay for Soviet weapons to enable the communist regime to kill the rebels in the north of the country. Forced collectivization of farms and short-sighted food relief plans have compounded an already impossible situation in many countries.

According to the 1988 Annual Study of the U.N. Population Fund, the amount of agricultural land is decreasing rapidly. New deserts are growing at the rate of 14.8 million acres every year. Over 26 billion tons of topsoil are lost each year and the tropical forests, which produce significant amounts of our planet's oxygen, are shrinking by 27 million acres per year. That distant sound you hear while you stand comfortably on the platform waiting for your train is not the oncoming train: it is the sound of banging, empty, rice bowls from the one-third of mankind who are approaching starvation.

Even in North America, the "greenhouse effect" which seems to be caused by our environmental pollution, is contributing to the worst drought in the last two hundred years. Many farmers will harvest no crops in areas which have previously yielded two or three ample crops in the past. In many areas of the Midwest over one third of the crops are rated very poor. The unprecedented increase in average worldwide temperature has been continuous during the last 100 years. Dale Robertson, the head of the U.S. Forest Service reports that 1987 was the worst year since 1917 for drought-caused forest fires. He predicted that 1988 will be much worse than 1987. Part of the problem is that in most of Europe and Asia there is almost no arable land which has not been cultivated. Therefore our challenge is to increase the yield on tired agricultural land which has been cultivated for hundreds of years. That is a difficult task.

The deadly effect of population growth is not a future problem; the disaster has already begun in Asia, Africa and South America. Can you hear the ghostly black horseman of the Apocalypse as he rides out from that dark forest where he has waited down through the centuries for that dreaded final trumpet call of worldwide famine? The appalling specter of widespread famine is already here and the black horse of the book of Revelation, who represents famine, has already begun his deadly ride.

The world population is growing at the rate of 220,000 people per day. However, of the one hundred and fifty additional babies born into the world during the next minute, 90 percent of them will be born in the Third World where the prospects for food growth are poorest. Rapid worldwide population growth, and its devastating aftermath, represents one of the most dangerous problems facing the world as we near the year 2000.

The average rate of population increase worldwide is approximately 2 percent, although it is much higher in those Third World countries that can least afford new hungry mouths to feed. A rich country like Austria will only double its population in the next three thousand years at its slow rate of growth, but Nigeria will double its already large population by the year 2000.

In order to place this average 2 percent growth-rate in perspective, consider the following:

Time Scale	Years	World Population
Beginning of man until Christ	?	300 million
Christ to Columbus A.D. 1492	1462	500 million
Columbus to World War 1- A.D. 1918	418	2 billion
World War 1 to A.D. 1962	44	3 billion
A.D. 1962 to A.D. 1980	18	5 billion
A.D. 1980 to A.D. 2000	20	6 billion (estimated)

At this rate of growth, in six hundred years there would be one person standing on every square meter of land on the globe. Obviously, catastrophe will overtake us long before that. Unless God intervenes, the correct image of the city of the future will be Calcutta, not Dallas.

Within two decades there will be more than six billion Africans, Latin Americans and Asians who will constitute some 85 percent of the world's population. The world population explosion and its resulting famine has developed because we have solved the "death rate" problem with D.D.T., antibiotics and sanitation measures before we brought in effective fertility control measures. The resulting imbalance is quickly creating a nightmare of massive starvation and famine in those countries we were assisting to achieve a better quality of life.

Meteorologists predict worldwide climatic changes leading to drastic reductions in the food growing capacity of Canada, U.S.A., Russia and France. Yet it is precisely these nations, excluding Russia, that produce the vital food surplus which supply the nations that can't feed themselves.

Our American and Canadian pioneers discovered a land with six to ten feet of topsoil which had been built up over thousands of years. Soil erosion has now brought us to the point where we are down to three inches of topsoil, on the average, throughout our North American farmland. Our soils are so depleted that enormous amounts of fertilizer are required on every acre of farmland to produce an economical yield. The moral tragedy is that an investment of less than 1 percent of the annual world expenditure on armaments – ten billion dollars – on building and running fertilizer plants would solve the world hunger problem within several years. The world food problem could be solved if only the political will was there to implement existing technologies.

Even in North America we stand only one harvest away from hunger. There is less food storage capacity today than in the 1920s when world food demand was much smaller than it is today.

"And I beheld, and lo a black horse; and he that sat on him had a pair of balances in his hand. And I heard a voice in the midst of the four beasts say, A measure of wheat for a penny, and three measures of barley for a penny; and see thou hurt not the oil and the wine" (Revelation 6:5-6).

In this vision, the prophet John sees a famine so destructive that an entire day's wages will only buy enough wheat to supply the needs of a single man. Another feature of this worldwide famine of the last days is that side by side with absolute poverty will be found the " oil and wine" of enormous wealth.

While the ultimate solution to this problem will only come with the return of Christ, each of us as Christians must respond as our brother's keeper with the resources He has given into our hands.

4. Pestilences

Christ said **"there shall be famines and pestilences"** (Matthew 24:7) and it is the tragic experience of this century that pestilence follows famine and war to compound their terrors.

Jesus warned that "pestilences" would be a sign that the last .days were upon us. Today we face incredible pollution and ecological problems which appear virtually unsolvable. Hazardous waste dumps are hidden in every community, leeching out their toxic elements into an unsuspecting city's water supply. Love Canal, in the United States of America, is only the tip of an enormous iceberg of similar hazardous dumps.

The problem of disposal of radioactive waste from nuclear reactors is still unsolved, yet we continue to produce radioactive materials in the vain hope that someday we will find a solution. Over sixty-five thousand new chemicals have been introduced into the biosphere during the last four decades. Only ten thousand of these chemicals have even been tested as to their effect on humans. When we add to this deadly concoction thousands of new, environmentally untested chemicals each year, we may well be creating problems and diseases for which there is no cure.

The continued heavy usage of pesticides has helped produce new strains of insects, "superbugs," which cannot be controlled. Studies have revealed that the children living in homes which use garden pesticides have a 600 percent greater risk of developing leukemia. Crossbreeding of African and South American bees has produced "killer bees" which are moving farther north each year toward the United States.

One of the reasons for Third World famine is that over one-third of all food produced is destroyed by rats and other pests. In many cities the rats outnumber the humans. Between chemical research and biological-genetic experiments for industry and the military, we will, unfortunately, see many more accidents such as that in Bhopal, India. The potential for terrorism in these areas is frightening.

The scourge of over fifteen sexually-transmitted diseases is a new form of pestilence which has now also introduced A.I.D.S., the deadliest plague in mankind's history. Thus far, this disease has developed a 100 percent death rate. It appears that A.I.D.S. is transmitted primarily through homosexual practices, but can then be transmitted from an A.I.D.S.'s carrier to a wider heterosexual group through shared intravenous drug needles, infected blood transfusions and to babies born to mothers with A.I.D.S. Studies indicate that over one and one-half million people in North America alone will die from this tragic disease, which so far shows no signs of a cure. In countries like Uganda, tragically, estimates are that up to 20 percent of the population is infected.

5. Earthquakes in various places

Earthquakes traditionally signaled political changes for ancient nations. Christ and the Old Testament prophets prophesied that the time leading up to the Battle of Armageddon would be characterized by increasingly severe earthquakes where they had previously been unknown (Matthew 24:7). This century has witnessed an unparalleled increase in the frequency and intensity of earth disturbances, and areas which never had quakes before are experiencing them for the first time. Each decade of this century has seen an increase in the number of earthquakes worldwide. More than one million minor quakes hit each year, and around one hundred thousand are strong enough to be felt with approximately one thousand causing some degree of damage.

To illustrate this phenomenon consider the earthquake results for just one year: **1976:**

Location	Death Toll
Turkey	6,000
China	1,100,000
Guatemala	23,000
South Pacific	22,000
U.S.S.R.	5,000

Many areas of North America are rated extremely hazardous for earthquakes -- Washington, California, Tennessee, New York and the Great Lakes region with a rating of 4 out of a maximum danger rating of 5.

The explosion of Mt. St. Helens in May 18, 1980 gave us a small example of the enormous power which God has prophesied that will be ultimately released in the last days. At 6:40 A.M., I was standing on the balcony of my condominium on a mountain in British Columbia, Canada. Even though I was over 200 miles away from Mt. St. Helens, I could hear the distant roar and in the following days we received a fall of white ash in southeastern B.C. When the mountain exploded, the force of the explosion was the equivalent of 500 atomic bombs. It vaporized one cubic mile of rock and devastated over 200 square miles of forest. That is equal to one ton for every human of this planet. For weeks the dust and ash were falling from the sky. To illustrate the magnitude of the explosion, scientists calculated that enough material was blown into the atmosphere to cover Manhattan Island to a depth of 400 feet if it had all landed in one place. That one blast was one indication of the incredible forces that God will unleash upon the planet in the time of the Great Tribulation.

In the "last days" the prophesied Russian attack on Israel will be marked by the strongest earthquake in history. Although it will be centered in Israel, it will destroy cities around the world. The prophet Ezekiel told us that it will be so catastrophic that men everywhere will recognize that it is God who has intervened in history (Ezekiel 38: 19-20). The prophet Haggai seems to indicate that this great earthquake will occur on the twenty-fourth day of the ninth month (December), the day before Hanukkah (Haggai 2: 6-7,18-21).

6. All these are the Beginning of Sorrows

Then Jesus tells His disciples that all these things are only the beginning of the birth pains of the Great Tribulation, that is quickly approaching its appointed hour (Matthew 24:8). Then Jesus gets more specific as to the details of the signs.

7. Then ye [Jews] shall be hated of all nations for my name's sake

The name Israel means "Prince of God" and was given to Jacob and his descendants forever. Jesus warned His Jewish disciples that one of the characteristics of the last days would be an evil hatred of the Jews by all nations (Matthew 24:9). Our generation has seen the appalling genocide which Hitler's S.S. committed against six million Jews. Persecution continues in the Soviet Union where some four to five million Jews still reside. Terrorist attacks worldwide have been focused on Jewish synagogues.

The United Nations is faced with hundreds of serious issues each year. However, during the last fifteen years the General Assembly has spent enormous amounts of time in debates and condemnation of one of its smallest member nations—Israel.

An automatic majority of Warsaw Pact and Third World nations can be counted on to vote in favor of any resolution condemning Israel, no matter how one-sided or unfair it is. For example, after a brutal terrorist car bombing that killed twelve Israeli soldiers near a border crossing in March, 1985, Israel retaliated with an attack on the terrorist base in Lebanon. Naturally, the majority in the General Assembly supported a United Nations resolution condemning Israel, with no mention of the terrorist attack.

8. The love of many will grow cold

Alienation has affected millions of people during these last few decades (Matthew 24:12). We have watched the breakup of the family to the point that the "nuclear family" of two parents and their children now represent a minority in North America. Transitory relationships are the norm for many, with divorces exceeding marriages in numerous communities.

Many North American hospitals register more abortions than live births. The head of the Soviet Union's medical establishment stated that, on average, seven million babies are aborted each year in Russia. It is not unusual to find Soviet women who admit to having eight or more abortions. In North America, the abortion figure exceeds one million annually.

The emotional toll of all these factors is reflected in the unwillingness of many to commit themselves to another person in unreserved love; yet, without real love, life becomes a mechanical drudgery that lacks the meaning which makes life precious. Christ said that this failure of natural love will be the precise state of things as man approaches the Great Tribulation period.

The increasing transitory nature of society breaks down the sense of community and mutual support that characterized the life of our parents. In forty years we have been transformed from a society in which our grandparents knew all their neighbors to our present, alienated society, where most of us do not even know the people next door.

Violent crime, child abuse, wife-battering and even abuse of aging parents by their children are sad fulfillments of that two thousand year old prophecy which said that as we enter the final countdown "the love of many will grow cold."

9. The Gospel of the Kingdom shall be Preached in all the world

The primary fulfillment of this prophecy will occur during the Great Tribulation when the Two Witnesses and the "144,000" Jewish witnesses will preach the same message as John the Baptist, **"Repent ye; for the kingdom of heaven is at hand."** Despite the terrible persecution, this gospel of the Kingdom will reach every tribe on earth.

Revelation 7:9-17 assures us that a great number from every nation will finally become believers during the Great Tribulation. They are gathered together as the returning Messiah's "elect," when the angels bring them from the four corners of the earth. Matthew 24: 31, 39-42 tells us that this gathering will occur at the end of the Tribulation period as Christ returns in power and glorify to defeat the armies of Antichrist in the Battle of Armageddon. When Christ appears, He will be accompanied by the pre-tribulation Christians who have been in Heaven. Jude 14 reveals that **"the Lord cometh with ten thousands [millions] of His saints."**

The second fulfillment of the gospel being preached in all the world is unfolding today in the explosion of distribution and expansion of the gospel message into every nation on earth (Matthew 24:14). In order that we might grasp the astonishing scope of world evangelism, consider the following facts:

	Year 1800	1890	1985
Number of languages in which the Bible was translated	50	250	*1,763
Number of missionaries	170	2,400	76,000

* 1,763 languages covers 97 percent of the world population

In 1984 more than 300 million Bibles, New Testaments and scriptural selections were distributed throughout the world. According to the best calculations, a total of <u>seventy-</u>

eight thousand new believers responded to the gospel worldwide each day in 1987.

Every week one thousand new churches are formed in Asia and Africa. These may meet initially in homes or outdoors, but as the churches grow, buildings are constructed.

In Santiago, Chile, Pastor J. Vasquez leads a church of more than 100 thousand members. In 1980, I had the pleasure of meeting this extraordinary man at the World Pentecostal Congress. His clear presentation of the gospel of Christ continues to touch the spiritual needs of his city and country.

In the troubled country of Guatemala, the church has grown from one thousand Protestant believers in 1930 to more than one and-a-half million in 1985. Over 25 percent of the country's citizens are now evangelical believers.

Reinhard Bonnke and his team travel throughout Africa with the largest tent meetings in the history of the world. Their tent seats around thirty-four thousand people who can listen to the gospel and receive healing. At the present growth-rate, over 50 percent of Africa will be born-again believers by the end of the next decade.

The spreading of the gospel message in Asia is as astonishing as in Africa. One hundred years ago, Asia was a spiritual wasteland. Today some estimate that 30 percent of South Koreans follow Jesus Christ.

Pastor Yonggi Cho has built the largest congregation in history with more than 500 thousand members. With seating for more than seventy thousand, seven services each Sunday will accommodate the 500 thousand believers. There are nineteen thousand trained home-cell leaders to work closely with each family. In addition, many spin-off churches have been formed from this mother church. Truly, God is working a miracle in church growth such as the world has never seen since the days of the early church. We are seeing prophecy fulfilled before our eyes.

Mainland China contained perhaps one million believers in 1949 when Chairman Mao and his Communist Party began their persecution of Christians. Many were killed, tortured or put into concentration camps. As a result, the Church went underground in the same way early

Christians hid from pagan Rome. In the last few years, China has partially opened the Bamboo Curtain to the West. The most conservative estimates are that China now contains between fifty and seventy-five million Chinese Christians. When my wife, Kaye, and I visited China in 1985 our hearts were touched by these Chinese people. Despite the opposition of man and Satan, men and women have searched for spiritual reality and found it in the person of Jesus Christ.

Almost two thousand years ago, when Christ told His disciples that one of the most significant signs of His return would be the preaching of the gospel to <u>all nations</u>, He added, **"And then shall the end come."**

10. Additional Signs of "The Last Days"

Paul wrote to Timothy and warned him of the following signs: **"This know also, that in the last days perilous times shall come. For men shall be lovers of their own selves, covetous, boasters, proud, blasphemers, disobedient to parents, unthankful, unholy, without natural affection, trucebreakers, false accusers, incontinent, fierce, despisers of those that are good, traitors, heady, highminded, lovers of pleasure more than lovers of God; having a form of godliness, but denying the power thereof: from such turn away" (2 Timothy 3: 1-5).**

This prophecy so accurately characterizes today's world that it could easily have been written as a synopsis to this morning's newspaper. This catalogue of the symptoms of our society precisely fulfills the prophecy of Paul as our nations stand one step away from disaster.

We are a nation addicted to tranquilizers, sleeping pills and drugs. Anxiety prevails throughout the world and even our children believe nuclear war is near. America has become a victim of self-indulgence, materialism and an overwhelming blasphemy to God expressed in both music and conversation. Child abuse, runaway children, childhood prostitution and widespread homosexuality are plagues upon our lands.

We are suffering an epidemic of ungratefulness and dishonesty in both word and deed. Our society is deluged with sensuality in the media and advertisements. Sadly, many churches have lost their first love and trust in their relationship with Christ. They have become empty, dried-out spiritual husks.

Your Personal Appointment With Destiny

The Apostle Paul said that God *"Now commandeth all men every where to repent: because he hath appointed a day, in the which he will judge the world in righteousness by that man whom he hath ordained; whereof he hath given assurance unto all men, in that he hath raised him from the dead"* (Acts 17: 30-31).

As we survey the exact precision of God's past and present appointments with Israel and the nations, we believe that these future appointments will be fulfilled as well.

Jesus told His disciples, **"When ye shall see all these things, know that it is near, even at the doors. Verily I say unto you, This generation shall not pass, till all these things be fulfilled"** (Matthew 24: 33-34).

In the preceding pages, attention has been focused on impending world events. As we turn to examine our personal future we shall see that these same incredibly accurate Scriptures have prophesied that each one of us also faces an appointment with God: **"It is appointed unto men once to die, but after this the judgment"** (Hebrews 9:27).

God has set an appointment with destiny with each of us which cannot be postponed or evaded.

The Apostle Paul wrote, **"For it is written, As I live, saith the Lord, every knee shall bow to me, and every tongue shall confess to God. So then every one of us shall give account of himself to God"** (Romans 14: 11-12).

The basis of this judgment will be our relationship with Jesus Christ, and this alone will determine whether you and I will spend an eternity with God in Heaven or an eternity without God in Hell.

Some people feel that if God is love, then somehow He will be "kind" and bend the rules to allow "good" people into heaven despite their rejection of Jesus Christ. Consider this proposition for a moment. If God allowed sinners who did not repent of their sins into heaven, He would not be our Holy God, and it would turn heaven into an annex of hell. If an unrepentant soul was allowed into Heaven, he would not only destroy the holiness of Heaven but would find its holiness repugnant to his sinful state. Others point to sincerity and ask, "Don't all roads lead to Rome?" A brief glance at a map will show you that in the same way that most roads do not lead to Rome; a man's "sincere" false beliefs will not lead his soul to an eternity with God. **"There is a way which seemeth right unto a man, but the end thereof are the ways of death" (Proverbs 14:12).**

The entrance requirements to heaven will be our righteousness and holiness before God. It is obvious that not one soul who has ever lived on this earth can meet these requirements on their own merits. As the scriptures said: **"For all have sinned, and come short of the glory of God" (Romans 3:23).**

Since God cannot ignore the fact that all of us have sinned, it was necessary that someone who was sinless should pay the penalty of physical and spiritual death as a substitute for you and me. The only person who could qualify was Jesus Christ, the Holy Son of God. **"For the wages of sin is death; but the gift of God is eternal life through Jesus Christ our Lord" (Romans 6:23).**

Christ's sacrificial gift of His life on the cross paid the price for our sins. Each one of us, by accepting His pardon, could now stand before the judgment seat of God clothed in Christ's righteousness: **"For he hath made him [Jesus] to be sin for us, who knew no sin; that we might be made the righteousness of God in Him" (2 Corinthians 5:21).**

This fact of Christ's atonement is perhaps the greatest mystery in creation. Jesus is the only one in history who, by His sinless life, was qualified to enter heaven. Yet He loved each one of us so much that He chose to die upon that cross to purchase our salvation. The marvelous and astonishing truth is that all that is required to make Jesus Christ your personal Savior from the guilt and power of sin, is to turn away from your sin in true repentance, accept Him as your Lord God and confess your belief to others.

John said, **"But as many as received him, to them gave he power to become sons of God, even to them that believe on his name" (John 1:12).**

Each one of us has our own "appointment with destiny." On an appointed day, we will stand before Jesus Christ. The choice is entirely up to us whether we will meet Him as our returning Savior or as our final Judge.

Moses addressed Israel, as they prepared to enter the struggle for the Promised Land, with words which equally apply to us as we hear the approaching hoofbeats of the Four Horsemen of the Apocalypse:

"I call heaven and earth to record this day against you, that I have set before you life and death, blessing and cursing: therefore choose life" (Deuteronomy 30:19).

As the prophetic clock ticks down to the final midnight hour, the invitation of Christ is still:

"Behold, I stand at the door, and knock: If any man hear my voice, and open the door, I will come in to him, and will sup with him and he with me" (Revelation 3:20).

Jesus Christ chose to die and then victoriously rise from the dead to win salvation for each of us who will accept Him as our Savior.

"God so loved the world that he gave his only begotten Son, that whosoever believeth in him should not perish but have eternal life." (John 3:16)

CHAPTER 16

The Temple of Gold

The following chapter, written especially for the Bantam edition of Armageddon: Appointment With Destiny, *features new, previously unpublished material.*

"He who has not seen Jerusalem in its glory has never seen a beautiful city" (Talmud Succah 51b).

"The land of Israel is at the center of the world; Jerusalem is the center of the land of Israel; the Temple is the center of Jerusalem" (Midrash Tanhuma, Kedoshim 10).

Many prophecies indicate that Israel will build its Third Temple after the Jewish people have returned from their worldwide captivity and before the return of the Messiah to set up His Kingdom. Today, as throughout history, Israel is strategically and spiritually the most important place on this planet. For four thousand years Jerusalem and the Temple Mount have been the spiritual center of the earth. The spiritual focus of Jerusalem even today is the Temple Mount and site of the Holy of Holies, the Foundation Stone. The *Mishnah* (Yoma 5:2 and 5:3b) describes that the "*Even Shetiyah*," the Foundation Stone, was the spot chosen by God upon which the Ark of the Covenant once rested. This flat bedrock is now located under the small Arab cupola, the Dome of the Tablets.

"Ten measures of beauty descended to the world. Nine were taken by Jerusalem—and one by the rest of the world" (Talmud Kiddushin 49b). Some have added, "In consequences of this; when ten measures of suffering were poured out upon the world, nine parts were given to Jerusalem and one to the rest of the world."

Jerusalem has a special quality of beauty all its own which affects almost every visitor to the city. Especially in the evening and morning a special golden glow gives a magical, almost mystical quality to the very air surrounding the ancient hills and the limestone buildings, which have a timeless beauty found nowhere else on earth. Yet paradoxically, here in Jerusalem, whose name means "city of peace," probably more blood has been spilled than in any other place in the history of this planet. Armies from a bewildering list of nations have fought and died here. There is probably not a single stone or foot of ground within the walls of Jerusalem which has not known the cry of a dying woman or child or the lifeblood of a soldier poured out to mix with the blood of the hundreds of thousands who have died before him on this spot fighting for possession of Jerusalem, the "city of peace."

Yet the eternal promise of God is: **"Thus said the Lord: I have returned to Zion, and I will dwell in Jerusalem. Jerusalem will be called the City of Faithfulness, and the mount of the Lord of Hosts the Holy Mount. . . . There shall yet be old men and women in the squares of Jerusalem, each with staff in hand because of their great age. And the streets of the city shall be crowded with boys and girls playing in its squares"** (Zechariah 8:3–5).

For millennia this spot has been the focus of the communion between God and Man, Spirit and Body, Eternity and Time. Here on this mountain, more than any other spot on Earth, are focused the hopes, fears, and prayers of billions of Muslims, Christians, and Jews. No one can be neutral about Jerusalem and the Temple Mount. Throughout history it has aroused the passions of millions. On this sacred mountain a bewildering succession of religious structures has been erected: Abraham's altar, Solomon's Temple, the Second Temple, a pagan Roman temple, the Muslim's Dome of the Rock, a Crusader church, and once more, a Muslim Dome of the Rock. The dust of Jerusalem contains the ashes of these millions of soldiers, priests, and worshipers who came here to meet their God.

The Bible records that God appeared to King Solomon when he had built the Temple and said, **"I have hallowed this house, which thou have built, to put my name there for ever; and mine eyes and mine heart shall be there**

perpetually" (1 Kings 9:3). Despite the fact that for thousands of years the majority of Jews were exiled from their homeland, righteous Jews have prayed daily with their faces turned towards Jerusalem, "May we behold Thy merciful return to Zion."

The ancient sages named this rock the Foundation Stone because they believed that this was the foundation upon which God built the entire world and, later, the very place where Abraham found the ram provided by God as a substitute sacrifice for his son, Isaac.

The Foundation Stone of the World

Four thousand years ago an old man and his young son, Isaac, walked slowly up a trail which led to the summit of a small mountain. Abraham and his son, born to him miraculously in his old age, carried wood, a knife, and other materials necessary for the special sacrifice that God had commanded. God, in order that he might test and prove Abraham's faith, had asked Abraham to offer his son as a sacrifice. Although Abraham did not understand God's ultimate purpose, he was obedient to the divine command to travel a three-day journey to Mount Moriah and there he prepared to offer the sacrifice of his son to his God.

Isaac naturally inquired, "Behold the fire and the wood; but where is the lamb for a burnt offering?"

His father, in one of the greatest statements of faith ever uttered, replied, "My son, God will provide himself a lamb for a burnt offering." Later, with the altar prepared, Abraham held the knife ready to obediently fulfill the command of his God. At the last possible moment, the Angel of the Lord called out to him to stop, that he had proved his total faith and obedience and that now the needed sacrifice would be provided. As Abraham and Isaac looked up from the altar, they saw a ram caught in a thicket by its horns.

There on the peak of Mount Moriah, which would become the most sacred spot on Earth, God intervened to provide the needed sacrifice to cover their sins. This holy mountain, which felt the touch of God, the footsteps of Abraham, and the presence of Melchisedek, the priest-king of the ancient city of Jerusalem, would become the focus of the spiritual energies and struggles of all mankind for the next four thousand years. This unique, rocky mountain became the foundation stone for the three great monotheistic religions which have shaped so much of human history. Almost a millennium later a direct descendent of Abraham, King Solomon, listening to the same voice of God, would choose this same mountain to be the foundation of the most magnificent Temple that the world has ever seen. Upon this sacred rock would rest the holy Ark of the Covenant upon which the sacred presence of God, the Shekinah glory of the God, would commune with man. It has been estimated by scholars that Israel invested more than one billion dollars in today's currency in building this incredible "Temple of Gold."

The Ark of the Covenant is the most important object in Israel's history. In the beginning of human history in the Garden of Eden, "God walked with man in the cool of the day." However, after the sinful rebellion of Adam and Eve, the precious daily communion between God and Man was lost. Except for those rare righteous men like Enoch and Noah who "walked with God," for thousands of years Man lost his close daily communion with the Lord. Then, during the miraculous deliverance of Israel in the wilderness, God appeared to His chosen prophet Moses face-to-face and promised that he now desired to commune with Man daily in a unique way. **"Let them make me a sanctuary, that I may dwell among them. According to all that I show thee, after the pattern of the tabernacle, and the pattern of all the instruments thereof, even so shall ye make it. . . . And they shall make an ark of acacia wood: two cubits and a half shall be the length thereof, and a cubit and a half the breadth thereof, and a cubit and a half the height thereof, and thou shall overlay it with pure gold within and without. . . . And there I will meet with thee, and I will commune with thee from between the two cherubim which are upon the ark of the testimony"** (Exodus 25:8–11, 22).

God's special Shekinah glory attached itself to the mercy seat upon the Ark of the Covenant and guided and protected Israel. Its holiness and divine presence were so overwhelming that the improper handling of the Ark resulted in death when King David violated the law of God regarding the correct manner for the Levites to carry the Ark with the golden staves provided. When the Ark was improperly carried on a cart, it began to fall, and Uzzah tried to prevent its fall by reaching out and touching it. This violation of the Ark's sanctity resulted in instant death. Earlier, when the Ark was returned from the Philistines to Israel the men of Bethshemesh violated the Ark's sanctity and opened it to satisfy their curiosity, more than fifty thousand people died of a plague. The Ark was continually used by Israel as it went forth to do battle against those tribes that opposed their settlement in the Promised Land. The armies of Israel conquered as Moses and other leaders sang the Psalm of the Ark (Psalm 68), "Let God arise and His enemies be scattered." The prophet Isaiah seems to prophesy that the Ark or Ensign, the "Nez," will play a significant role in the future deliverance of Israel from her enemies. He talks about this Nez or Ensign being a rallying point for Zion during the final battles of this age.

A thousand years passed from the time of Abraham and now King David was led by God to this rock, the threshing floor of Araunah, to choose it as a place where his son, King Solomon, would build the most beautiful and massive Temple the world has ever seen. When Solomon began to build his place of worship to the north of the City of David, Jerusalem, he faced the challenge of building a huge Temple on a small mountain with two high points one hundred yards apart on a north-south axis. In order to prepare a suitable basic platform for his Temple, Solomon instructed his masons to build an enormous plaza with containment walls around the mountain, and then fill up the interior with huge stones to create a base for the largest temple enclosure in the ancient world.

The entire Temple Mount is undergirded by stone arches and tunnels which created a honeycomb of empty passages. The purpose of this unprecedented design was to preserve the spiritual sanctity of the Temple by ensuring that if any impurity existed due to the presence of a dead body buried on the spot, it would be effectively sealed off by the intervening air passages of these tunnels and arched domes. Solomon's workmen dug an incredibly long tunnel directly through the mountain to the north of the Temple, which would provide a secure water supply for the vast water needs of the sanctuary. This tunnel was sealed off a thousand years later by the workmen of King Herod while they were completing their reconstruction job on the

Second Temple during the life of Jesus Christ, and remained secret until this year. This phenomenal tunnel was not mentioned in any of the known literature on the Temple and was discovered just a few weeks before my fascinating journey into the incredible tunnels being dug along the Western Wall.

Archaeologists have been digging for over twenty years, since the 1967 recapture of Jerusalem, along the underground sections of the Western Wall of the Temple Mount. In this amazing excavation, which few people have been allowed to enter, I was able to get some extraordinary photos of this underground Western Gate, the burnt stones, and two-thousand-year-old ashes from the burning of the Temple by the Romans on the tragic ninth day of Av in A.D. 70. Along this tunnel we came to the ancient Western Gate used by the Levites and priests during the time of the Second Temple. As I stood by this sealed, sacred entrance to the Temple, an old Rabbi stood there praying for the coming of the Messiah and the rebuilding of the Temple with his hands resting on a Torah Scroll. This is the closest he could come to the most sacred Holy of Holies. The Western Gate once opened into a large tunnel system which led underneath the Temple Mount as a special gate for the Levites and priests.

When they discovered this Herodian gate the archaeologists requested permission from the Chief Rabbi to explore further. Before they could commence, a violent Arab riot broke out. Muslim authorities falsely claimed that the Israelis were attempting to undermine the foundation of the Dome of the Rock. Tragically for scholarly research, the tunnel's gate was sealed to avoid further riots and bloodshed. It remains sealed to this day.

Further along the Western Wall tunnel we came to the point in the tunnel directly opposite the Eastern Gate and the Arab Dome of the Tablets which stands on the site of the Foundation Stone, the ancient Holy of Holies.

Dr. Asher S. Kaufman, an Israeli archaeologist from Hebrew University, completed some fascinating original research which has uncovered traces of the foundations of the Second Temple. An excellent article by Dr. Kaufman in the respected Biblical Archaeological Review (March–April 1983) developed additional evidence and arguments, which support his conclusion that the Temple stood to the north of the present Dome of the Rock. While the majority of scholars and certainly the Muslim writers have assumed that the original Temple site is under the Dome of the Rock, Dr. Kaufman and others believe that the archaeological remains he has discovered on the Temple Mount prove that the correct site is some three hundred feet north of the Dome, directly opposite the sealed Eastern Gate. Sadly, some of this archaeological evidence which proves the precise location of the ancient Temple is being destroyed by recent Arab construction trenches on the Temple Mount. Fortunately, Dr. Kaufman was able to photograph the position of these valuable remains of cisterns and walls in place, prior to this destruction.

When someone would enter the Temple Mount in the days of Christ by way of the Eastern Gate he would find himself facing gates leading directly in a straight line into the sacred Inner Temple, toward the Holy of Holies. This section in front of the sealed Eastern Gate is now a flat, completely empty area which you can walk across directly towards the small Arab cupola, known as the Dome of the Tablets. As illustrated in the diagram (see figure 4, chapter 8), the Dome of the Rock is far to your left, to the south of the east-west line between the Eastern Gate and the Dome of the Tablets. In the Commentary Halachah 6 in the Mishneh Torah the great Jewish scholar Maimonides states, "The Temple Courtyard was not situated directly in the center of the Temple Mount. Rather, it was set off further from the southern wall of the Temple Mount than from the wall of any other direction." (In other words, the Temple was placed in the northern part of the Temple Mount, not the center, where the Arabs built the Dome of the Rock.) The Mishneh's detailed measurements also state that there were precisely 213 cubits (320 feet) between the Temple Courtyard and the Eastern Wall. According to these and other detailed measurements the Temple could not have been built on the site of the present Dome of the Rock because it is too close to the Eastern Wall to meet these specifications.

Additionally, the great Jewish scholar Rambam in censored sections of the Mishneh Torah, the Hilchos Bais Habechirah, states that the Temple was directly opposite the Eastern Gate. "The Eastern Gate was twenty cubits high. . . . For this reason, the wall above this (Eastern) gate was low. Thus, the priest [who offered the Para Aduma—the sacrifice of the Ashes of the Red Heifer] could see the opening of the Temple when he sprinkled its blood, while standing on the Mount of Olives." The Commentary Halachah 5 states that "the five gates were placed in a straight line: The Eastern Gate, the gate to the Chayl (rampart), the gate to the Woman's Courtyard, the gate of Nicanor, and the gate to the Entrance Hall (of the Sanctuary)." This is only possible if the Temple was directly opposite the Eastern Gate, not if the Temple was to the south on the site of the Dome of the Rock.

The Sacrifice of the Ashes of the Red Heifer

According to God's command to Moses regarding the special sacrifice of the Red Heifer, found in Numbers chapter 19, the priest was to take a "pure" Red Heifer, which had never had a yoke or hand laid upon it, outside the camp and sacrifice it. The blood was to be sprinkled opposite the front of the Tabernacle while they were in the Wilderness, prior to bringing the Tabernacle and Ark to Jerusalem. Once the Temple was built in Jerusalem this sacrifice of the Red Heifer took place on the western slope of the Mount of Olives in view of the Holy of Holies, directly opposite the front of the Temple and the Eastern Gate. During my last research trip to Israel I followed the precise description found in the Mishneh Torah, and found the precise spot described as the place for this sacrifice. According to the Rabbis this sacrifice of the ashes of the Red Heifer occurred only seven times in history. Each of the seven times the remaining ashes of the last sacrifice were added to the new sacrifice ashes to provide continuity. These ashes were sprinkled on the surface of the water of a large cistern to provide "waters of purification" to purify people from ritual defilements. According to the Copper Scroll of the Dead Sea Scrolls found in cave number 3, the last ashes of the Red Heifer were burnt just prior to the burning of Jerusalem by the Roman army in A.D. 70 and then taken from the Temple by the priests and secretly buried so they could be recovered in the last days.

A "pure" Red Heifer is highly unusual as almost one hundred percent of cattle have imperfections in their coloring. The Talmud states that even one white hair would disqualify the Heifer from being used for this sacrifice. Additionally, the Red Heifer must never have had a yoke laid upon its neck. While in Israel in the spring of 1989, I heard rumors that a Red Heifer had been born which met the detailed Talmudic and Biblical qualifications, and was being raised in secret by some orthodox rabbis.

Obviously the entire Temple Mount has been defiled both by ritual impurity and by the deaths of literally hundreds of thousands of soldiers, priests, and others during the tragic burning of the Temple on the ninth day of Av in A.D. 70. These dead bodies and thousands of years of religious desecration have made the Temple Mount incapable of being used today for the worship as demanded by laws of God in the Old Testament. It would be necessary to cleanse the Temple with the waters of purification produced only from the ashes of the Red Heifer to enable a reconstituted Sanhedrin to resume the entire Temple sacrifice system and the rebuilding of the Temple once the Ark and these ashes were found.

Many Christian and Jewish students of prophecy believe that these ashes will be recovered from their secret hiding place just prior to the building of the Third Temple. I am aware of several intensive archaeological investigations in Israel which are seeking to locate the lost Ark of the Covenant and the ashes of the Red Heifer. The Chief Rabbis of Israel have expressed serious interest in these investigations because they believe that these ashes and the Ark of the Covenant are the keys to the rebuilding of the Temple.

One Christian archaeologist, Vendyl Jones, has been searching in a cave near Jericho for several years for these ashes and further scrolls which would indicate the location of the lost Ark. Several months ago, in a nearby cave, his party discovered a clay jar which contains a highly unusual incense oil. It has been scientifically dated to the time of the Second Temple and appears to contain the five special ingredients the Bible describes as being used for the "oil of anointing" for kings. The evidence at this point in time is inconclusive, but if this proves to be "the oil of anointing," which is described in the Copper Scroll, it is a very important discovery. This find would lend credence to the other material in the Scroll about the secret location of the Kalal (a vessel made with clay and dung from the Red

Heifer), which holds the last remaining ashes of the Red Heifer.

Curiously, a reputable source alleged that Vendyl Jones and his search for the ashes and the Ark was one of the inspirations for the famous movie Raiders of the Lost Ark, which has a character named "Indiana" Jones who searches for the lost Ark. Interestingly, the movie fictionally displays the Nazis' fascination with the Ark and other sacred objects and shows them searching for the Ark in Egypt. The truth is that both the Nazis and the Italian Fascists, led by the dictator Mussolini, were fascinated by the Ark and other rare religious objects, and one of the war aims of the Italian army which invaded Ethiopia in 1935 was the capture of the Ark of the Covenant for Mussolini. A special unit of the German SS, the Ahnenerbe, was formed with enormous resources by the occult-minded Nazi leadership led by Heinrich Himmler and Adolf Hitler. This group was sent searching for such religious objects as the Ark and the Holy Grail throughout Europe and especially Tibet, from the early 1930s till the end of the war. The Ark was moved to safekeeping in the mountains of Ethiopia during Mussolini's 1936 invasion, and escaped capture by the Italian dictator's troops who were assigned to steal it from its underground Temple in the ancient capital of Aksum. The Jewish Christian Emperor of Ethiopia, Haile Selassie, fasted and prayed for three days as the Italian invasion began, and was assured that God would again grant Ethiopia the final victory. As had occurred during numerous other invasions over the last three thousand years, God honored these Ethiopian remnants of the tribe of Judah who protected the Ark and caused the mighty Italian army to fail in its objectives. Once the Italian army had retreated from Ethiopia, the Ark was safely returned to its underground Temple in Aksum where it remains to this day.

The Holy of Holies in Ethiopia

Deep within the complex of underground passages beneath the ancient Church of Zion, in Aksum in northern Ethiopia, lies a special secret passage which leads to the most sacred object in human history. For three thousand years this passage to the Holy of Holies has been guarded by the royal priestly guards of the ancient Jewish monarchy, led by Emperor Haile Selassie, who called himself "the Conquering Lion of Judah." Within the underground Temple are seven concentric rings of interior circular walls. An Ethiopian Coptic priest can worship within the areas of the first to fourth rings. Only the highest priests and the Emperor can enter the fifth and the sixth innermost rings. The final, seventh, central walled circular room is the Holy of Holies. Within this sacred room is kept the holy Ark of the Covenant which contains the Mercy Seat and the Shekinah Glory of God. Only one person is allowed to enter this room and that is the Guardian of the Ark. This is a man chosen at the age of seven, the age of understanding, from the priestly family. He has been trained as a child and agrees to guard the Ark for the rest of his life. He fasts 225 days every year while he prays, meditates, and guards the sacred Ark. He never leaves this Holy of Holies until the day of his death, when he is replaced by another seven-year-old Guardian. Each day the High Priest enters the sixth innermost ring to meet him and give him his food and take care of his needs. For three thousand years the Ark of the Covenant has been guarded continuously by these Guardians and Temple priest guards.

From the rebirth of Israel in 1948, the Israeli government enjoyed very close relations with Emperor Haile Selassie and provided considerable technical support and advice to Ethiopia. The royal family has told me that the Mossad, the Israeli secret service, assisted Ethiopia on numerous occasions and that Israeli agents repeatedly talked to the Emperor about the Ark of the Covenant in Aksum. The Israelis suggested that since Israel had returned from the captivity in 1948 and had recaptured the Temple Mount, the time had finally come for the Ethiopians to return the Ark to its ancient resting place in a rebuilt Temple in Jerusalem. The Emperor is reported to have replied, "In principle, I agree that the Ark should be returned to the Temple, but the correct time has not yet come." He felt that God would reveal the correct time for the return of the Ark to Jerusalem.

The Ethiopian monarchy is the oldest continual royal dynasty in history, beginning with the Queen of Sheba and her son, Menelik I, the offspring of her marriage to King Solomon of Israel, and extending for three thousand years until the reign of the late Emperor Haile Selassie. Although the army coup in 1974 overthrew the monarchy and later killed the Emperor, several of the princes have survived and are living in exile today. Prince Stephen Mengesha, the great-grandson of the Emperor, was fortunately outside the country, studying in Canada, and thus escaped the imprisonment or death which was the fate of most of the royal family. For fourteen years his mother, aunts, and uncles were imprisoned by the Marxist regime. Three of the royal princes remain in prison to this day. Despite the revolution and fourteen years of civil war, the Ark of the Covenant remains safely hidden within the Holy of Holies. Prince Stephen has become a friend of mine, and his sources state that the Ark is still guarded by the Ethiopian black Jewish priest guards, and neither the central Communist government nor the Tigre rebel forces will enter the sacred Church of Zion in Aksum due to fear of repercussions from the population and a deep, foreboding, historical superstition about the tremendous supernatural power surrounding the sacred Ark of the Covenant. Since the publication of the first edition of this book, the rebel Tigre army forces in northern Ethiopia were victorious and forced the Communist government army out of the province for the first time, in the spring of 1989. Shortly after this decisive defeat an aborted coup attempt by army officers, frustrated by years of unsuccessful war, was defeated by the current government. Prince Stephen's father, Prince Mengesha Sevoum the former governor-general of Ethiopia, is now the director of Ethiopian relief operations out of the Sudan. He appeared on national T.V. programs in the United States in the fall of 1988, after the release of this book (confirming the accuracy of my research), and confirmed that the Ark was still protected in Ethiopia. He showed pictures of his trip in 1965, taking Emperor Haile Selassie, Queen Elizabeth II, and Prince Philip to Aksum to visit the repository of the ancient Ark of the Covenant.

The Ark of the Covenant

The Ark is a prototype of Jesus Christ, the promised Messiah. More than any other element of the ancient Jewish liturgy of Tabernacle and Temple worship, the Ark symbolized the person of Christ, the Messiah. As the Ark displayed the actual Divine Shekinah Presence of God and contained the Law, the stone tablets of the Ten Commandments given to Moses by God directly, Jesus Christ in His claim, "My Father and I are One," embodied the Divine Presence of God and claimed to have come "not to abolish, but to fulfill the Law." The prophet Jeremiah tells us not only that the Ark of the Covenant will play a pivotal role in these coming end-time events, but also says that once Christ has ushered in His millennial reign in Jerusalem, the Ark, though still there, will no longer be the central focus of the Temple, because the Messiah Himself will be there to display the Divine Presence.

The word *ark* comes from the Hebrew word *aron*, which means a chest, box, or coffin. Its dimensions are described by the Bible as 2.5 cubits by 1.5 cubits by 1.5 cubits (45 inches by 27 inches by 27 inches). Curiously, this is the exact volume of the stone chest or porphyry coffer in the King's Chamber in the Great Pyramid in Egypt. This coffer was the only object within the King's Chamber, as the Ark was the single sacred object within the Holy of Holies, in the Temple. Also the laver, or basin, that the priests used to wash their feet had the identical cubit dimensions.

In addition, the cubit dimensions of the inner chamber of the Temple, the Holy of Holies, are precisely identical in size to the King's Chamber in the Pyramid and the same volume as the molten sea of water on the Temple Mount as prepared by King Solomon. Since the Pyramid was built and sealed long before the days of Moses, when he built the Ark and the Holy of Holies, and had remained sealed for over twenty-five centuries until the ninth century after Christ, there is no natural explanation for the phenomenon of both structures having identical volume measurements. The coffer in the pyramid contains exact measurements representing tremendous scientific knowledge as does the entire Great Pyramid. A small example of this data is that the height of the pyramid is precisely one billionth the distance of the Earth to the Sun.

God continually warned the Hebrews about the necessity for exact and fair measurements, and stated that false measurements were an abomination to Him. The Lord warned, **"Thou shall not have in thy house strange measures, a great and a small. But thou shall have a perfect and just weight, a perfect and just measure shall thou**

have" (Deuteronomy 25:14, 15). Obviously, the Lord could not demand that Israel keep exactly to just and consistent measurements unless He had provided an unchanging standard which could not be tampered with and could be appealed to as an ultimate check of accuracy. Some rabbinical sources have suggested that the rod of Aaron and the pot of manna were probably also used as final standards of measurements as we do today with precise samples being kept at a Bureau of Standards. The measurements of the Ark of the Covenant would be the ultimate standard of measurement. Unchangeable for all time. It was essential that they be kept in such a well guarded and safe place that they could never be tampered with. Considering the many secular, mercantile, and legal matters which were resolved by the various committees, including the Sanhedrin on the Temple Mount, the presence of the Ark in the Holy of Holies of the sacred Temple served as the ultimate repository until it disappeared during the reign of King Solomon, as discussed in detail in chapter 8.

While working on this final chapter I discovered a wonderful book on the Temple in a rabbinical bookstore in the Old City of Jerusalem. Rabbi Eliyahu Touger is the editor of the 1987 translation of the Mishneh Torah volume by Rambam, which deals with the rebuilding of the Temple by the Messiah in the last days. He naturally, as a Jewish scholar, approaches the matter from a different perspective than I do. However, I share his anticipation and deep longing for the coming of the Messiah to finally bring peace to Israel and the world. In his introduction he says that his fellow scholars often told each other, "Work faster. At any moment, Moshiahch may come and rebuild the Temple. Who knows how the book will sell then!"

As the world increasingly turns its eyes to the Middle East, the cradle of both our civilization and of the great spiritual beliefs of mankind, there is a growing sense of anticipation that we are approaching the key turning point in human history. Arthur Clarke wrote in *The Children of Icarus,* "We are living at a time when history is holding its breath, and the present is detaching itself from the past like an iceberg that has broken away from its icy moorings to sail across the boundless ocean." The tiny land of Israel is once more poised to play a decisive role in the unfolding story of Man. Jerusalem and the Temple of Gold, which have played so pivotal a role before in world history, will once more experience a profound meeting between God and Man. This age-old struggle between good and evil for the very soul of Man will finally come to its predestined conclusion in Jerusalem as foretold by the ancient biblical prophets. The promise of God is certain. When the Messiah comes, the prophecy of joy and peace for Jerusalem and the world will finally be fulfilled. **"For, behold, I create new heavens and a new earth; and the former shall not be remembered, nor come into mind. But be ye glad and rejoice for, behold, I create Jerusalem a rejoicing, and her people a joy" (Isaiah 65:17, 18).**

APPENDIX A

The 360 Day Prophetic Year of the Bible

It is vital that, if we are to correctly understand the precision of biblical prophecy, we must determine the precise length of the biblical (or prophetic) year which is used in the Scriptures.

Our modern world calendar is based on the solar cycle, and consists of 365.25 days. The modern Jewish calendar is calculated according to both the lunar and solar cycles. Their twelve months are currently calculated as containing 354 days, which leaves their year eleven-and-one-fourth days short of the true solar year. This is corrected by adding a "leap month," known as Ve-Adar, seven times during a nineteen-year cycle.

However, when we turn to the Scriptures we discover that the biblical-prophetic year consisted of 360 days. Abraham, the father of Israel, continued to use the 360-day year, which was known in his home in Ur of the Chaldees. The Genesis account of the flood in the days of Noah illustrated this 360-day year by recording the 150-day interval till the waters abated from the earth. The 150 days began on the seventeenth day of the second month, and ended on the seventeenth day of the seventh month (Genesis 7:11,24 and 8:3-4) In other words, the five months consisted of thirty days each; therefore, twelve months would equal 360 days (12 x 30 = 360 days).

Sir Isaac Newton stated, "All nations, before the just length of the solar year was known, reckoned months by the course of the moon, and years by the return of winter and summer, spring and autumn; and in making calendars for their festivals, they reckoned thirty days to a lunar month, and twelve lunar months to a year, taking the nearest round

JEWISH CALENDAR 1997

	JAN.	FEB.	MAR.	APR.	MAY	JUNE	JULY	AUG.	SEPT.	OCT.	NOV.	DEC.
1	Tebeth 22	24	22	23	24	25	26	27	29	29	Cheshvan 1	Kislev 2
2	23	25	23	24	25	26	27	28	30	Tishri 1	2	3
3	24	26	24	25	26	27	28	29	Elul 1	2	3	4
4	25	27	25	26	27	28	29	Av 1	2	3	4	5
5	26	28	26	27	28	29	30	2	3	4	5	6
6	27	29	27	28	29	Sivan 1	Tamuz 1	3	4	5	6	7
7	28	30	28	29	30	2	2	4	5	6	7	8
8	29	Adar 1	29	Nisan 1	Iyar 1	3	3	5	6	7	8	9
9	Shebat 1	2	30	2	2	4	4	6	7	8	9	10
10	2	3	2 Adar	3	3	5	5	7	8	9	10	11
11	3	4	2	4	4	Pentecost	6	8	9	Atonement	11	12
12	4	5	3	5	5	7	7	9	10	11	12	13
13	5	6	4	6	6	8	8	10	11	12	13	14
14	6	7	5	7	7	9	9	11	12	13	14	15
15	7	8	6	8	8	10	10	12	13	14	15	16
16	8	9	7	9	9	11	11	13	14	Tabernacle	16	17
17	9	10	8	10	10	12	12	14	15	16	17	18
18	10	11	9	11	11	13	13	15	16	17	18	19
19	11	12	10	12	12	14	14	16	17	18	19	20
20	12	13	11	13	13	15	15	17	18	19	20	21
21	13	14	12	14	14	16	16	18	19	20	21	22
22	14	15	Purim	Passover	15	17	17	19	20	21	22	23
23	15	16	14	16	16	18	18	20	21	22	23	24
24	16	17	15	17	17	19	19	21	22	23	24	25
25	17	18	16	18	18	20	20	22	23	24	25	26
26	18	19	17	19	19	21	21	23	24	25	26	27
27	19	20	18	20	20	22	22	24	25	26	27	28
28	20	21	19	21	21	23	23	25	26	27	28	29
29	21		20	22	22	24	24	26	27	28	29	30
30	22		21	23	23	25	25	27	28	29	Kislev 1	Tebeth 1
31	23		22		24		26	28		30		2

JEWISH CALENDAR 2000

	JAN.	FEB.	MAR.	APR.	MAY	JUNE	JULY	AUG.	SEPT.	OCT.	NOV.	DEC.
1	Tebeth 23	25	24	26	27	27	28	29	Elul 1	2	3	4
2	24	26	25	27	28	28	29	Av 1	2	3	4	5
3	25	27	26	28	29	29	30	2	3	4	5	6
4	26	28	27	29	30	Sivan 1	Tamuz 1	3	4	5	6	7
5	27	29	28	30	Iyar 1	2	2	4	5	6	7	8
6	28	30	29	Nisan 1	2	3	3	5	6	7	8	9
7	29	Adar 1	30	2	3	4	4	6	7	8	9	10
8	Shebat 1	2	2 Adar 1	3	4	5	5	7	8	9	10	11
9	2	3	2	4	5	6	6	8	9	Atonement	11	12
10	3	4	3	5	6	7	7	9	10	11	12	13
11	4	5	4	6	7	8	8	10	11	12	13	14
12	5	6	5	7	8	9	9	11	12	13	14	15
13	6	7	6	8	9	10	10	12	13	14	15	16
14	7	8	7	9	10	11	11	13	14	Tabernacle	16	17
15	8	9	8	10	11	12	12	14	15	16	17	18
16	9	10	9	11	12	13	13	15	16	17	18	19
17	10	11	10	12	13	14	14	16	17	18	19	20
18	11	12	11	13	14	15	15	17	18	19	20	21
19	12	13	12	14	15	16	16	18	19	20	21	22
20	13	14	13	Passover	16	17	17	19	20	21	22	23
21	14	15	14	16	17	18	18	20	21	22	23	24
22	15	16	15	17	18	19	19	21	22	23	24	25
23	16	17	16	18	19	20	20	22	23	24	25	26
24	17	18	17	19	20	21	21	23	24	25	26	27
25	18	19	18	20	21	22	22	24	25	26	27	28
26	19	20	19	21	22	23	23	25	26	27	28	29
27	20	21	20	22	23	24	24	26	27	28	29	Tebeth 1
28	21	22	21	23	24	25	25	27	28	29	Kislev 1	2
29	22	23	22	24	25	26	26	28	29	30	2	3
30	23		23	25	26	27	27	29	Tishri 1	Cheshvan	3	4
31	24		24				28	30	Feast			5
									of Trumpets			

numbers, whence came the division of the ecliptic into 360 degrees."[1]

This truth about the biblical 360 day year as mentioned by Newton was quoted by Sir Robert Anderson in his book, The Coming Prince, page 68. This was not a new discovery by Sir Isaac Newton in the late 1600's or even by Sir Robert Anderson in 1895. It was clearly discussed in detail by the Christian, Julias Africanus in his Chronography in his explanation of the fulfillment of Daniel's Seventy Weeks, written about A.D. 240.

The book of Esther (1: 4) indicates the same 360-day length of year by recording the six-months-long feast of Xerxes as continuing exactly 180 days.

The prophet Daniel recorded that the time of the absolute power of the Antichrist over the nations will last three-and-one-half years (Daniel 7:25). John, in the book of Revelation, described this same three-and-one-half year period (Revelation 13:5-7) as consisting of forty-two months of thirty days each, totaling 1260 days (Revelation 11:2-3; 12:6). The biblical writers used the ancient 360-day biblical year in both the historical and predictive parts of Scripture.

THE BIBLICAL CALENDAR

JEWISH MONTH		OUR EQUIVALENT MONTH
Order	**Name**	
1.	Nisan	Mar - April
2.	Iyar	April - May
3.	Sivan	May - June
4.	Tammuz	June - July
5.	Ab or Av	July - Aug
6.	Elul	Aug - Sept
7.	Tishri	Sept - Oct
8.	Bul	Oct - Nov
9.	Chisleu	Nov - Dec
10.	Tebeth	Dec - Jan
11.	Sebat	Jan - Feb
12.	Adar	Feb - Mar

Ve - Adar - Intercalary Month - Leap Years

The Date of Christ's Nativity, Ministry and Crucifixion

The Date of Christ's Nativity

Our current system of numbering years (e.g. A.D. 1988) was developed in the sixth century by a monk named Dionysius Exiguus. He calculated the birth of Christ as having occurred in the Roman year 754. He computed the New Year, beginning January 1 of the year following Christ's birth as recorded by Luke, as the year A.D. 1 of his new calendar (Anno Domini--"Year of God-Christ"). He based this calculation on the historical records available to him in Rome, plus the clear chronological statements of the historian Luke (3:1-2). The Christian historian, Eusebius, in A.D. 315, appealed to existing Roman government records (the census of Cyrenius and Caesar Augustus) to prove that Christ was born in Bethlehem when Joseph and Mary went there to be enrolled in the census, as mentioned in Luke 2:1-6. Justin Martyr also stated that census records were still available to prove the truth of Christ's prophesied birth in Bethlehem (Apology chapter 1, verse 34). It is therefore probable that the monk, Dionysius, had access to accurate records to determine that the birth of Christ occurred in the year before A.D. 1, which would be the fall of the year 1 B.C., since there is only one year between 1 B.C. and A.D. 1.

Scholars discovered evidence several hundred years ago that caused them to adjust the date of Christ's nativity back to 4 B.C., or even 6 B.C. One reason was that they believed that the governor of Syria, Cyrenius (who administered the taxing in Luke 2:1-3), ruled in that position from 7 B.C. to 4 B.C. However, more recent archeological evidence has proved that Cyrenius was twice governor of Syria, and that his first period of rule was from 4 B.C. to 1 B.C.

In his book The Coming Prince, page 92, Sir Robert Anderson said:

> In his Roman history, Mr. Merivale . . . says (vol. iv, page 457), 'A remarkable light has been thrown upon the point by the demonstration, as it seems to be, of Augustus Zumpt in his second volume of Commentationes Epigraphicae, that Quirinus (the Cyrenius of St. Luke ii) was first governor of Syria from the close of A.U. 750 (B.C. 4), to A.U. 753 (B.C.1).'

Therefore, there is no contradiction with the time of Cyrenius's first Syrian governorship (4 B.C. to 1 B.C.) and the census of Luke 2:1-3 occurring during 1 B.C., as stated by the early Christian writers.

Another factor which caused the date of Christ's birth to be adjusted back several years to 4 B.C. was that some scholars believed that King Herod's death (which followed Christ's birth) must have occurred in 4 B.C. The reason for assigning 4 B.C. for the death of Herod was that the Jewish historian, Flavius Josephus, recorded that Herod died just before Passover in the same year that there was an eclipse of the moon. Astronomers knew of a partial lunar eclipse in Jerusalem on March 13, 4 B.C.; therefore, scholars were certain this proved that Herod had died and Christ was born in 4 B.C.

However, additional astronomical evidence has revealed that the date of Herod's death could be as late as 1 B.C. or A.D. 1, allowing Christ's birth to have occurred in 1 B.C. We now know that a full (not a partial) lunar eclipse took place on January 9, 1 B.C., which could well be the one referred to by Josephus in Antiquities of the Jews (book xvii, chapter 6). Astronomical records reveal that eclipses of the moon were visible in Jerusalem during several years from 5 B.C. to A.D. 4, for example: March 23, 5 B.C., September 15, 5 B.C., March 12, 4 B.C. and January 9, 1 B.C. (Bible Encyclopedia and Scriptural Dictionary, page 423, by Rev. Samuel Fallows).

In the light of these facts, Christ's nativity could have occurred as early as 4 B.C. or as late as 1 B.C. This author believes the weight of evidence leans toward the Fall of 1 B.C., which agrees with the understanding and tradition of the early Church.

The traditional date set for Christmas, December 25, is almost certainly an error. Around A.D. 320, the church adopted the date of December 25 to officially celebrate the nativity, under the direction of the first Christian Roman emperor, Constantine. Apparently, the reason for picking this particular day was to replace the already existing pagan festival to the sun, known as Saturnalia. The information given in Luke 2:8, about the **"shepherds abiding in the field, keeping watch over the flock by night,"** indicates that it could not have been in late December because the cold weather would force the flocks and the shepherds to take shelter during that season.

The Scriptures give a hint that the actual date of Christ's birth could have been the fifteenth day of Tishri, the Feast of Tabernacles, which occurs in our September-October. The Gospel of John (1:14) states, **"And the Word was made flesh, and tabernacled [dwelt] among us."** John would certainly be in a position to know Jesus' birthday and it is probable that he is hinting at the Feast of Tabernacles as the actual date by using the unusual word "tabernacled" to describe Christ's birth. The fact that some forty other key events in the spiritual history of Israel have occurred on biblical anniversaries of feast days would indicate a high probability that the birth of the Jewish Messiah would also occur on a feast date (in this case the Feast of Tabernacles, 1 B.C.).

The Feast of Tabernacles was one of the annual Feasts on which all Jewish males were required to go to the Temple in Jerusalem to worship. This would cause a huge pilgrimage and thus a temporary increase in the population close to Jerusalem, and would help to account for the fact that **"there was no room in the inn"** in Bethlehem on the night of Christ's birth. This census also would contribute to the overcrowding.

The Date of Christ's Ministry and His Crucifixion

In all of Scripture the clearest, most definitive chronological statement is found in the beginning verses of Luke (3:1-2), which describes precisely the actual year in which John the Baptist began his ministry. Luke recorded that the beginning of Christ's teaching ministry started with

His baptism (Luke 3:21-22), and that Jesus, when He began His ministry, "was about thirty years of age" (Luke 3:23, RSV).

Luke's chronological statement is this: **"Now in the fifteenth year of the reign of Tiberius Caesar, Pontius Pilate being governor of Judaea, and Herod being tetrarch of Galilee, and his brother Philip tetrarch of Ituraea and of the region of Trachonitis, and Lysanias the tetrarch of Abilene, Annas and Caiaphas being the high priests, the word of God came unto John the son of Zacharias in the wilderness" (Luke 3:1-2).**

The Roman emperor, Tiberius Caesar, ascended his throne as Emperor on the nineteenth day of August A.D. 14. This date was as well known in Luke's day as the date of the assassination of President John F. Kennedy is known in our day. Therefore, the fifteenth year of Tiberius Caesar began on the nineteenth day of August, A.D. 28 Historical records confirm that all of the above named officials ruled in the year A.D. 28. It thus approaches historical certainty that Christ's ministry began in the fall of A.D. 28.

It is obvious that many Bible commentators have assigned several earlier dates for the commencement of Christ's ministry, from A.D. 24 to A.D. 27. The reason they ignore the clear date of A.D. 28, described with such precision by the Gospel historian Luke, is probably due to their previous commitment to an early (7 B.C. to 4 B.C.) dating of the nativity of Christ.

Since Christ was "about thirty years of age" at the time of his commencement of public ministry, they are forced to ignore Luke's clear historical dating. The way they accomplish this is to imagine that the first year of the reign of Tiberius Caesar refers to A.D. 12, when Caesar Augustus promoted General Tiberius for his victories in Germany, not to the actual official coronation of Tiberius Caesar as Emperor, on August 19, A.D. 14, following the death of Caesar Augustus. They imagine a kind of co-regency of the two men for the last two years of the reign of Caesar Augustus.

An analogy would be for a historian to count the years of President Johnson's presidency from January, 1960 when President Kennedy was inaugurated; instead of from the date of the death of President Kennedy in November 22,

1963 when Vice-President Johnson was elevated to the presidency. Such a calculation would be a total distortion of historical dating and no reasonable person, let alone a historian, would do it.

The problem with such an interpretation of a co-regency from A.D. 12 is simply that there is not one single shed of evidence in any other contemporary historical writing, which dates the reign of Tiberius Caesar from any date other than the true start of his reign, August 19, A.D. 14. It is inconceivable that an accurate historian such as Luke, in writing to the Gentile Roman officer Theophilus (Luke 1:1-4) would have adopted such a peculiar way of counting the years of Tiberius Caesar's reign that would certainly confuse him as to the correct date of the beginning of Christ's ministry.

Our conclusion, therefore, is that Christ's public teaching commenced in the Fall of A.D. 28. The first Passover of His ministry would have then taken place six months later on the fourteenth of Nisan, A.D. 29 (John 2:12-23).

There is a further confirmation of this thesis that Christ's public ministry began in the fall of A.D. 28. The Apostle John records that while attending this Passover Feast six months later in the Temple, Christ prophesied that He would be killed and would rise again in three days. The Jews did not understand that He was referring to Himself, not the Temple, and replied to Jesus, **"Forty and six years was this temple in building, and wilt thou rear it up in three days?"** (John 2:19-20).

The historical records of that time, including Flavius Josephus in his War of the Jews tell us that Herod the Great began the restoration of the Temple in 18 B.C. The year of Christ's first Passover of His public ministry, A.D. 29 is exactly 46 years from the commencement of Herod's restoration program in 18 B.C. (Note: only one year exists between 1 B.C. and A.D. 1).

Jesus continued His ministry over a period of approximately three-and-one-half years. Dr. Pusey, in his excellent book, Daniel, on pages 176 and 177, states, "It seems to me absolutely certain that our Lord's ministry lasted for some period above three years." According to the Gospel of John, Jesus attended at least three Passovers, and if the Feast mentioned in John 5:1 is also a Passover, then it is certain that the crucifixion occurred on the date of His final Passover in A.D. 32. The Feast described in John 5:1 must be either the Feast of Passover or Purim and, since Purim was a social feast celebrating the events described in the book of Esther, it is unlikely in the extreme that Jesus would specifically go up to Jerusalem for a non-religious holiday. The evidence supports the contention that this Feast was also a Passover. Thus, Christ's ministry extended from the Fall of A.D. 28, three-and-one-half years, to end with His final Passover and crucifixion in A.D. 32.

SELECTED BIBLIOGRAPHY

Anderson, Robert. *The Coming Prince*. London: Hodder & Stroughton, 1894.

Auerbach, Leo. *The Babylonian Talmud - In Selection*. New York: Philosophical Library, 1944.

Barnes, Albert. *Notes on the Book of Daniel*. New York: Leavitt & Allen, 1855.

Baylee, Rev. Joseph. *The Times of the Gentiles*. London: James Nisbet & Co. 1871.

Besant, Walter & Palmer, E.H. *Jerusalem*. London: Chatto & Windus, 1908.

Blackstone, Wm. E. *Jesus is Coming*. London: Fleming H.Revell Co., 1908.

Blackstone, Wm. E. *The Millennium*. New York: Revell Publishing Co.

Bloomfield, Arthur. *Where Is the Ark of the Covenant and What Is Its Role in Bible Prophecy?* Minneapolis: Dimension Books, 1976.

Bradley, John. *World War III – Strategies, Tactics and Weapons*. New York: Cresent Books, 1982.

Bullinger, Ethelbert W. *Number In Scripture*. Grand Rapids: Kregel Publications, 1978.

Burnett, Bishop. *The Sacred Theory Of The Earth*. London: 1816.

Butterfield, Herbert. *Christianity And History*. New York: Charles Scribner and Sons, 1949.

Calder, Nigel. *Unless Peace Comes*. Victoria: Penguin Books, 1968.

Chaldler, Bishop Edward. *A Defence of Christianity from the Prophecies of the Old Testament*. London: James and John Knapton, 1725.

Culver, Robert Duncan. *Daniel and the Latter Days*. Chicago: Moody Press, 1954, 1977.

Cummings, John. *Lectures on the Book of Daniel*. Philadelphia: Lindsay and Blakiston, 1855.

Cummings, John. *Apocalyptic Sketches*. London: Hall, Virtue and Co., 1850.

Davidson, John. *Discourses on Prophecy*. London: John Murray & Co. 1825.

Dimont, Max I. *Jews, God And History*. New York: New American Library, 1962.

Edersheim, Alfred. *The Temple*. London: The Religious Tract Society, 1912.

Edersheim, Alfred. *The Life and Times of Jesus the Messiah*. Vol. 2 New York: Longmans, Green, and Co., 1896.

Edersheim, Alfred. *Bible History - Old Testament*. Grand Rapids: William Eerdmans Publishing Co., 1982.

Eusebius. *Eusebius' Ecclesiastical History*. Oxford: The Clarendon Press, 1881.

Fabun, Don. *The Dynamics of Change*. Englewood Cliffs: Prentice-Hall, Inc., 1967.

Freeman, Hobart E. *An Introduction to the Old Testament Prophets*. Chicago: Moody Press, 1968.

Gaster, Theodor H. *Festivals of the Jewish Year*. New York: Morrow Quill Paperbacks, 1953.

Gilbert, Martin. *The Arab-Israeli Conflict - Its History In Maps*. Jerusalem: Steimatzky Ltd., 1985.

Graham, Billy. *Approaching Hoofbeats - The Four Horsemen Of The Apocalypse*. Waco: Word Books, Inc., 1983.

Guinness, H. Grattan. *The Approaching End of the Age*. 8th ed. London: Hodder & Stoughton, 1882.

Hallifax, Dr. Samuel. *Twelve Sermons on the Prophecies Concerning the Christian Church*, London: T. Cadell, 1776.

Harrison, William K. *Hope Triumphant - Studies on the Rapture*. Chicogo: Moody Press, 1966.

Hawley, Charles A. *The Teaching of Apocrypha and Apocalypse*. New York: Association Press, 1925.

Heinish, Dr. Paul. *History Of The Old Testament*. St. Paul: The North Central Publishing Co., 1952.

Jarvis, Rev. Samuel F. *The Church of the Redeemed*. Boston: 1950.

Josephus, Flavius. *Wars of the Jews*. Kingston: N.G.Ellis, 1844.

Jones, Alexander. Editer *The Jerusalem Bible*. Garden City: Doubleday & Co., 1968

Kellogg, Dr. Samuel. *The Jews or Prediction and Fulfillment*. New York: Anson D.F.Randolf & Co., 1883.

Kidron, Michael and Smith, Dan. *The War Atlas*. London: Pan Books Ltd., 1983.

Larkin, Clarence. *The Book o Daniel*. Philaoelphia: Clarence Larkin, 1929, 1949.

Lewis, David Allen. *Magog 1982 - Cancelled*. Harrison: New Leaf Press, 1982.

Lindsay, Hal. *The Late Great Planet Earth*. Grand Rapids: Zondervan Publishing House, 1970.

Lockyer, Herbert. *All The Messianic Prophecies Of The Bible*. Grand Rapids: Zondervan Publishing House, 1973.

Ludwigson, R. *A Survey of Bible Prophecy*. Grand Rapids: Zondervan Publishing House, 1951.

Marsh, Rev. John. *An Epitome of General Ecclesiastical History*. New York: J. Tilden and Co., 1843.

McCall, Thomas S. and Levitt, Zola. *The Coming Russian Invasion Of Israel*. Chicogo: Moody Press, 1976.

McDowell, Josh. *Evidence That Demands A Verdict*. San Bernadino: Here's Life Publishers, Inc., 1979.

Mesorah Publications. *Daniel - A New Commentary Anthologized From Talmudic, Midrashic And Rabbinical Sources*. Brooklyn: Mesorah Publications, Ltd., 1980.

Messing, Simon D. *The Story of the Falashas*. Broooklyn: Balshon Printing, 1982.

Misorah Publications. *Ezekiel - A New Commentary Anthologized From Talmudic, Midrashic And Rabbinical Sources*. Brooklyn: Mesorah Publications, Ltd., 1980

Newton, Bishop Thomas. *Dissertations on the Prophecies*. 2 Vol. London: R & R Gilbert, 1817.

Payne, J. Barton. *Encyclopedia of Biblical Prophecy*. Grand Rapids: Baker Book House. 1980.

Pentecost, Dwight. *Things to Come*. Grand Rapids: Dunham, 1958.

Peters, Joan. *From Time Immemorial - The Origins of the Arab-Israeli Conflict Over Palastine*. New York: Harper & Row, Publishers, 1984.

Pusey, E. B. *Daniel The Prophet*. Plymouth: The Devonport Society. 1864.

Rosenau, Helen. *Vision of the Temple*. London: Oresko Books Ltd. 1979.

Sale-Harrison, L. *The Remarkable Jew*. London: Pickering & Inglis, 1928.

Schell, Johnathan. *The Fate Of The Earth*. New York: Avon Books, 1982.

Scofield, C. I. *The Scofield Reference Bible*. Oxford: Oxford University, 1909.

Siegel, Richard and Rheins, Carl. *The Jewish Almanac* . New York: Bantam Books, Inc., 1980.

Smith, Wilbur M. *Israeli/Arab Conflict and the Bible*. Glendale: Regal Books, 1967.

Seiss, Joseph. *The Apocalypse*. Philadelphia: Approved Books, 1865.

Suborov, Victor. *Inside The Soviet Army*. London: Granada Publishing Ltd., 1984.

Szyk, Arthur. *The Haggadah*. Jerusalem: Massadah and Alumoth, 1960.

Taylor, Gordon R. *The Biological Time Bomb*. London: Thames and Hudson, 1968.

The Ante-Nicene Fathers. 10 Volumes. Grand Rapids: Eerdmans Publishing Co., 1986.

Tinbergen, Jan. *Reshaping The International Order - A Report To The Club Of Rome*. Scarborough: The New American Library Of Canada, 1976.

Ussher, Archbishop Jacob. *Chronology Of The Old And New Testaments*. Verona, 1741.

Walvoord, John F. Daniel, The Key to Prophetic Revelations. A Commentary. Chicago: Moody Press, 1971.

Walvoord, John F. *The Rapture Question*. Findlay: Dunham Publishing Co., 1957.

Strassfeld, Michael. *The Jewish Holidays - A Guide And Commentary*. New York: Harper And Row, Publishers, 1985.

Weber, Timothy P. *Living In The Shadow Of The Second Coming*. Oxfo/New York: Oxford University Press, 1979.

West, Gilbert. *Observations on the History and Evidences of the Resurrection of Jesus Christ*. London: R. Dodsley, 1747.

White, John Wesley. *World War III*. Grand Rapids: Zondervan Publishing House, 1977.

Yadin, Yigael. *Masada*. London: Sphere Books Ltd., 1973.

Zlotowitz, Rabbi Meir. *Bereishis - Genesis*. Brooklyn: Mesorah Publications, Ltd., 1980.

Hal Lindsey has taken his millions of faithful readers
on a fabulous journey...